IPv6 Network Administration

Other resources from O'Reilly

Related titles

802.11 Wireless Networks: The Definitive Guide

BGP

Cisco Cookbook

Cisco IOS in a Nutshell

DNS and BIND, Fourth Edition

Ethernet: The Definitive Guide

Internet Core Protocols: The Definitive Guide

IP Routing

IPv6 Essentials

SSH, The Secure Shell: The Definitive Guide

TCP/IP Network Administration

---

oreilly.com

oreilly.com is more than a complete catalog of O'Reilly books. You'll also find links to news, events, articles, weblogs, sample chapters, and code examples.

oreillynet.com is the essential portal for developers interested in open and emerging technologies, including new platforms, programming languages, and operating systems.

Conferences

O'Reilly brings diverse innovators together to nurture the ideas that spark revolutionary industries. We specialize in documenting the latest tools and systems, translating the innovator's knowledge into useful skills for those in the trenches. Visit *conferences.oreilly.com* for our upcoming events.

Safari Bookshelf (*safari.oreilly.com*) is the premier online reference library for programmers and IT professionals. Conduct searches across more than 1,000 books. Subscribers can zero in on answers to time-critical questions in a matter of seconds. Read the books on your Bookshelf from cover to cover or simply flip to the page you need. Try it today with a free trial.

IPv6 Network Administration

Niall Richard Murphy and David Malone

O'REILLY®

Beijing · Cambridge · Farnham · Köln · Paris · Sebastopol · Taipei · Tokyo

IPv6 Network Administration
by Niall Richard Murphy and David Malone

Published by O'Reilly Media, Inc., 1005 Gravenstein Highway North, Sebastopol, CA 95472.

O'Reilly books may be purchased for educational, business, or sales promotional use. Online editions are also available for most titles (*safari.oreilly.com*). For more information, contact our corporate/institutional sales department: (800) 998-9938 or *corporate@oreilly.com*.

Editor:	Mike Loukides
Production Editor:	Colleen Gorman
Cover Designer:	Ellie Volckhausen
Interior Designer:	David Futato

Printing History:

March 2005:	First Edition.

 This book uses RepKover™, a durable and flexible lay-flat binding.

ISBN: 0-596-00934-8
[M]

This book is dedicated to the late John Lewis,
mathematician and academic, who enriched
the lives of the many people he touched
with his ability, humility, and good humor.
Rest in peace.

Table of Contents

Foreword

IPv6 has evolved during the last dozen years or so, and the road has not been easy. The process has been driven primarily by the shortage of address space under IPv4, but also by the desire for new applications that don't fit within the older protocol's limitations. The address space crisis has been delayed by several new approaches to IP addressing, the most important of them being CIDR, NAT, and RFC1918 private address space. At the same time, it was clear that these solutions only postponed the inevitable, so efforts began to redesign the IP protocol. These efforts led to IPv6.

Although CIDR, NAT, and private address spaces have been successful, they didn't solve the problem—they only put it off. Today, the Regional Internet Registries have IPv4 address allocation policies that scare away those who would like to get public address space. IPv4 address space has become a scarce resource, and getting a public address block requires too much paperwork and bureaucracy. We can stretch out the IPv4 address space for 5, 10, or 50 years, but if the result is that only a privileged few can get public address space, what's the point?

Enter IPv6. IPv6 provides a clean fix to the fundamental problem: too few bits in the IP address. The increased length of IPv6 addresses means that they can be assigned freely and used comfortably; they're not a scarce resource that needs to be conserved. IPv6 also makes it possible to deploy new types of applications that rely on public address space, or that encode information in the IP address itself, such as multihoming and verifiably secure local networking.

The IPv6 specifications are now reasonably stable. Dozens of implementations have been deployed and used for years; if you want to use IPv6, you no longer need special software or patches. Most operating systems include IPv6 support, and some vendors even turn it on by default. IPv6 has arrived at a state where almost everyone can use it. The problem is now that they don't know how.

Therefore, the most important work at the moment is enabling IPv6 deployment, and creating an atmosphere where IPv6 applications can be created and flourish. That's where we'll really see the benefit of IPv6: in new applications that go beyond the client-server paradigm, and take advantage of IPv6's end-to-end addressing and connectivity features. That's where this book comes in: it gathers knowledge scattered across the Internet about deployment and applications. There are many ways to deploy IPv6, and the more complex the network you have, the more possibilities you have. This book helps you to understand those possibilities and deploy IPv6 on your network.

Have the Internet users, application developers, and vendors grown too comfortable with short-term patches to counter the problem caused by NATs and address space shortage, instead of choosing the longer-term solution, IPv6? We'll see.

IPv6 is ready for deployment. For *you* to deploy, use, and write applications for. This book shows you how; don't let inertia hold you back. Have fun doing that!

—Pekka Savola
IETF IPv6 Operations (v6ops) working group co-chair

Preface

The chief thing is not to study, but to do.
—Sayings of the Fathers, 1:17

IPv6 has been overhyped, undersold, rubbished, acclaimed, scuppered, and resurrected—often several times a day by the same person in different conversations. It's been talked up and talked down, misunderstood, ignored and defended; but it is overcoming barriers and finding growing acceptance and support within the Internet community. For an obscure networking protocol of current interest to a small fraction of the population of our planet, this combination of passion and ignorance seems remarkable. You might ask, 'So why all the fuss?' The motivation behind IPv6 is the need to fix the most difficult problems that the Internet faces today: address exhaustion, network management, scalability issues, and multi-homing. It is the promise of addressing* these issues that has sparked the interest it has aroused, and that same promise is and will drive its adoption and eventual deployment. In fact, about the only thing that IPv6 *hasn't* been is widely deployed enough to justify this attention! We hope to do our small part to change that by providing this book to help you make your own judgement, ignoring the gain-sayers and the hype, and focusing on what IPv6 can do for you.

We of course know that technical merit or promise alone is not enough to make something successful, so besides an excellent design and good intentions, what else does IPv6 have going for it? Well, it's been adopted as a standard by organizations such as the 3GPP† and well-known industry players such as Cisco, Microsoft, and Sun, it's seen an increasing amount of commercial deployment from organizations such as Microsoft and NTT, and confidence is increasing that the rightful successor to IPv4, the most popular internetworking protocol in the world, has arrived just when we need it the most.

---

* Pun intended.

† The 3rd Generation Partnership Project, a group set up to work on standards for third generation mobile telecomunications.

No authors come without bias, this we accept, but in this book we hope to show you what is good, what is bad, and what is practical, acknowledging the faults and praising the innovations. Rather than presenting a protocol design manual or reference work (an endeavour tackled by many others previously) we will present a distillation of what IPv6 *means in practice*, directly relating it to the hands-on experience of network administrators. We take this approach both when describing IPv6 itself and when discussing how to use it—this means we don't hesitate to leave things out if they are of marginal utility, but do try to cover processes and procedures in detail.

You might be surprised to know that you get IPv6 functionality for free in a growing number of operating systems; pains have been taken by the designers of IPv6 to make it easy to experiment and work with, and some early adopters are now using it for their day-to-day business.

There are, of course, those who doubt that a serious transition will ever happen, who think that "the devil you know" is better than risking instability of their network. We confess a certain sympathy with that view. However, there are so many precedents for rapid change—and necessary change—in this industry. We think it is foolish to ignore what is the only candidate for the future IP protocol of choice. After all, not many people were running a HTTP in 1993.* Installed bases are relative things, especially in an industry that can change radically in a year.

Finally, a word on the ultimate success of the IPv6 process. There's no question that of the time of writing, it is mainly the adventurous who are deploying commercial production services over this protocol. Is there room for a sober, conservative approach? Predicting the future of technology is always a risky business. However, it is our contention that the slow growth of frustration with IPv4, the unavoidable issue of address exhaustion, together with the benefits of IPv6 outlined above will eventually cause a critical mass of deployment to accumulate. One point to keep in mind is that the projected IPv4 addressing requirements of China are larger than the total amount of free address space *now*! Eventually something will have to be done about the crises IPv4 faces—it's just a question of when, and IPv6 is the best shot we've got.

What This Book Is … and Is Not

This book tries to take IPv6 into the real world. It is not about understanding dry analysis of header formats and new protocols—although those are obviously fundamentally important—it is about understanding what those header formats mean for a real organization today; it is about trying to use those headers on *your* network, and warning you of the dangers and opportunities you will face. It is about helping

---

* To find out who, see the archived copy of Tim Berners-Lee's list of W3 servers from November 1993, available at *http://jmason.org/WWW-servers.txt*.

---

you to turn IPv6 into something real, something that can be useful to you, and something you feel comfortable with.

In detail, we begin in Chapter 1 and Chapter 2 by describing IPv4 in terms of its successes and failures, as these have influenced much of the motivation for and design of IPv6. Chapter 3 discusses the eventual results of the design process: the core elements of IPv6. Of course, most of us who operate IPv4 networks don't have the full details of IPv4 to hand, so we work with a simplified picture of IPv4 for day-to-day purposes. Consequently, we avoid some of the fine details covered in other IPv6 texts. For those who want to find out more of the details, we have included references allowing you to find out more when you need to.

Chapter 4 deals with planning IPv6 deployment. This includes thinking about how to get connectivity, address space, and how to make your IPv6 infrastructure fit well within your existing network.

The basics of how to configure IPv6 are covered in Chapter 5. We review a selection of popular operating systems, explaining the extent of their support for IPv6 and their basic commands and configuration procedures. We include references to vendor documentation where the detail is distracting.

The later chapters deal with making IPv6 do useful things in your network. Chapter 6 deals with typical operations you might perform on an IPv6-enabled network. The main subjects in this chapter are DNS, IPsec, firewalling and routing; network infrastructure and support services can be found here. Chapter 7 deals with providing services that end-users and customers are actually interested in. Naturally, the main focus here is HTTP and SMTP. Chapter 8 deals with the modifications to the sockets API to deal with IPv6, and should provide a starting point for those who want to port their local network applications to IPv6.

As we've said above, we hope to provide you with the general principles first and specific details later, when their consequences can be properly appreciated. This has translated into the structure of the book as separate sections for operating system and application specific detail, so they can be used more as reference material than as narrative.

For material where the current status of the feature in question is unclear, we've highlighted this. We've also included our guesses as to how things may eventually turn out in Chapter 9.

History and Background

No major change to the core protocols of the Internet could be introduced without its share of controversy, and IPv6 has had history controversial enough to fill a book on its own. We'll only cover the crudest outline here; for more detail, we suggest you consult Christian Huitema's book *IPv6, The New Internet Protocol* (Prentice Hall), or, alternatively, *IPng Internet Protocol Next Generation*, edited by Bradner and Mankin (Addison-Wesley).

To properly understand how IPv6 came into being requires more than a passing familiarity with the organizations that are behind the technical and administrative existence of the Internet. Readers who are already familiar with these can skip ahead; others please continue, for though the acronyms are fast and furious, they are all relevant.

The IETF and friends

The IETF (Internet Engineering Task Force) are the ultimate networking geeks. Responsible for the standards on which the Internet is based, the "members"* of the IETF engage in protocol design, protracted discussions and incessant, mostly cynical, joking. Their guiding principle as engineers is to create protocol standards that work: "rough consensus and running code" is mentioned as the IETF's credo in RFC 2031.† There is an interesting Ph.D waiting to be written on IETF culture, but we shall confine ourselves to commenting on its methodology. IETF standards, generally arising from motivations like "This protocol is broken because X is really hard to do—we need to fix it," or "Hey, wouldn't it be nice if we could do Y?" start as discussions on mailing lists which are categorized by Working Group.

A Working Group is a collection of people and technical resources aimed at considering (usually) a quite specific topic. Working Groups are themselves sorted by subject *Area*. So, for example, the effort around getting IPv6 up and running is conducted in several working groups, including IPv6 WG, v6ops WG, and multi6 WG. The IPv6 WG is under the Internet Area in the IETF (dealing with design), and v6ops and multi6 is under the Operations and Management Area (making protocols operable).

Working Groups and Areas have people who are responsible for their upkeep. Areas have Area Directors making decisions about items of concern to the Area. Most commonly, they decide whether a working group be created or disbanded. In turn, Working Groups have *chairs*. These chairs, in co-operation with Area Directors and the members of the Working Group (WG for short), decide what work items the group will adopt. (If all of this sounds bureaucratic, we apologize for misleading you, for although its structure has been well established, the IETF is one of the most successful decentralized organizations permitting public participation in the world.)

Work generally happens on documents known as *Internet Drafts*. These are basically documents that present information in a standard way. Internet Drafts are passed between the members of a group for comment, feedback, and analysis. Some

---

* Members is in quotes since the only current pre-requisite of membership is a desire to be one.

† This phrase seems to have originated with Dave Clark, a founding figure of the Internet. We'll explain what an RFC is in a moment.

drafts, if they meet the "rough consensus and running code" benchmark, then work their way up to the hallowed status of RFC (Request For Comments).* An RFC is a document that encapsulates the thinking of the Working Group on a particular topic. RFCs are the official "documents of record" of the IETF. Often, they are definitive statements on how certain kinds of network communication must happen; sometimes, they describe operational constraints or other peripherally related topics. You would expect them to have some connection to networking, but apart from that, they could be about literally anything.

RFCs themselves can have different statuses: an RFC on the standards track can work its way from Proposed Standard to Draft Standard to Standard as its maturity grows and its volatility decreases. RFCs that are not intended as standards can be classified as Informational (contains something worth noting), Experimental (something people are trying out), BCP (a codification of Best Current Practice), and Historic (obsolete or superseded). RFC 2026 contains more details about the standardization process.†

The IESG (Internet Engineering Steering Group) is a group consisting of all the Area Directors. It has a steering function in terms of setting strategy, but also in terms of resolving disputes arising in the course of IETF work. We may have given you the impression above that all is happy-go-lucky in Internet-land; not so, of course, and when disputes arise, there are procedures for dealing with that too.

The IAB (Internet Architecture Board) is where geeks go when they grow up. The IAB's main job is to oversee the development of standards by the IETF. They can suggest the setup of new Working groups and even propose the creation of longer running research projects. They also appoint the IESG from a list provided by the IETF. (This is a purely formal, rubber-stamping exercise; they perform no selection themselves.)

More details about how the IETF fits together are available in RFC 3160. As it happens, the body giving the most momentum to the IPv6 effort is the IETF.

Chronological overview

IPv6 is the culmination of over a decade's worth of work, initially inspired by one of the biggest problems still facing the Internet today: address exhaustion.

It was clear from early on in the development of the Internet that IP addresses, although finite, were perhaps rather more finite than desired. Way back then, it only took approximately two years to go from 10,000 to 100,000 hosts (from the end of 1987 to 1989). At around the same time, the original constituency of military and

---

* It's interesting to note in passing that, officially, every finished RFC is simply asking for people to review itself!

† The section "A Note on RFCs and Internet Drafts," later in this chapter, tells you how to find RFC documents—they are available free on the web.

academic sites had been joined by commercial efforts, as well as an expanding number of countries. The phenomenal growth that was occurring, coupled with the inefficiency of the then-current *class-based* address allocation method was already starting to arouse concern in the technical community.[*]

The earliest records of a formalized search for a replacement for IPv4[†] are found in the proposal to create an IETF Working Group called "ROAD," in November of 1991. ROAD's brief was to investigate the possible solutions to the near-term scaling problems identified above. ROAD was not a standard IETF Working Group—it existed for a short time only, and membership was not open; this was done because of the urgency of the scaling problems and the necessity of a quick practical response to it. In March of 1992 ROAD made its final set of recommendations, documented in RFC 1380, that *classless interdomain routing*[‡] should be used to get around the immediate problems of class B address exhaustion and routing scalability, but that more research was needed into future routing and addressing models for the Internet. In other words, the mid- to long-term problems could not be solved within the context of the group.

Dave Crocker[§] of Brandenburg Consulting summarized the situation nicely with this paragraph from his 1992 paper on "The ROAD to a new IP:"

> Concern about IP address exhaustion and routing table size explosion has created a sense of crisis within the IETF community. Almost 2 years ago, a special effort, called the ROAD (ROuting and ADdressing) group was formed to consider solutions. It gravitated towards one option, but did not see quick adoption of its recommendation. But time had passed and urgency grew. There has been pressure to select a solution immediately, without extensive exploration and development of options. The Internet Engineering Steering Group (IESG) divided the concerns into short-term, mid-term and long-term. Class-B exhaustion and routing table size explosion fall into the first category. IP address space exhaustion falls into the mid-term timeframe. The IESG feels that other issues of general enhancement to IP, such as quality of service, security/authentication, mobility, resource allocation, accounting, and high packet rates can be deferred for "long term" consideration.

After the delivery of the ROAD recommendations, another Working Group was formed in 1993, called ALE (Address Lifetime Expectation), whose job was to establish the probable lifetime of IPv4 address space given current policies and practices. ALE decided that there was indeed a very short lifetime for the remaining space: one year! Efforts were redoubled to get CIDR out in the real world—in this case, getting it into CIDR-capable backbone routers—and in administration of address allocation policies.

---

[*] For example, Vint Cerf's comments in various discussions in the TCP/IP list at the end of 1988. See *http://www-mice.cs.ucl.ac.uk/multimedia/misc/tcp_ip/8813.mm.www/0144.html* for more detail.

[†] IPv4 was itself was a replacement for a protocol called NCP.

[‡] Classless interdomain routing, or CIDR for short, is explained in more detail in the "CIDR" section of Chapter 1.

[§] Author of RFC 822 on email headers, amongst many other things.

While this work was highly urgent and necessary, it did not escape the IAB's and the IESG's notice that the larger problem of a future replacement for IPv4 still needed attention. Thankfully, the resounding success of CIDR bought enough time for the establishment of a "next-generation" directorate in the IETF. Oddly enough, the IAB recommended that work should begin as soon as possible on integrating OSI CLNP* type addresses into the next version of IP, then called IP version 7.† Although this was neither the first nor the last time the integration of aspects of OSI with IP was proposed, it met with as approximately the same amount of success as all the other efforts—none.

In retrospect, it seems the crisis had pushed the IAB into recommending a path, any path, rather than not reacting at all. However, the IAB made it clear that this was not supposed to shortcut the normal IETF process of evaluating and discussing as many proposals as could be found; accordingly, RFC 1550 in December 1993 solicited white papers from the community about what they felt IPng, the next generation of IP, should look like. This was an active attempt to engage all the possible stakeholders, from electricity companies to national research agencies. The Call For Papers wasn't a carte blanche to send in your favorite research protocol though; the reviewers of this process were looking for genuine contenders to the throne, and as such were going to examine proposals for such intangible but nonetheless vital qualities as vision and longevity as well as practical assurances of functionality.

Based on this work, the IPng Working Group very quickly assembled a list of proposals for IPv4 replacements, some of which we examine in more detail below. At the "IPDecide BOF" meeting held at the Amsterdam IETF meeting in July 1993, it was clear that direction from a higher body was necessary in order to help focus and direct efforts because so many complicated issues were involved. The decision was made that the IPng Area Directors should recommend a candidate to the IESG, who would henceforth ratify the decision. There was a retreat by the IESG to discuss the proposals with the IPng Area Director in May 1994; the process as a whole was documented in RFC 1752, "The Recommendation for the IP Next Generation Protocol." Eventually this was approved, consensus was achieved, and it was made a Proposed Standard in November 1994, to be followed by finalized versions in 1995.

Contenders for the throne

Let's now take a quick look at some of the contestants paraded during the selection process. It is often said that the thing the IETF does best is devising acronyms, and the contenders for IPng were no exception.

TUBA (TCP, UDP with Bigger Addresses or TCP/UDP over CLNP Addressed Networks)
    TUBA left the transport layer (TCP and UDP) essentially unchanged, but replaced IP with CLNP. The transition strategies planned to allow the move

---

* CLNP, or the ConnectionLess Network Protocol is the approximate equivalent of IP in the ISO networking stack.

† RFC 1347 describes how it was envisaged this would operate.

from IPv4 to TUBA were very similar to the strategies used in IPv6 today: dual-stack, no flag day, et cetera. Initially, the protocol was attractive because of the notion that there could be a final convergence between the OSI networking holdouts and the Internet. However, there wasn't any attention paid to correcting the deficiencies of CLNP, or in particular, the *right* of the IETF to correct these deficiencies within the context of the IPng effort.

CATNIP (Common Architecture for the Internet)

An interesting attempt to merge the three most important networking protocols of the day, namely IP, the OSI ISO protocols, and the Novell networking stack (IPX and friends). It decoupled the transport from the other layers such that it was theoretically possible for an end host using IPv4 to communicate transparently via TCP (or other arbitrary transport protocol) to an end host using IPX.

The unification of these protocols was CATNIP's central aim. It was a relevant idea for the time, but in view of the almost complete domination of IP everywhere today, it is much less relevant now. Other aspects, such as transition mechanisms and mobility, were not so well specified, so CATNIP ultimately floundered on too much complexity.

SIPP (Simple Internet Protocol Plus)

SIPP was the merging of two earlier suggested protocols: Steve Deering's SIP and Paul Francis's PIP, with 64 bits for addresses by default. It had also adopted parts of other proposed protocols, such as IP-in-IP.

SIPP was well documented, but the transition plan had problems and the addresses were thought to be too small. Routing was also felt to be insufficiently reworked, a concern that still persists today.

In the end the decision was to use SIPP as the basis of the next version of IP, but with some changes, including widening the address space to 128 bits.

Why 128 Bits?

There are many occasions in computer science and networking where the fixed-but-fast philosophy has warred with the flexible-but-slow; it is, in a very particular sense, a religious (and hence timeless) debate. In this particular case, 128 bits came about because the IPng directorate decided that a length of 64 bits (the size in the original SIP[P] proposals) was too small, but the proposed mechanism for extending it, to wit, arbitrary chained headers providing arbitrary length addresses (!) was too complicated. So 128 bits was the compromise that was made.

People

We'll stop for a moment to mention some of the people you may hear mentioned in relation to IPv6. Naturally, if we were to mention every name this would be a very long section.

Probably the most influential person in the IPv6 community, although he would probably be the first to engage in self-deprecation, is Steve Deering, a Cisco fellow. He, together with Bob Hinden and Margaret Wasserman were co-chairs at the time we started working on this book. However, in October 2002 Steve took sabbatical leave. The v6ops Working Group has been chaired by Jun-ichiro itojun Hagino, Bob Fink, Margaret Wasserman, Jonne Soininen, and Pekka Savola, to name a few. Some of these characters, such as Itojun* and Margaret have been members of the IESG and/or IAB.

Christian Huitema is a former member of the IAB and has worked in an impressive variety of places (e.g., INRIA, Bellcore, and Microsoft). We've already mentioned his book on the IPv6 protocol. He's not the only member of the IAB to have taken a special interest in IPv6 though, others include Tony Hain, Robert Elz, Jun Murai, Brian Carpenter, and so on.

Many others have also contributed—just look at the names of RFC authors for a small, small subset of those engaged in the overall IPv6 project.

Adoption

Adoption of any new protocol is a multiple stage process. First, it has to be designed! This in itself is often a protracted process,† requiring standards committees or IETF standardization efforts to converge on a stable definition. Then the entire specification, or enough of it to usefully implement, has to be written down and expressed clearly enough that the various manufacturers can write the code they need to and put it in their hardware. In the case of IPv6, the policies and addressing models also have to be defined and be operating before adoption can commence. Finally, of course, people have to begin *using* it.

IPv6 has only recently emerged into the final stage of the process described above, so, unsurprisingly, in comparison to IPv4, adoption is currently low, but it is growing and accelerating. Let's look at some of the reasons for this growth.

The adoption of IPv6 was given a major boost in May 2000 with the acceptance by the 3GPP of a Nokia proposal to use it within certain portions of 3G networks. Specifically, it is required to be used within the IMS portion of the core network—essentially

---

* Itojun is also part of the KAME development team.

† Though hopefully not infinitely prolonged...

the component that provides applications and higher-level infrastructural services for handsets. (You can read more about this in Chapter 9.) This, combined with a re-engineering of IPv6 address allocation policies worldwide* has fixed two of the most problematic issues preventing adoption. First, the issue of having no confidence in a new protocol, easily solved when a major body steps up to endorse it. Second, the old, Byzantine and unfriendly address request process. Thankfully, since these impediments have been removed, things have been growing rapidly, fuelled by (for example) the announcement of Japanese government, as part of the "e-Japan" project, setting a deadline of 2005 to have Internet infrastructure and technology running on IPv6, a mandate which is expected to further stimulate network upgrades and application development, already making steady progress in Japan. There is even tax relief available for IPv6 deployment in Japan! We can only hope this progressive attitude will be repeated elsewhere.

Imagine What You Can Do!

The shortage of IPv4 addresses around Asia has meant that Asian countries are at a more advanced stage of IPv6 deployment than many other parts of the world. For example, one Japanese project made taxis IPv6 capable so that they could report their location and speed automatically and feed this information back to base. This allows other taxis to avoid traffic jams and so forth.

There is a rumor in circulation that when one Japanese electronics company decided to begin incorporating IPv6 into its forthcoming products it was so eager that it asked why Japan was being so slow to adopt IPv6! Where this leaves the rest of us, we're not quite sure.

Even more recently, the US Department of Defence announced that it would only buy IPv6 capable technology from October 2003, aiming for full IPv6 implementation by 2008. Their reasoning is simple: to be ready for IPv6 in 2008 they need to make sure that equipment and projects that start now and operate for several years will be IPv6 capable when they come to fruition. The huge spending power available to the US DoD can only further help IPv6.

Commercial Services

You know that a technology is becoming viable when someone tries to make money out of it. Accordingly, we'd like to highlight some of the companies out there who are attempting to sell this bundle of joy. This is of course a non-exhaustive list, and

---

* Up until recently, one of the most badly crafted bits of IPv6.

you might be surprised to find your favorite ISP is already in a position to offer you paid service!

NTT/Verio

NTT launched their commercial IPv6 service in Japan in April 2001, in Europe in February 2003 and in the U.S. around the end of 2003. They offer services to ISPs and also provide web hosting.

XS4all.nl

The well-known Dutch ISP XS4all has been offering its DSL customers IPv6 tunnels for some time.

IXPs

IXPs (Internet Exchange Points) worldwide are offering IPv6 services including AMS-IX, LINX, and LAIIX. There are also some IPv6 specific exchange points, such as UK6x.

Hexago

Hexago is a French-Canadian company specializing in IPv6 migration.

Abilene

Abilene, the research-only network in the United States, exchanges native IPv6 traffic with research networks worldwide, including KREOnet2 in Korea, SURF-net in The Netherlands and HEAnet in Ireland.

GÉANT

The pan-European research network has essentially completed the rolling out of native IPv6 support.

Microsoft

Microsoft's *three degrees* is a piece of groupware allowing friends and family to share files, music, photos and so on. As three degrees is a peer-to-peer technology, Microsoft have decided that it is best to base it on IPv6. While it is a free piece of software available from *http://www.threedegrees.com/*, it is easy to see the value in the software.

Internet2

Don't confuse IPv6 and Internet2. Internet2 is a US based consortium led by Universities looking at new networking technology and applications. IPv6 is a networking protocol designed to be the successor of the current versions of IP, IPv4. In fact, IPv6 is one of the new networking technologies used by Internet2 in its backbone network Abilene.

While we are at it, we should also mention the 6bone, which was the original test network for IPv6 formed by connecting IPv6 users via network tunnels. Now that there's a live IPv6 Internet the 6bone is connected to, the 6bone tunnels are gradually being phased out.

Conventions Used in This Book

The following typographical conventions are used in this book:

Plain text

> Indicates menu titles, menu options, menu buttons, and keyboard accelerators (such as Alt and Ctrl).

Italic

> Indicates new terms, URLs, email addresses, filenames, file extensions, path-names, directories, and Unix utilities.

`Constant width`

> Indicates commands, options, switches, variables, attributes, keys, functions, types, classes, namespaces, methods, modules, properties, parameters, values, objects, events, event handlers, XML tags, HTML tags, macros, the contents of files, or the output from commands.

`Constant width bold`

> Shows commands or other text that should be typed literally by the user.

`Constant width italic`

> Shows text that should be replaced with user-supplied values.

 This icon signifies a tip, suggestion, or general note.

 This icon indicates a warning or caution.

In some parts of this book we show the changes to a configuration file or C code in *unified diff* format. In this format, only the sections of the file that changed are shown. Lines that are prefixed with a '-' have been removed, and lines that have are prefixed with a '+' have been added. Each section is introduced by a line starting '@@'; this shows the line numbers in the new and old version of the file.

For configuration file or command examples where you encounter italicized text, it means "insert the appropriate value for your site here."

Using Code Examples

This book is here to help you get your job done. In general, you may use the code in this book in your programs and documentation. You do not need to contact us for permission unless you're reproducing a significant portion of the code. For example, writing a program that uses several chunks of code from this book does not require

---

permission. Selling or distributing a CD-ROM of examples from O'Reilly books *does* require permission. Answering a question by citing this book and quoting example code does not require permission. Incorporating a significant amount of example code from this book into your product's documentation *does* require permission.

We appreciate, but do not require, attribution. An attribution usually includes the title, author, publisher, and ISBN. For example: "*IPv6 Network Administration*, by Niall Richard Murphy and David Malone. Copyright 2005 O'Reilly Media, Inc., 0-596-00934-8."

If you feel your use of code examples falls outside fair use or the permission given above, feel free to contact us at *permissions@oreilly.com*.

Comments and Questions

Please address comments and questions concerning this book to the publisher:

> O'Reilly Media, Inc.
> 1005 Gravenstein Highway North
> Sebastopol, CA 95472
> (800) 998-9938 (in the United States or Canada)
> (707) 829-0515 (international or local)
> (707) 829-0104 (fax)

We have a web page for this book, where we list errata, examples, and any additional information. You can access this page at:

> *http://www.oreilly.com/catalog/ipv6na*

To comment or ask technical questions about this book, send email to:

> *bookquestions@oreilly.com*

For more information about our books, conferences, Resource Centers, and the O'Reilly Network, see our web site at:

> *http://www.oreilly.com*

The authors also have a companion web site for the book, where updates, articles, and tips and tricks can be found. It's at *http://www.deployingipv6.net*.

Safari Enabled

 When you see a Safari® Enabled icon on the back cover of your favorite technology book, that means the book is available online through the O'Reilly Network Safari Bookshelf.

Safari offers a solution that's better than e-books. It's a virtual library that lets you easily search thousands of top tech books, cut and paste code samples, download chapters, and find quick answers when you need the most accurate, current information. Try it for free at *http://safari.oreilly.com*.

Contacting the Authors

You can contact the authors at by email via *authors@deployingipv6.net*, or via the web site *http://www.deployingipv6.net/*, if you have any comments or notice errors. We welcome feedback.

A Note on RFCs and Internet Drafts

In many sections of the text we refer to documents known as Internet Drafts and RFCs. In general, if we refer to RFC 2545, then it can be found at *http://www.ietf.org/rfc/rfc2545.txt*. There's also an overall index of all RFC documents available at *http://www.ietf.org/rfc/rfc-index.txt*. You can use this to check if an RFC has been updated by a more recent document.

Internet Drafts are living documents and may or may not become RFCs at the end of their lives as drafts. A draft will usually have a name like *http://www.ietf.org/internet-drafts/draft-ietf-ipv6-flow-label-07.txt*. The digits "07" at the end the end of the draft name is the current version of the draft, and this could be incremented at any time. If we refer you to a draft which is no longer available at the location we specify, try increasing the version number to find the current version of the draft. Sometimes, if a draft is abandoned entirely, it may become unavailable on the IETF site. If you are still interested in such a draft then your best hope is to pop its name into your favorite search engine.

Acknowledgments

Books don't happen without quite a lot of help. We've lots of people to thank, but we should single out Mike Loukides from O'Reilly, who helped to make this a reality, followed by everyone at our publisher.

Contributors

We'd like to thank Robert H Zakon for reference to his Internet Timeline, at *http://www.zakon.org/robert/internet/timeline/*. We'd also like to thank David Wilson of HEAnet Ireland for significant contributions to the routing-relevant sections of this book. Go, Dave! HEAnet and the Dublin Institute for Advanced Studies also provided us with access to hardware and people. Ken Duffy managed to resist the temptation to edit our manuscript, and we can only admire his restraint.

Various others contributed comments, corrections or clarifications to this book. In no particular order, we'd like to thank John Walsh, Colm MacCárthaigh, Sharon Murphy, Wayne Sullivan, Glynn Foster, Juliana Breithaupt, Ian Dowse, Niall Brady, Orla McGann, Christine Hogan, Willie O'Connor, Ross Chandler, Jennie O'Farrell, Tadhg O'Higgins, Gary Coady, Eoin Lawless, Sharon Jackson, Mike Norris, Leo Vegoda, John Nisbet, Susan Quinn, Alex French, Jennifer Alexander, Peta Spies, Eoin Kenny, Phil Bradley, Peter Bieringer, John Tobin, Ruadhri Power, Ronan Kelly, and Pekka Savola.

Support

The authors would like to acknowledge the support of their respective organizations, without which pens would never have been lifted in anger. (That was, of course, a figure of speech: no pens were harmed during the making of this book.)

David would like to thank the Communication Networks Research Institute for its support, Niall for having the enthusiasm to get this book off the ground, Sharon for advice on book writing, Trinity College Dublin for being his primary IPv6 guinea pig and all those who have offered us advice, corrections and suggestions.

Niall would like to thank Léan, for believing in him when he did not, and Dave Wilson, for inviting him in. Kate Murphy and the Gray family provided welcome familial support, and tribute is due to his friends and the technical community in Ireland for rallying around and helping so generously.

Donations

We'd like to thank HEAnet for their kind loan of a 26xx and the facilities of their test lab for us to crash during the preparation of this book. We'd also like to thank EsatBT and Eircom, local Irish ISPs, for implementing IPv6 support for their customers sufficiently well that we could use it, also during the preparation of the book.

PART I
The Character of IPv6

## CHAPTER 1

The Unforeseen Limitations of IPv4

Those who cannot remember the past
are condemned to repeat it.
—*George Santayana*

So—if you were sitting down to design what was to become the most popular networking protocol in the world, what would *you* do?

Well, if you're anything like us, you probably still feel a chill on cold nights when you remember the more exciting times you've had debugging weird problems with IPv4. Consequently, we'd guess you'd try to create a protocol that, whatever other deficiencies it had, definitely *didn't* have the problems that kept you up until 3 a.m. last Saturday. The designers of IPv6 have done their best to address the well-known limitations of IPv4, while avoiding introducing new ways to keep you awake at night.

That's what this chapter is: an attempt to distill some of the more notable (some might say, broken) characteristics of IPv4, pointing out the motivations thereby deriving that drove the design of IPv6. Some of you might find this material familiar enough to skip; we don't mind. Others might find a refresher useful, or would like to know what tack we take on their favorite issue. For those and others, please read on.

Addressing Model

An IPv4 address is 32 bits long. They are usually written in *dotted quad* form, a.b.c.d where each of a, b, c and d are decimal numbers in the range 0–255. So the addresses range from 0.0.0.0 to 255.255.255.255. This means that there is an upper limit of 4,294,967,296, or about 4 billion, addresses. Since the address is, in truth, just a number, people sometimes refer to IPv4 addresses as IP numbers.

The whole space was originally split into fixed chunks, called *classes*, that had particular meanings. Class A, B and C networks are the best known divisions of the range. A single class A address had 8 bits of network and 24 bits of host addresses, a class B address had 16 bits of network and 16 bits of host address and a class C address had

24 bits of network address. You knew what class of network you were looking at by what range that address fell into. (Table 1-1 shows these ranges.) As it turned out, doing classful allocation was horribly inefficient, and led to the development of a better way of doing network boundaries, called CIDR, which we discuss below.

Table 1-1. IPv4 traditional address ranges

Class	Range	Netmask/Comment
A	0.0.0.0 – 127.255.255.255	255.0.0.0
B	128.0.0.0 – 191.255.255.255	255.255.0.0
C	192.0.0.0 – 223.255.255.255	255.255.255.0
D	224.0.0.0 – 239.255.255.255	Multicast
F	240.0.0.0 – 255.255.255.255	Future use

As can be seen from Table 1-1, a range of addresses was later set aside for multicast. For a variety of reasons, multicast in the IPv4 world has remained a rather fringe activity, as we discuss in the "Broadcast Versus Multicast" section later in this chapter.

In each of the A, B, and C ranges, a certain address space was set aside as "private" address space, to be used by those who wanted to use IP networking but wouldn't need their hosts to be publicly addressable by the Internet. These are the well-known ranges 10.0.0.0–10.255.255.255, 172.16.0.0–172.31.255.255 and 192.168.0.0–192.168.255.255, currently described in RFC 1918. Note that these aren't the only ranges of IPv4 addresses reserved for special purposes; RFC 3330 gives a summary of the special use blocks.

IPv4 allows for broadcasts, and there was initially some confusion about what address within a range should be used to symbolize the broadcast address. Some implementors used the first address (all 0s for the host part) and others used the last address (all 1s). The standard practice is now to use the all ones address, and the all zeros address is considered to be reserved as the network's address.

CIDR

Classless Inter-Domain Routing (CIDR) was a break from the notion that you could determine the network size by knowing it was class A, B or C. It's central idea was to do away with separating network and host parts of an address on byte (8-bit) boundaries only.

With CIDR, the boundary between network and hosts can fall on any of the bits of the address, and networks can be described by the all-zeros network address followed by the number of bits in the host part. For example, the old 10.0.0.0 class A network would be written 10.0.0.0/8, where 8 refers to the number of bits in the network part of the address. The class C network 192.168.1.0, which previously was the smallest network that could be allocated, could be now be subdivided. For example, it could be split into 4 networks: 192.168.1.0/26, 192.168.1.64/26, 192.168.1.128/26 and 192.168.1.192/26. The number on the right can range from 32, meaning a single host, to 0, meaning every possible host, or "match everything." The important thing to note is that every decrement of this number doubles the size of the relevant network. For example, 10.0.0.0/23 is twice as big as 10.0.0.0/24, and contains it! This is an important idea. It means that a collection of multiple networks can often be represented by a single CIDR block instead of an explicit list of candidate networks. This means multiple adjacent networks can be *aggregated* into a single CIDR block, allowing more efficient description in routing protocols, access lists and the like.

With CIDR the smallest normal network that can be allocated is a /30, because the all zeros and all ones addresses are reserved and you need to have space for at least one host. This means that for the network associated with a point-to-point link, 4 IPv4 addresses are usually consumed. (RFC 3021 discusses how /31 networks work, but this requires that the devices at both ends of link support it.)

CIDR addressed several problems. First, it allowed smaller allocations of IP addresses, slowing the rate at which IPv4 addresses were consumed. Second, it allowed routing tables to be more compact as routes to several adjacently numbered networks could be merged into a single representation. Aggregation, as this is called, is an extremely powerful technique for making routing more efficient. Indeed, on backbone networks where default routes are not available,* it is aggregation that makes routing possible at all.

CIDR has been quite successful in preventing classful IPv4 from exploding at the seams, but isn't perfectly efficient, and is in essence a delaying tactic. Its guiding principle, assignment of network and host boundaries within an address, is accommodated within IPv6 already.†

We'll see that in IPv6 there are different ways to address "all hosts on a subnet." Consequently, there's no necessity to waste space in every allocation on addresses with special meanings, as is done in IPv4.

NAT

Network Address Translation (NAT) is a technique that has arisen in response to the shortage of globally routable IPv4 addresses. It allows a single IP address to provide connectivity for a large number of hosts. The usual deployment of NAT involves a network of hosts using one of the private address ranges mentioned in the "Addressing Model" section earlier in this chapter, routing traffic to a gateway or proxy with a private IP address on the inside of the network, and a real IP address on the outside

---

* Often called "the default-free zone."

† IPv6 has a boundary at 64 bits between the network part of the address and the host part.

facing the Internet. For outgoing traffic, this gateway replaces the private IP address with its public IP address and uses port numbers to remember the private IP address to which replies should be directed.

For incoming traffic, the gateway looks up the port numbers in a table, the original private IP address is determined and the packet is forwarded to the host in the private network. The details of traditional NAT are discussed in RFC 3022.

Because of the economics of IPv4 addresses, NAT has proven extremely popular with small businesses and home users. While one cannot strictly speaking *sell* IP addresses, ISPs commonly attach a charge for routing and other services to make these addresses useful. This cost is often prohibitive for many users of the SOHO persuasion. NAT has provided a way to connect an entire office to the Internet using a single, cheap dialup connection – it might even be cheerful if you're lucky.

NAT has also been used* by some organizations as a form of protection against having to change the addresses of their network. This *renumbering* of a network might be required because of a change of ISP, or because the organization was using IP addresses unsuitable for use on the general Internet. Renumbering in the IPv4 world is quite a tricky process and the use of private addresses has actually made renumbering *more* common, as distinct groups can, and often will be using the same private address range, creating problems if they merge. As we will see later, IPv6 goes to some effort to make renumbering less painful.

NAT is a mixed blessing. It has certainly reduced the demand for IPv4 addresses. However, certain protocols cannot operate over NAT without special treatment, particularly those ones that embed addresses of endpoints within the protocol; the canonical example of this being FTP, and another important one being IPsec, of which more later.

NAT is also a more complex and CPU-intensive operation than simply forwarding traffic. Even in the post-dot-com days, the growth of Internet traffic is outstripping the increase in CPU speeds, and so the cost of performing NAT at high speeds is greater than the cost of a faster (but dumber) router. A network reliant on NAT may find that its growth is limited, not by the cost of network capacity, but by the cost of the NAT device.

NAT also hinders hosts on the Internet making incoming connections to hosts in the private network, as there is no easy way to create suitable state on the gateway to allow this. Some consider this a feature, as it acts as a simple form of stateful firewalling. Others consider it a violation of the *end-to-end* principle of the Internet—the idea that any host should be able to talk to any other host. This end-to-end principle has been important in the creation of new applications on the Internet, so the general view is that NAT is currently a useful and necessary evil in the IPv4 world.

---

* A third use of NAT is for load-balancing; we consider this beyond the scope of this book.

Security

IPv4 was designed with a network of relatively trusted users in mind where the network infrastructure was likely to be relatively secure and the information that was being transmitted was relatively public. Consequently, it did not seem important at the time to include security features, like non-repudiation or authentication, directly into the protocol.

But over its lifetime, the way the IPv4 Internet has been used has changed radically. The huge number of users of the Internet mean that trusting them all is simply not an option. The network infrastructure itself now involves cooperation between a large number of public and private organizations, with wildly differing agendas. Most significantly, the data that is being transmitted on the Internet now is often commercially, financially or personally sensitive. From a security perspective, IPv4 is way out of its depth.

As a consequence of its origin, security in the IPv4 world has not been provided by the basic, underlying transport protocol. Instead, as the need has arisen, application level security (one time passwords, SSH, TSIG, etc.) or manipulation of the protocols (packet filters and firewalls) have been introduced to provide security. These solutions have often had an ad-hoc character, and have suffered the attendant limitations: different management schemes, different levels of security provided, and duplicated effort. SSL, the most successful of these compromises, has been designed in such a way that it can be applied in situations other than HTTP, for which it was originally devised.[*]

We'll briefly consider the implications of security not being provided by IPv4 itself—particularly in the case of DNS—but the same issues apply to most IP-based protocols, and protocols underlying IP, such as ARP (see the "MAC Layer Address Resolution" section later in this chapter).

DNS

From a security perspective, the gods have not smiled on DNS over IPv4. Most queries are conducted over UDP. The UDP protocol, while being lightweight and kind to small CPUs, is easily tampered with. The protocol fields can be guessed in many cases, and where they can't, it's possible to use a flooding technique to populate the wire with candidate packets, one of which may be mistaken for the real one. DNS itself has a few additional protections, but they do not amount to much. To fake a response to a DNS request you must correctly guess an ephemeral port number and a query-ID. In the case of DNS the port numbers are often easy to determine and some DNS implementations produce guessable query-IDs.

---

[*] This light re-working of SSL is called TLS.

If you can fake DNS responses,* it is then possible to direct people to the wrong host. If a convincing enough fake of some e-commerce site has been put up on an attacker-controlled web page, passwords or credit card numbers might then be stolen very easily. In the case of the web, some protection is possible if you are using SSL, but if a mail server were impersonated for example, few would notice that email had gone to the wrong destination until it was too late.

Layers of Networks

Networks are often thought of as being layered, where complex services are built up based on protocols stacked on top of each other. The canonical model that is dragged out to explain this is the 7-layer OSI model, shown in Table 1-2. This model is used to classify and analyze network protocols. As is the case with IP, there may not be a clean mapping from each of the seven layers to a specific protocol.

From this model, a few phrases have become common. We will often mention link-layer, layer 2 or MAC addressing—this is the low level addressing that allows IP to be carried over Ethernet, token rings, firewire and similar technology. We will mention layer 3, which is the level of IP packets. This is really where the big changes between IPv4 and IPv6 lie; the upper layers are largely unchanged.

Some people have extended the 7-layer model to a 9-layer model, which includes Layer 8, money, and Layer 9, politics. We would like to be able to tell you that IPv6 solves problems in these areas too, but IPv6's contribution to Layer 9 has so far been limited to making IPsec mandatory.

Table 1-2. 7 Layer OSI model

Layer	Name	Description	Example
7	Application	Applications and associated protocols	HTTP
6	Presentation	Data syntax and semantics	XDR
5	Session	Session management for applications	
4	Transport	Packetization, retransmission, ...	TCP
3	Network	How subnets interoperate	IP
2	Data Link	Management of interface	Ethernet (upper level)
1	Physical	Physical operation of the medium	Ethernet over UTP

* Doug Song's dsniff tools are designed to demonstrate some of the DNS and ARP vulnerabilities we talk about in this chapter. More information about dsniff can be found at *http://naughty.monkey.org/~dugsong/dsniff/*.

MAC Layer Address Resolution

IPv4 Ethernet networks require a mechanism for nodes to find out which link-layer addresses correspond to which layer three addresses. In other words, how does a machine locate the link-layer address for a given IP address that is on your network? In the vast majority of conventional networks today, this is done using a protocol called ARP, defined in RFC 826.

The protocol works as follows: hosts maintain a table of the link-layer addresses corresponding to IPv4 addresses. When a packet needs to be transmitted, the host checks this table and uses the link-layer address, if it is present. If not, the host broadcasts an ARP request message saying, "Here are my IP and link-layer addresses, who knows the link-layer address for X?" The target host is expected to construct a reply and send it to the requester. Note that the ARP request is a broadcast and contains the information needed to form a table entry for the requesting host. Crucially, this allows the reply to be sent without issuing any further ARP requests.

Although ARP works very well when no-one is fiddling with it, it has a number of key deficiencies when it comes to security. First, when you receive an ARP reply, there is *no* guarantee that it has actually come from the correct system. Anyone who is on the same medium can fake this reply if desired, and there is nothing that can easily prevent this. Sophisticated attackers, having targeted a key machine, can perform a DoS attack or otherwise disrupt the network interface of that machine. They then can bring up a virtual address or alias on another machine, and ARP will take care of the rest, redirecting new connections to the replacement machine. (This kind of attack is often referred to as *ARP poisoning*.) If the attackers have replaced key infrastructure servers like DNS or proxy servers it's entirely possible they can begin to use this foothold to obtain more authentication "tokens," whether they be usernames, passwords or off-site accounts.

Second, on most systems, it is possible to specify the mapping from IP address to MAC address in a configuration file, allowing you to hardwire addresses in the ARP table. Although this allows you to mitigate the effects of ARP poisoning, this is a very inflexible configuration, and will eventually cause problems when someone forgets that the old MAC address has been hardcoded into many arbitrary systems within their network. We can't recommend it as a technique in large networks.

Although this is a problem which isn't easy to fix, it's rarely encountered in networks which are under the one administrative control (unlike, say, web site hosting networks) and we therefore note in passing that IPv6 considerably improves on the basic host-to-address mapping mechanism.

Broadcast Versus Multicast

Another feature of ARP is that it is a broadcast protocol, which means its transactions are heard network-wide. Every time a host receives a broadcast, it must process the packet, even if, as must be the case in sufficiently large networks, the packet has nothing to do with the host. This can add up to phenomenal amounts of traffic on (badly-designed) flat networks. (There are urban legends floating around of a network on which it is impossible to plug in machines of below a certain specification, because they do not have the processing power to deal with the volume of ARP and other broadcast packets. If you find such a network, let us know.)

Multicast is an entirely more sensible way to hold multiway conversations. Multicast allows you to address a group of hosts interested in a particular type of network traffic without disturbing uninterested bystanders. The section "Multicast" in Chapter 3 talks more about IPv6 multicast.

Unfortunately multicast never really took off on IPv4 networks. There are a variety of likely reasons for this: it's not enabled by default, it takes significant work to configure and most of the target applications for multicast involve cooperation across multiple administrations. This is a pity, as multicast is useful and well-designed.

Quality of Service

Quality of service (QoS) refers to the ability to give guarantees that the network traffic you send gets there on time (there's a longer discussion of QoS in the section "Quality of Service" in Chapter 3). One of the earliest approaches to guaranteeing a certain level of QoS in IPv4 networks was a field called "Type of Service" in the IP header. This field is included in the RFC 791 definition of IP, and clarified further in RFC 1349. In this model, the IPv4 header itself contains fields that are set to particular values depending on what kind of treatment the packets "want" from routers; the idea being that packets proclaiming themselves to be worthy of immediate forwarding will be plucked out of queues by routers and preferentially dealt with. Unfortunately this was a rather crude approach, not widely implemented, and in its first revision died a death. Perhaps the two biggest problems with it were that it provided no mechanism for authenticating the request for a particular QoS, and that there was no flexible way to assign priorities within a particular set of flows, such that certain ones could be designated *lower* priority. In essence, we have the rather contradictory result that a mechanism introduced to allow for more appropriate and fairer treatment of packets leads to unfairness!

There have been various efforts to retrofit more complete QoS features to IPv4, especially now that some people consider IP networks 'mission critical' and others want to run their telephones over their IP infrastructure. There has been a significant amount of work designing frameworks such as DiffServ (RFC 2475, …) and IntServ

(RFC 1633, ...), and protocols such as RSVP (RFC 2205, ...) to deal with QoS. It's unclear whether we will ever see wide ranging public deployment of these mechanisms, as they require significant cooperation between networks. Some potential adopters discover that, rather than invest time and equipment into deciding which packets to drop, it is cheaper to buy more bandwidth so that all the traffic gets through! There is no question, however, that a well-implemented mechanism to offer QoS guarantees would be of immense value to IP users in the future. This is what IPv6 attempts to provide the infrastructure for; only time will tell if it succeeds.

Routing

Of all the sections we cover here, this is probably the one where IPv4 has survived best. It is certainly true to say that the routing infrastructure of the Internet has scaled beyond anyone's original expectations, and it continues to work quite well, with only the occasional continent-sized hiccup.

Internal Routing Protocols

Dynamic routing, after all, is what sets IP apart from its circuit-switched cousins in the telco world. Within an administrative domain (an organization, campus, or any entity that has control over a "single" network) there are a few options available when the time comes to deploy a routing protocol.

Until the mid-1990s, the no-brain choice for internal routing was RIP. Its main attraction? It was, and it remains, extremely easy to configure. It's still out there, and not just in legacy installations, but the list of factors that make it less than optimal for use on the Internet at large has grown over time. For one, RIP was designed for a classful world. This is the reason most frequently trotted out by rabid anti-RIP fanatics like, well, us, but it's also the least convincing—classless routing was retrofitted, along with a bunch of other stuff, into RIPv2.*

Much as we would like to dispense with it, RIP is still around in the IPv6 world, and we deal with it in more detail in the "Routing" section in Chapter 3 and the "Routing Protocols" section in Chapter 6. Thankfully, there are much better internal routing protocols available these days†—ones which do not limit the growth or management capabilities of your network quite so much. Apart from mentioning that IPv6 has been defined for these protocols also, we don't need to talk about it in any more detail until Chapter 3. As much as we might wish them to, however, neither RIP nor its link-state cousins will scale to encompass the wider Internet.

---

* The current definition of RIPv2 is RFC 2453.
† OSPF and IS-IS being two examples.

BGP: The External Routing Protocol

BGP is the protocol that is used to route between large networks on the Internet. It works (for complex values of works) by communicating information about who can reach which CIDR prefixes (in essence, which addresses) via which networks.[*]

The key to BGP is summarization. Our networks are complex, intricate things *internally*, but when we have a limited number of ways in and out, it's natural to represent our network as a single entity. This is precisely what happens—each network is assigned an Autonomous System (AS) Number. All the blocks of IP addresses within the network are advertised as belonging to that AS. Each network may then exercise a large degree of control over the routes it sends to and receives from its peers; filtering unwelcome routes, tuning their preferences, even to some extent changing their "distance" from each other.

This, then, is perhaps why IPv4 has scaled so well, and it is no coincidence that the routing protocols are the one part of the Internet architecture that has survived mostly intact in the switch to IPv6. Of course they have their weaknesses, and everyone has a theory on how these may be fixed in conjunction with IPv6, but this is largely a separate exercise. At the moment the focus is on making IPv6 routing work "right" and in time people will move on to making it work better.

Limits to Success of BGP

Sadly, there is one critical problem that IPv4 and BGP are in fact contributing *to*, by their very nature. This is the problem of routing table growth, and in particular the growth of multihomed, nontransit end sites.

Under the current routing model, these end-sites have a choice: they can get provider-independent address space and a new Autonomous System number,[†] or they can get provider-aggregable address space. Provider Independent (PI) address space is assigned to the end organization and does not change if the organization changes ISP. Provider Aggregate (PA) space is drawn from a group of addresses belonging to the ISP.

Unsurprisingly, many larger organizations try to get PI space, if they can possibly get away with it. There are many motivations for this. Perhaps the most powerful is that renumbering is not necessary if their ISP changes. This does not come without its cost, and that cost is another entry in the global routing table, which really should not be necessary for nontransit end sites.[‡] After all, they're not actually routing any traffic for other people, they're just reachable via two (or more) paths.

---

[*] The details of BGP are complicated, if you need more details you should consult a book such as Iljitsch van Beijnum's *BGP: Building Reliable Networks with the Border Gateway Protocol* (O'Reilly).

[†] You can get an AS number moderately easily if you connect to multiple sites. See Chapter 4 for more details.

[‡] A nontransit site is a site that only carries traffic for itself. See the Glossary for a slightly longer definition of transit.

An absolutely key goal of IPv6 is to allow as much aggregation as possible. To this end the restrictions surrounding who can have entries are much more demanding. It is hoped that IPv6's provision for easy renumbering will remove much of potential pain associated with provider aggregatespace. Multi-homed sites will usually just assign one address *per provider* to their hosts. We'll talk more about this in Chapter 4.

Summary

IPv4 has problems. Some of them can be worked around, some not; but as time goes on, new applications will pile increasing amounts of cruft on top of the venerable protocol, making a new start even more attractive. We've outlined some of the ways in which IPv4 has been overstretched, primarily in the security and traffic management arenas, and next we will cover the things that IPv4 has done well.

## CHAPTER 2

The (Un)foreseen Successes of IPv4

If we want things to stay as they are,
things will have to change.
—Il Gattopardo, Giuseppe Tomasi di Lampedusa

Before we talk about how well-designed IPv6 (and how it fixes all the broken things in IPv4, honest!) it's worth pausing for a little bit to understand exactly what we can learn from the more successful elements of IPv4. These elements have informed and guided the design of IPv6, so it's worth examining in detail both the principles behind the design decisions, and the results of them. In many ways, the design of IPv6 can be said to have started when IPv4 was first created; so it, and we, will be beneficiaries of the hard work done and the lessons learned from over 20 years of deployment.

Simplicity

This first element is the most important consideration, and also quite a strange one. Initially you might think that simplicity was quite a philosophical or aesthetic principle, with no practical implications. Perhaps surprisingly, the opposite is actually the case; the desire for simplicity springs not solely from the human desire to create the elegant or the beautiful, but rather from sound engineering principles. The simpler a thing is, the easier it is to understand, the easier to control, the faster to operate, and the simpler to build upon. Put this way, simplicity in protocol design seems like such an obvious criterion, it's difficult to see who could argue for the opposite.*

IPv4 itself was substantially simpler than its competition when it was created—that primarily being the somewhat top-heavy OSI protocols—although it did use some of the more abstract concepts behind OSI to advantage, in particular the notions of layering protocols, and abstracting transport from the particular way in which it happened

---

* Of course no one *argues* for the opposite. It is always just adding "one little bit more."

to be implemented (say, connectionless or connection based communication, for example.) There were also attempts to deal with anticipated problems like QoS with the ToS field; in this case, perhaps a case of being too simple for the job at hand.

IPv6 has a similarly simple basic design. It has dropped some features that were seldom used in IPv4 and added some simplifying features, such as *stateless address autoconfiguration*.* In some areas IPv6 has retained complexity though, such as mobile IP and IPsec. This complexity is probably unavoidable if we want to actually do something about the problems of mobility and security.

Resiliency

By resiliency, we mean two things.

First, consider an average network. At any given time, there may be various adverse conditions present. These conditions may be environmental, inherent or of some other form. Regardless of these, IPv4 can often continue to work. For example, network congestion, error-prone lines, memory overload, and so on, are all problems IPv4 has proven able to cope with.

Second, the specification for IPv4 is written in such a manner that it admits of "reasonably" coherent definition, and can be implemented in a finite amount of time, by a finite number of people, for a finite amount of money. Not all networking standards have had such felicitous specifications. It's a real testimony to the robustness of IPv4 that the stack has made it into an incredible array of computing equipment, and particularly into embedded systems, tiny machines with barely a single kilobyte to spare that somehow squeeze in a full IPv4 stack. Indeed, if IPv4 had an overly vague specification, the economics of embedded systems would have made it impossible to produce embedded devices supporting IPv4.†

Accordingly, in IPv6, we would like for the specification to be coherent, complete, and not contain any hidden "gotchas" that only emerge under unusual circumstances, such as heavy load or limited memory availability.

Scalability

IPv4 has scaled to support the whole Internet—surprising or self-evident as that statement may be, it is still a useful observation. IPv4 has definitely had growing pains, but the Internet operates remarkably well for a global network run by

---

* To be fair, IPv4 does have autoconfiguration mechanisms, as we mention in the section "Autoconfiguration" later in this chapter, but they are a bit of a post-facto affair.

† With embedded systems, you usually only get one chance to get something right. If the system contains an error, replacing it will frequently not be an option.

hundreds of thousands of organizations in cooperation. There are few things that work as well internationally.

Why might this be? The reasons for this are partially administrative and partially technical. From a technical perspective, we would have to highlight the distributed nature of DNS, the CIDR addressing architecture, followed by independence of the underlying hardware as important features that allowed the Internet to grow to its current size using IPv4.

Administratively, the fact that IPv4 networks can be run independently by organizations, with cooperation along the network's borders, means that the problem of a central administration becoming the bottleneck for growth is reduced. In fact, this has resulted in the Internet being divided into many distinct routing domains, called Autonomous Systems, and using BGP means that each network can avoid having to know the internal details of every other network.

Given the above, IPv6 should scale at least as well as IPv4—and in fact, there's every reason to believe it can do much better than IPv4.

Flexibility

One final point to note is that IPv4 has proved to be flexible, allowing it to accommodate solutions to problems as they arise. CIDR increased the yield of a given portion of address space, NAT reduced the demand on address space, and BGP evolved to accommodate the needs of the routing community. In one respect this is bad, as you could view these as hacks fixing problems in the original IPv4 design. On the other hand, future-proofing is almost impossible without flexibility, and this is something the design and deployment of IPv6 needs to account for.

Autoconfiguration

In the early days of IPv4, host (re)configuration was something that required the intervention of a skilled operator. Even in the early days of the Internet boom, end-users were required to enter IP addresses and other configuration details manually. However acceptable this might have been to early adopters at the time, automatic configuration was absolutely necessary in getting less technically savvy people online. Even today, *re*configuration of a host can be tricky if it has the same IP address for a long time, as an address can gradually appear in more and more configuration files, forgotten about until that crucial moment.

The two main protocols that perform this configuration, DHCP for corporate networks, and PPP for dialup, have played large parts in getting us to the Internet penetration levels we see today. DHCP helps to centralize IP configuration details for networks, making it possible for end-users to "plug-and-play" without having to ring the hapless network administrator to find out their DNS settings. PPP, and its cousins PPPoE and PPPoA, have relieved the consumer ISP's end users of almost any configuration work* beyond typing a username and password.

This is a particularly key element for deploying large networks and IPv6 aims to improve autoconfiguration even further—providing large networks with limited support staff should be possible with IPv6.

Extensibility

It is fair to say that the uses to which the Internet is put today were not foremost in the minds of the designers of IPv4. The open and simple nature of IPv4's design means that it has been possible to build applications such as remote-login, the Web and peer-to-peer file sharing without repeatedly returning to the drawing board. We mentioned before the notion of networking "layers," originating with the OSI 7-layer model described in Chapter 1, which is partially responsible for this, but it's a testimony to good engineering that there are so few hidden dependencies between levels. IPv6 also preserves this decoupling.

The simplicity of IPv4, discussed in the "Simplicity" section of this chapter, is almost certainly another reason why it has been extended and pushed in unusual directions. It works on the principle of giving people simple building blocks, which can be assembled in weird and wonderful ways.

In Short...

IPv4 is simple enough that people can understand and implement it. It is flexible and robust enough that it has been possible to apply it in areas it was not originally intended for, and change it without breaking everything. It has even become relatively easy for nontechnical users to configure. Hopefully, IPv6 has picked up these good qualities of its older sibling.

---

* Of course the PPP-based services have to be configured by ISP technical staff, but the end user doesn't generally get involved.

CHAPTER 3

Describing IPv6

Perfection, of a kind, was what he was after.
—*Epitaph on a Tyrant, W.H. Auden*

In this chapter we'll cover the features of IPv6 and the basics of its design. This will be a quick tour, addressing the topics of immediate relevance to those using or about to use IPv6. Our intention is to present the information in an easy-to-understand overview format first, and then to get down to the juicy details later in Chapters 4 and 6.

Designed for Today and Tomorrow

When we talk about networking protocols in general it's important to understand the difference between specification and implementation. Specifications are written in IETF RFCs and are hotly debated. Implementations are prepared to those specifications, generally by coders or systems people. If you had to choose which one of these to get right, it should of course be the specifications. Broken implementations that misbehave or don't interoperate can always be rewritten, or even gradually refined; but if your design is inherently broken, you might as well throw away all your work and start again. Since (at the time of writing) we are in a relatively early stage of adoption, we expect that implementation quality will vary across different stacks, but the design is definitely right. Lessons learned during the last few decades of networking have been incorporated into the architecture of the protocol, and so the existing problems with IPv4 have been addressed. In fact, some of the problems with IPv4 will only grow worse over time, and if IPv6 didn't take them into account, it might flounder even before IPv4 reaches the end of its life.

Perhaps the biggest and most important problem facing IPv4, which will only grow over time, is address space exhaustion.

Address Space Exhaustion

Address space is, with both IPv4 and IPv6, a finite resource. There are only so many addresses that can be allocated from any fixed range. Furthermore it's a hard limit, pending a change in the meaning of addresses as they are currently understood; one day, you will reach into your "address bag" to assign some new addresses, and there won't be any more there. Perhaps this won't be a problem for you immediately—who can say when you might need to grow your network—but it will certainly be a problem for the people you need to communicate with, so it thereby becomes everybody's problem.

So what's the scale of this risk? Well, prior to CIDR,* IPv4 address allocation, based on class A, B and C addresses, had been over-generous to some users, and address space allocation was running out of control. Today, allocation policies are much stricter, and address space is assigned more frugally. So, the end has not been deferred indefinitely, but the process is definitely under much better control. However, time is inevitably running out: only 36% of the total IPv4 address space remained in 2002, and, depending on whose extrapolations you believe, the remaining space runs out some time between 2005 and 2035. Recent measurements by Geoff Huston suggest that stricter policies have helped considerably, and we may be looking at the upper end of that range. However, even if IPv4 addresses remain available for the next 200 years, but obtaining them requires you to write longer and increasingly baroque essays on why you deserve them, that's little good to anyone.

Figure 3-1 shows the Internet Systems Consortium's host count. This count is based on DNS records, which gives data only loosely related to the actual number of live hosts,† but does grow proportionally to the amount of address space that has been allocated. We can see that even though growth stalled a little in the last few years, the clock is still ticking.

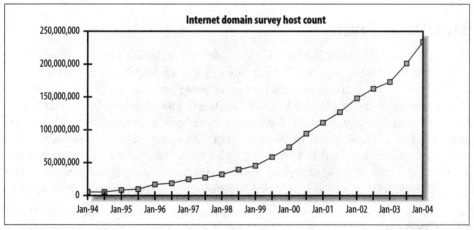

Figure 3-1. Internet Systems Consortium's host count (source: www.isc.org)

---

* CIDR is described in the "CIDR" section in Chapter 1.

† There are large numbers of hosts hidden behind NAT and it does not account for hosts without DNS records, of which there are a sizable number.

Optimization

Optimization in this context means two things. First, the design of IPv6 takes into account the problems of IPv4, focusing, in particular, on the consequences for the end user. In other words, the lack of certain desired features is addressed. Management features are one thread in this part of IPv6 tapestry that we choose to isolate for attention. There are serious problems with the way that IPv4 is managed today in enterprises, and IPv6 has the potential to fix those problems. Potential, mind you; no one is pretending that immediate benefits will accrue to any organization implementing IPv6 right now. We shall explain more about this later.

The second aspect of optimization in IPv6's design is to simplify the mechanisms on which IP is built; for example, the basic IP headers have all been slimmed down to the necessary minimum. This should, in theory, lead to higher performance and lower cost routers, since less processing needs to be done to forward an IPv6 packet than an IPv4 packet. This should also help in areas such as header compression.

Packets and Structures

The IPv6 packet structure is, in most ways, very similar to the IPv4 packet structure. Some fields have been removed and some have been added, but the most obvious change is the size of the addresses. While the IPv4 source and destination addresses are 32 bits each, IPv6 addresses are 128 bits each. The reason for 128 bits is discussed in the following sidebar, "Is 128 Bits Enough?"

Basic Header Structure

Overall IPv6 actually simplifies the basic header, by including only the information needed for forwarding a packet. This results in a fixed-length header, unlike IPv4. Fixed-length headers are important for router designers and for coders, because it allows more efficient memory allocation strategies and algorithm implementation. Other information, which might traditionally have been stored in the IPv4 header or as IPv4 options, is now stored within a chain of subsequent headers, identified by the *next header* field. The final header will usually be a TCP, UDP or ICMPv6 header. This way the task of forwarding can be accomplished by dealing with the first few bits of the packet that you have received. Figure 3-2 compares IPv4 and IPv6 headers.

Many familiar fields have equivalents in IPv6: Version, ToS/Traffic Class, Total Length/Payload Length, Time to Live/Hop Limit, Protocol/Next Header, source address and destination addresses. Note the removal of IPv4 fragmentation fields (ID, Flags, Offset), and header checksum. The Traffic Class field is also augmented by the presence of Flow Label field, both used for quality of service, discussed in the "Quality of Service" section later in this chapter.

Is 128 Bits Enough?

People who remember the second law of thermodynamics (or who have worked in large organizations) know that it is impossible to have a perfectly efficient system. As it is with heat exchangers, so it is with network protocols.

In particular, when addressing endpoints in a real network, from any limited pool, there is a certain amount of the addresses that will be "lost," or inefficiently allocated. This is not simply due to factors in the protocol itself (for example, wasting addresses on the broadcast address in point to point links) but is also due to real world concerns like administrative error, customer churn, aggregation, and so on. It turns out that this error is actually measurable, and we do it using a metric called the host density ratio, or *HD* ratio. This is a number that increases from zero to one as the address space fills. For reference, it's defined as:

$$HD: = \frac{\log(\text{number of allocated objects})}{\log(\text{maximum number of allocatable objects})}$$

Empirical calculations for telephone number allocation and network address assignment show that a *HD* value of 0.8 is reasonable but a *HD* value of 0.85 is overcrowded. RFC 3194 goes into more detail.

Having examined common real-world ratios, let's ask how well can IPv6 do by comparison. One might think that although the size of the address is so much larger, perhaps the inefficiency is larger too, and we might well be back in an IPv4-type address crunch in 10 years time.

Well, let's look at the numbers. For IPv4 a *HD* ratio of 0.8 corresponds to $2^{32 \cdot 0.8}$, or about 50 million hosts. The Internet Domain Survey, *http://www.isc.org/ds/*, suggests that we passed this point some time ago and are now at a point where $HD > 0.85$. A comfortable density of 0.8 for IPv6 would correspond to $2^{128 \cdot 0.8}$, or about 1,000 hosts for every gram of the Earth!

We can see that even with relatively mediocre allocation policies, IPv6 can still number all the projected end devices for at least the next few decades. After that, it's either time for a new protocol, or time to ship people off to another planet (with, of course, a non-bridging firewall).

TCP and UDP remain unchanged from IPv4, although individual application protocols that hard-code address sizes may have unpleasant surprises waiting for them in the new world. (We deal with that specific topic in Chapters 7 and 8.)

Addressing Concepts

The use of IPv6 addresses is covered in RFC 3513. To begin with, you need to know that IPv6 addresses come in different types (Unicast, multicast, anycast) and different scopes (link, global, and so on). The type of the address determines if packets are destined for one or for many machines. The scope of the address determines which

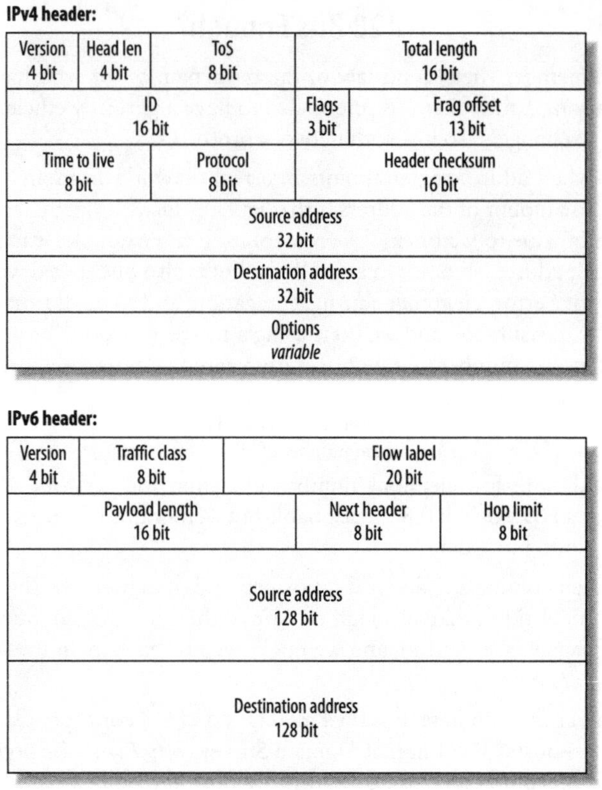

IPv4 header:

Version 4 bit	Head len 4 bit	ToS 8 bit	Total length 16 bit		
ID 16 bit			Flags 3 bit	Frag offset 13 bit	
Time to live 8 bit		Protocol 8 bit	Header checksum 16 bit		
Source address 32 bit					
Destination address 32 bit					
Options *variable*					

IPv6 header:

Version 4 bit	Traffic class 8 bit	Flow label 20 bit		
Payload length 16 bit		Next header 8 bit	Hop limit 8 bit	
Source address 128 bit				
Destination address 128 bit				

Figure 3-2. IPv4 versus IPv6 packet header

contexts the address makes sense in. We'll explain more about types and scopes shortly.

RFC 3513 also makes the point that IPv6 addresses are assigned to interfaces on nodes, not to the nodes themselves. This is a big change from IPv4, where very often the address associated with a machine's interface *is* that machine. Instead, IPv6 interfaces commonly and usefully have more than one IPv6 address.

In fact, IPv6 allows *scoped* addresses, which only have meaning within a certain context. For example, most interfaces have a link-local address which is only unique on that specific link. This means that two interfaces on a node could have the *same* link-local address if they were attached to different links! If all of this seems confusing, just think of the IPv4 loopback address. It is an example of a scoped address because 127.0.0.1 indicates a different destination on each host.

Another important concept in IPv6, covered in the RFC, is that of an *interface identifier*. In the IPv4 world, we split addresses into a network part and a host part; an example in CIDR notation is 137.43.0.0/16. In the IPv6 world the host part is now called the *interface ID*, and is used to pick out a particular interface within the specified network, in the same way that the host part of an IPv4 address picks out that host on a particular subnet.

The separation has a number of useful properties. Perhaps the most interesting is the potential for automatic assignment of interface IDs. This is one of the nicer features of IPv6, discussed in the "Neighborhood Watch" section later in this chapter. Naturally, manually configuring interface IDs and addresses or using DHCPv6 is still an option, and indeed might be preferable for certain kinds of services.*

RFC 3513 also covers the notation used for IPv6 addresses, which we'll now explain.

Notation

The notation for IPv6 addresses has changed greatly from IPv4. Given a greatly enlarged address space, using or describing IPv6 addresses efficiently becomes much more important than in IPv4, where you are never more than 16 keystrokes from the end of an address. The main differences are outlined below.

Hex digit notation

Instead of ordinary decimal, IPv6 addresses are encoded in hexadecimal, a base-16 numbering system common in computing and networking. (See the following sidebar, "Decimal, Binary, and Hexadecimal," for more details). For the moment, it is sufficient to note that the individual "digits" of an IPv6 address can range not only from 0–9, but also from A–F. Hence an address could begin 2002, for example, and also 20FE or even BD59. Though RFC 3513 uses capitalized addresses in its examples, IPv6 addresses are case-insensitive.

Grouping and separation

In IPv4 notation, addresses are "grouped" typographically on octet boundaries with a dot (.). In IPv6, addresses are grouped typographically on 16 bit boundaries with a colon (:). Since addresses are 128 bits long, this means there are 8 groups, every group using 4 hexadecimal digits. For example, 2001:0DB8:5002:2019:1111:76ff: FEAC:E8A6.

Elision

A lot of IPv6 addresses will contain repetitious elements, particularly zeros. There are ways provided to avoid writing, or *elide* these in order to speed up the description of

---

* With DHCPv6 it is possible for a client to request non-address–related configuration information (such as DNS resolvers) while obtaining their addresses via the autoconfiguration of interface IDs.

Decimal, Binary, and Hexadecimal

The usual scheme we use for writing numbers, where 1984 means one lot of a thousand plus nine lots of one hundred plus eight lots of ten plus four, is called Arabic system. It has this name because it was learned by Europeans from Arabs when the Europeans were still playing around with Roman numerals.

This system is base 10, because there are 10 "digits:" 0, 1, 2, 3, 4, 5, 6, 7, 8, 9. The places also increase in significance by factors of 10: the rightmost is lots of 1, the next lots of 10, the next lots 100, and so on. It is likely 10 was chosen because we have 10 fingers. 12 was also a popular choice for counting, possibly because we have 12 finger segments and a thumb for pointing at them.

Computers, on the other hand, do not have fingers. Computers have grown from devices with two states, which we usually consider as "on" and "off." For this reason, the natural counting system on computers is the binary system, where we have 2 digits, 0 and 1, with each place increasing in value by 2. Thus, the binary number 11001 is the decimal number $1*16 + 1*8 + 0*4 + 0*2 + 1*1 = 25$. Where there is ambiguity about the base of a number, you can clear it up by saying $11001_2 = 25_{10}$. The confusion that arises leads to the well known joke: "There are 10 types of people in the world, those who understand binary and those who do not."

Writing numbers in binary is quite longwinded. For 1984 in binary is 11111000000. On the other hand, converting numbers from binary to decimal is quite a chore, because ten has prime factors other than 2. For this reason, when humans deal with binary, they often convert it to base 8 (octal) or base 16 (hexadecimal). Here the conversion is easier, because each three "digits" of binary corresponds exactly to one "digit" of octal, and similarly four binary digits (bits) corresponds to one hexadecimal digit.

One problem arises when we move to hexadecimal—we need more symbols than we have been provided with by our base 10 system. The usual solution here is to draft in a few letters to provide the missing six digits: $a = 10$, $b = 11$, $c = 12$, $d = 13$, $e = 14$, and $f = 15$.

We should also mention that there is another representation of IPv6 addresses in base 85 defined in RFC 1924. Why 85? Well, to represent 2^{128} using the usual printable ASCII symbols requires at least 20 ASCII "digits." The smallest number of symbols that can represent 2^{128} in 20 digits is 85 and so base 85 was chosen. For some reason, probably the date it was published, RFC 1924 representation has fallen by the wayside; if humans grow a extra hand with 17 fingers, it may become more popular.

these addresses. You can avoid writing all of the elements of an address under the following conditions:

1. Whenever an address element in a grouping begins with one or more zeros

2. Wherever there is one or more groups of zeros

In the first case, the leading zeros may be dropped providing at least one hexadecimal digit is left in the group. In the second case, a run of groups of zeros may be replaced with a ::. This second elision can only be performed once, otherwise the address becomes ambiguous.

For example, we can write:

```
0237:0000:ABCD:0000:0000:0000:0000:0010
```

as 237:0:ABCD::10. How? First remove the leading zero from 0237. Then remove the leading zeros from the next group giving 0. Next, compress the run of zero groups into :: and finally remove two leading zeros from 0010. We could also have written the address as 237::ABCD:0:0:0:0:10. Like most things, reading and writing these addresses gets easier with practice.

There are certain classes of address space for which it makes sense to return to the old IPv4 ways, but we'll talk more about those shortly. Suffice it to say that:

```
::137.43.4.16
```

is also a valid IPv6 address, and could be written:

```
0000:0000:0000:0000:0000:0000:892b:0410
```

Example 3-1 shows some perl code that uses these rules and expands IPv6 addresses to their full form. Example 3-2 shows example inputs and this program which you might want to compare to the expanded forms in Example 3-3 to see this compression in action.

Example 3-1. Perl code for expanding elided IPv6 addresses

```perl
#!/usr/local/bin/perl

while(<>) { print &expandv6($_), "\n"; }

sub expandv6 {
        local ($_) = @_;
        local (@parts, @newparts, $part);

        s/\s+//g; # Get rid of white space.
        s/%.*//g; # Get rid of MS/KAME scope ID, if there is one.
        if (/:(\d+)\.(\d+)\.(\d+)\.(\d+)$/) { # Expand trailing IPv4 address.
                $part = sprintf ":%02x%02x:%02x%02x", $1, $2, $3, $4;
                s/:\d+\.\d+\.\d+\.\d+$/$part/;
        }

        @parts = split(/:/, $_, -1);
        $short = 8 - $#parts;
        @newparts = ( );

        foreach $part (@parts) {
                if ($part eq "" && $short >; 0) {
                        while ($short-- >; 0) { push @newparts, "0000"; }
                } else {
                        push @newparts, (sprintf "%04x", hex($part));
```

Example 3-1. Perl code for expanding elided IPv6 addresses (continued)

```
            }
        }

        return join ":", @newparts;
}

1;
```

Example 3-2. Some IPv6 addresses

```
::
237:0:ABCD::10
::137.43.4.16
2001:770:10::
::0
::ffff:0.0.0.0
200::
2000::
fe80::
fec0::
ff00::
2001:1200::
ff05::1:3
ff02::1:ffab:cdef
ff02::2
fe80::134.226.81.10
2001:770:10:300::134.226.81.11
```

Example 3-3. Expanded form of some IPv6 addresses

```
0000:0000:0000:0000:0000:0000:0000:0000
0237:0000:abcd:0000:0000:0000:0000:0010
0000:0000:0000:0000:0000:0000:892b:0410
2001:0770:0010:0000:0000:0000:0000:0000
0000:0000:0000:0000:0000:0000:0000:0000
0000:0000:0000:0000:0000:ffff:0000:0000
0200:0000:0000:0000:0000:0000:0000:0000
2000:0000:0000:0000:0000:0000:0000:0000
fe80:0000:0000:0000:0000:0000:0000:0000
fec0:0000:0000:0000:0000:0000:0000:0000
ff00:0000:0000:0000:0000:0000:0000:0000
2001:1200:0000:0000:0000:0000:0000:0000
ff05:0000:0000:0000:0000:0000:0001:0003
ff02:0000:0000:0000:0000:0000:0001:ffab:cdef
ff02:0000:0000:0000:0000:0000:0000:0002
fe80:0000:0000:0000:0000:0000:86e2:510a
2001:0770:0010:0300:0000:0000:86e2:510b
```

Scope identifiers

As mentioned in the "Addressing Concepts" section earlier in this chapter, IPv6 allows scoped addresses which are only meaningful in a particular context. The most common of these addresses is the link-local address, which is only meaningful on a particular network link. Suppose you want to ping a link-local address like fe80::1, and your computer is connected to several links. The address fe80::1 could be on any one of those links, so how does IPv6 know which one to use?

One way to solve this problem is to add a flag to programs like ping, to allow the specification of an interface. For example, the KAME and Microsoft stacks allow the specification of link as part of the address, by including a *scope identifier*. On a KAME-derived stack, as found on BSD systems, fe80::1%en0 means the address fe80::1 on the network attached to interface en0. On Microsoft derived stacks the scope-id is usually given as a number, so fe80::1%7 means address fe80::1 on IPv6 interface 7.

Subnetting

In IPv4, *subnetting* allows you to take pieces of your existing address space and divide it, to provide either more networks or to make more addresses available to certain people. One common example of using subnetting to provide more networks is an ISP assigning a subnet of their address space to a customer. An example of using subnetting to make more addresses available is when a company finds that its sales team have run out of addresses, but R&D have some spare. If R&D are using less than half of the 256 addresses in their /24 say, then a /25 could be reclaimed and assigned to sales.

IPv6 can subnet too. It uses the CIDR notation developed for IPv4 as well, which is a way of specifying the size of a network in addition to the actual network number. An example from IPv4 is 137.43.0.0/16, which is the old "class B" network of University College Dublin. Similarly, 2001:770:10::/48 is the IPv6 network of Trinity College Dublin. In IPv6 these blocks of addresses are often referred to as prefixes. Single hosts in IPv4 are called /32's, and consequently single hosts in IPv6 are /128's. (A calculator that can do CIDR calculations on IPv4 and IPv6 addresses is available at *http://www.routemeister.net/projects/sipcalc/*; you might find it useful for getting up to speed on IPv6 network numbering.)

In IPv6, subnets are supposed to be at least 64 bits wide, even for point-to-point links. Since an individual /64 has space for over a billion hosts, it is expected that re-subnetting to provide more addresses for an individual network will no longer be necessary. This is an important point: possibly the best way to understand it is to take the example of an IPv4 server farm that has outgrown the 256 addresses (only 254 of them being usable of course) in its /24. With IPv4 you have no choice but to subnet, creating another piece of network either contiguous or discontiguous to the original addresses, and add your new servers there, with consequent impact on the routing within your organization. In contrast, with IPv6, since the servers can all have a different interface ID, they can all live in the same subnet. This would allow large groups of machines, say Beowulf clusters, to happily fit within any subnet.

Therefore, the main reason for subnetting becomes the assignment of networks for different administrative or technical purposes, such as security or routing. To try to simplify this process, it is expected that organizations requiring internal subnetting will always be assigned a /48.* This means that everyone has 16 "network" bits to work with, or 65536 different subnets. This should be enough for anybody.†

Address Architecture

Those of you who are familiar with IPv4 networks may have encountered the notion of private versus public address space. Private address space is address space used within an organization's network, and in theory it cannot be reached from the outside world (often people like to pretend that this gives them additional security, see "NAT" in Chapter 1). These addresses are an example of address spaces with special properties—and often (but not always) these types of address space can be inferred by glancing at the address.

Examples of special addresses from the IPv4 world include the private class A space 10.0.0.0/8, which is discussed in the "Addressing Model" section in Chapter 1, and would be familiar to those building enterprise networks. Similarly 127.0.0.0/8 is the "localhost" space, which hosts use to contact themselves.

 One interesting IPv4 special address is the "broadcast" address in IPv4, 255.255.255.255, because it has no direct equivalent in IPv6. Broadcasts no longer exist in IPv6, and multicast is used as the transport for contacting multiple hosts simultaneously.

Similarly in IPv6 there are a number of address spaces, usually expressed as a prefix with CIDR network length. The official breakup of this space is documented on the IANA web site *http://www.iana.org/*, but we summarize the allocations in Table 3-1.

Table 3-1. The breakup of the IPv6 address space

Prefix	Intended use
::0/96	Unspecified/loopback/compatible-IPv4 address
::ffff:0.0.0.0/96	Mapped IPv4 addresses
200::/7	Reserved for NSAP Allocation (RFC 1888)
400::/7	Reserved for IPS Allocation
2000::/3	Global Unicast (RFC 3587)
fe80::/10	Link-Local Unicast
fec0::/10	Site-Local Unicast (deprecated in RFC 3879)

---

* See RFC 3177 for further details.

† As Bill Gates is alleged to have said, "640k should be enough for anybody."

Table 3-1. The breakup of the IPv6 address space (continued)

Prefix	Intended use
fc00::/7	Local IPv6 Unicast addresses (proposed)
ff00::/8	Multicast

A few of these types of addresses are worth explaining in more detail.

Global Unicast Addressing

These addresses are the analogue of the normal public IPv4 address space. Most of these addresses are still reserved, but the allocation of this space to users has begun. The blocks that have been allocated are listed in Table 3-2.

Table 3-2. Allocated IPv6 Global Unicast addresses

Prefix	Intended use	RFC
2001::/16	Production via Regional Internet Registries	RFC 2450
2002::/16	6to4transition mechanism (see Chapter 4)	RFC 3056
3FFE::/16	6bonetest network	RFC 2471, RFC 3701

Some of the production address space is being allocated to Regional Internet Registries* in large chunks. The RIRs are in turn then responsible for allocating smaller blocks to Local Internet Registries, who are usually Internet Service Providers. Finally, ISPs assign addresses directly to their customers.

This hierarchical address allocation scheme is expected to be the normal way that end users get IPv6 addresses.

Link-Local Addressing

The link-local prefix contains addresses that are only meaningful on a single link. In fact, this prefix is used for on almost *every* link that IPv6 is configured on. This means the link-local address fe80::feed will refer to a different computer depending on which network you are using, much like 127.0.0.1 refers to a different computer depending on which one you're using.

In this context, a link is a group of machines who may communicate directly without requiring an IPv6 router. This link may be a point-to-point, a broadcast link or something more esoteric, but packets addressed using link-local addressing will

---

* We'll talk about the RIRs and their address allocation policies in the "RIRs" section of Chapter 4.

never pass through a router.* Addresses that are only valid on the local link may not seem very useful, but they form a part of the IPv6 autoconfiguration process.

It's important to note that hosts generate link-local addresses by virtue of being connected to a link; no router or involvement by any outside agency is necessary for these addresses to be generated and used. So, a small office with one switch and a few computers connected can use link-local addressing for simple networking.† This is one of the major contributions of IPv6 to ease of management, especially for small organizations. (We'll get to how link-local addresses are actually generated in a moment.)

It is also possible to use link-local addresses when "real" addresses are not strictly required. For example, a point-to-point link between two routers could operate with only link-local addresses, without having to allocate any global Unicast addresses. However, IPv6 has been designed so that there should be no shortage of addresses and this sort of address conservation should be unnecessary. Also, routers may require real addresses for sending ICMP error messages or for remote management.

Automatically configured link-local addresses are in some ways quite similar to the IPv4 169.254.0.0/16 addresses that are sometimes used if no DHCP server is available or if only link-local communication is required. IPv6 autoconfigured addresses differ here in that they are intended to be unique and constant, whereas the IPv4 addresses are prone to collision and may vary as a consequence of collision resolution.

Site-Local Addressing

Site-local addressing is an interesting idea somewhat reminiscent of the IPv4 private address spaces discussed above. These addresses are meant to be used within a site,‡ but are not necessarily routable or valid outside of your organization. Opinions vary as to the definition of a site, but think of it as being an organization to which an address space allocation might be made. The reason for this is that as the use of site-local addressing mirrors the use of global addressing, it should simplify management of addresses and encourage sensible use of both.

Unlike link-local addresses, which are only required to be unique on a link, these site-local addresses require a router to be configured to avoid duplication of site-local addresses within a site.

---

* Of course, the link may involve tunnelled or encapsulated traffic, using MPLS or some other mechanism, but these operate in the layers below IPv6.

† Note well that IPv6 NetBIOS is not possible with Windows—which means your hostname resolution may well have to be done by Active Directory, Dynamic DNS or IPv6's node information queries. Complications in naming and addressing mean that link-local addressing alone is a bad idea for more complex networks.

‡ Like a business campus or university, not a web site!

At the moment the practical details of if and how site-local addressing should be deployed are still being discussed. There is a general wish to avoid the sort of problems associated with merging private networks (as discussed in "NAT" in Chapter 1). What this probably means is that there will be "site-local" addresses that are *globally* unique. However, it seems that site-local addresses, as originally considered for IPv6, have been abandoned and the details of this new "unique local IPv6 Unicast addressing" are being finalized. Given the clear need for stable in-site addressing in the face of provider allocated global addresses, considerable effort is being invested in getting the replacement for site-local addresses right. (We'll comment more on the future of site-local addresses in Chapter 9.)

Enough address space has actually been dedicated to site-local and unique local addressing to assign unique addresses to most organizations in the world. Thus it is possible that these addresses could actually end up being globally valid and routable! The main problem with this is that it is not clear how to solve the technical problems associated with routing such a large, unstructured address space.

For now, the best thing to do with local addressing is to ignore it. Once its future is clearer it may be useful to some people, but for now most people can survive with a combination of link-local and global addressing.

Multicast

Let's consider applications where conversing with many hosts at once is the norm. How can you make this happen as efficiently as possible? Unicasting data to many hosts is inefficient, because you have to send the data once for each host. Broadcasting to many hosts is also inefficient, because many hosts will not be interested in the data you are sending, and will waste resources processing the packet. *Multicast* is the solution allowing you to send a packet efficiently to an arbitrary collection of machines. It aims to be a compromise between Unicast and broadcast; hosts can sign up to receive messages destined to specific groups, and these *multicast groups* are identified by multicast addresses.

The usual example of a multicast application is streaming multimedia; lots of end stations need to receive the same rock video/party political broadcast from a single source. From an application point of view you send packets to a single group address, but everyone who has registered as being in that group receives the data. Naturally this requires the cooperation of routers and switches within the network.

Multicast exists in the IPv4 world; IGMP, defined in RFC 3376, is used to manage IPv4 multicast groups. However, multicast, although useful, has never really had wide deployment. By contrast, in IPv6, multicast is compulsory. Indeed, multicast is central to the operation of IPv6; IGMP has been merged into ICMPv6 (RFC 2710) and multicast is used to implement IPv6's equivalent of ARP. We talk more about this in the "ICMPv6" section later in this chapter.

Multicast requires no configuration if it is confined to a single network (i.e., a single link). However, for multicast traffic to cross routers a multicast routing daemon must be configured. For now we'll concentrate on link-local multicast.

Multicast addressing in IPv6

The IPv6 multicast address space described in Table 3-1 is split up into into chunks mirroring the different types of Unicast addresses. Multicast addresses are of the form ffXY:... where X is 4 bits of flags and Y is the scope of the multicast.

The top bit of the flags are currently reserved and should be zero. The final bit is 1 if the multicast address is a transient multicast address, rather than a well-known one.[*] For well-known addresses the other flags must be set to 0, the other values being reserved for later use.

The situation for transient addresses is a little more complex, but we only need to review it briefly. Here the value of the two middle flags is important. A middle flags value of 00 indicates an arbitrary assignment of addresses, where the addresses are assigned by those operating the link/site/network matching the scope of the address. Middle flags of 01 indicates assignment based on *Unicast prefix*, where by virtue of using a block (prefix) of IPv6 addresses, there is automatically a block of IPv6 multicast addresses available. Finally, middle flags of 11 is another assignment based Unicast addresses, but this time the address of a *rendezvous point* is also encoded in the multicast address. A rendezvous point is a place in a multicast network that acts as a distribution point for a particular multicast stream. Locating a rendezvous point is a tricky problem in some types of multicast routing, so including it in the address makes life easier.

The scope values are shown in Table 3-3, as are prefixes for well-known and simple transient addresses with this scope. There are similar blocks of addresses for the other flags values too.

Table 3-3. Multicast scope values

Scope	Value	Well-known	Transient
reserved	0	ff00::/16	ff10::/16
node-local	1	ff01::/16	ff11::/16
link-local	2	ff02::/16	ff12::/16
site-local	5	ff05::/16	ff15::/16
organization-local	8	ff08::/16	ff18::/16
global	E	ff0e::/16	ff1e::/16
reserved	F	ff0f::/16	ff1f::/16

---

[*] A well-known multicast address is one for some well-known service, like "all DHCPv6 servers." A transient address is one that is created dynamically, for example to send a specific audio stream to a group of users.

Within each of the well-known ranges, some addresses have been assigned for specific uses. Some assignments are *variable scope*, meaning that they are assigned for any valid scope value. For example, ff0X::101 is assigned to NTP servers with scope X.

Other assignments are only valid within certain scopes, for example DHCPv6 servers are assigned the site-local scope address ff05::1:3.

In some cases, ranges of addresses have been assigned. In particular, ff02::1:ff00:0/104 is the range for *solicited node multicast*. If a node has a Unicast address ending in, say ab:cdef, then it must be part of the multicast group ff02::1:ffab:cdef. Since an interface can have several Unicast addresses, this may mean several solicited node multicast addresses on that interface. However, if the interface ID is the same for all the Unicast addresses, then the interface will only need to join one solicited node multicast group.

The list of assigned multicast addresses is available on the IANA web site *http://www.iana.org/*, and is relatively long. However, there are two multicast address everyone should know about: ff02::1 and ff02::2. The first is the link-local all-nodes address, the rough equivalent of the non-routed broadcast address 255.255.255.255 in IPv4. The second is the link-local all-routers address, which is important in the IPv6 autoconfiguration process.

Hardware support

One final thing to note is that some sort of support is required in the end networks to support multicast. For example, in Ethernet networks certain destination MAC addresses are set aside for multicast. For IPv6 these addresses have the two high bytes set to 33:33 and the remaining four bytes taken from the low four bytes of the IPv6 multicast address.

This means that to receive multicast you need an Ethernet card that can pass up packets addressed to the relevant layer two address. Modern cards often have a facility called *multicast filters*, which allow only relevant multicast packets to be passed up to the driver, which means that the driver can avoid processing every multicast packet that the card receives.

If the card doesn't have this hardware support, the necessary filtering can be done in the Ethernet driver. Some hosts may actually want to receive all multicast packets. This is implemented with multicast promiscuous support that passes up all Ethernet frames that have a multicast destination address. If your Ethernet driver has to process all multicast frames, either because it does not support multicast filters or because it is operating in multicast promiscuous mode, it will obviously consume more of the computer's resources.

All this configuration of Ethernet multicast filters should automatically be done by the IP stack and Ethernet drivers, so you shouldn't have to worry about it. However, occasionally it doesn't work. We talk about what can go wrong with Ethernet multi-cast support in the "Gotchas" section of Chapter 5.

Anycast

An anycast address is an address half way between a Unicast address and a multicast address. Unicast addresses are assigned to one machine and each packet is delivered to that machine. Multicast addresses are assigned to many machines and each packet is delivered to all such machines. Anycast addresses are assigned to many machines, but each packet is delivered to only one of these machines. The use of anycast is still settling down, so we discuss it in Chapter 9.

ICMPv6

TCP and UDP have both remained unchanged from IPv4 to IPv6. ICMP is a very different story, as ICMPv6 encompasses the roles filled by ICMP, IGMP *and* ARP in the IPv4 world. Some aspects of ICPMv6 will be familiar to those who have worked with their IPv4 equivalents: ICMP Echoes and Errors, for example. However, the most important changes are in the area of *neighbor discovery*, which will be unfamiliar to IPv6 newcomers. We discuss this in the "Neighborhood Watch" section later in this chapter.

ICMP Echoes and Errors

RFC 2463 covers the part of ICMPv6 that is most similar to the familiar parts of ICMPv4. It covers ICMP Echo Requests and Replies, which are used to implement the well-known ping program. It also covers ICMP errors, which are returned when there is a problem with a packet: Destination Unreachable (because of routing, packet filtering or other unavailability), Packet Too Big, Time Exceeded (when the packet has travelled too many hops) and Parameter Problem (unknown or bad headers).

Out of Time

The original Time to Live field in IPv4 was supposed to be the maximum number of seconds a packet could live in the network before being discarded. In practice, this field was decremented by one by every router that forwarded the packet, regardless of how long the router had held the packet for. Thus, Time to Live is really the largest number of hops a packet can travel.

This has been recognized in IPv6, and the field is now called Hop Limit. However, the ICMPv6 message generated when a packet is discarded as a result of the Hop Limit being overrun is still called "Time Exceeded." *Plus ça change.*

ICMP messages have often been filtered out in the IPv4 world, which usually results in the failure of tools such as ping and traceroute or delays while waiting for the arrival of discarded "destination unreachable" messages. IPv6 will be even less forgiving in this respect, as correctly operating ICMP is absolutely essential to the protocol. In particular, Packet Too Big messages are now necessary for the valid operation of TCP and UDP because IPv6 routers are not permitted to fragment packets. Nodes need to be told to reduce the size of a packet if it will not fit within the MTU of a link. The process of figuring out the largest packet that can be sent to a particular destination is called *path MTU discovery*. IPv6 path MTU discovery is described in RFC 1981. IPv6 nodes are not required to use path MTU discovery, but if they don't, they must not send packets larger than 1280 bytes, the minimum permitted IPv6 MTU.

ICMP error messages are also explicitly rate-limited by the stack. This will usually restrict the number of error messages sent either per-period-of-time or to a fraction of link bandwidth (there are details of some suggested schemes in RFC 2463). This avoids repeating some mistakes IPv4 made with respect to overzealous, or overly-compliant, ICMP message generation.

Neighborhood Watch

Address resolution in IPv4 uses ARP, but in IPv6 a mechanism known as *neighbor discovery* is used. Neighbor discovery also provides additional features that are not provided in IPv4. Neighbor discovery is defined in RFC 2461.

Unlike ARP, ICMP neighbor discovery is an IP protocol, which means that it can be secured with IPsec (the "Security" section later in this chapter introduces IPsec). As a precaution, most neighbor discovery packets are also only acted on if they have not been forwarded by a router. This is achieved by checking the hop-limit field has its maximum value and makes it difficult to inject them into remote networks.

Like ARP, neighbor discovery explicitly includes the link-layer addresses within the body of messages, rather than peeking at the packet's link-layer header. This makes for easier implementation and also leaves the option of proxy neighbor discovery open for situations such as Mobile IP.

Address resolution

Neighbor Solicitation and Neighbor Advertisement are two types of ICMPv6 neighbor discovery packets. They have several uses, but the one that we will mention here is the equivalent of ARP in IPv4.

A neighbor solicitation packet is very similar to an ARP request packet. It is sent when a node wants to translate a target IPv6 Unicast address into a link-layer address. Basically it says, "Can the owner of this IPv6 address please get in touch?" Since we don't actually know the link-layer address of the target host, the neighbor solicitation packet is sent to the solicited-node multicast address* corresponding to the target address, and the target address is included in the ICMP message. The sending node will also usually include its link-layer address, to make replying easier.

A neighbor advertisement packet is the logical response to these solicitations. It is sent back to the requesting system, including the source address of the solicitation, the link-layer address of the target system and some flags.

An example of neighbor solicitation between two hosts is shown in Figure 3-3. Host 1 wants to talk to address 2001:db8::a00:2 on host 2, so it calculates the solicited node multicast address ff02::1:ff00:2 and sends the packet to the corresponding Ethernet multicast address. It includes its own Ethernet address in the packet. Host 2 responds with a neighbor advertisement sent directly to host 1's Ethernet address.

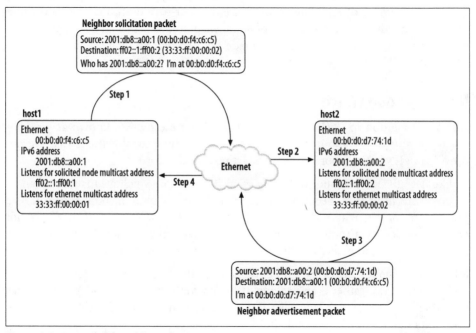

Figure 3-3. Example of neighbor solicitation

In the same way that hosts had an ARP table in IPv4, there is a table of neighbors maintained on a node in IPv6 called the *neighbor cache*. This cache manages the results of previous queries to avoid repeating requests too often.

Unlike ARP, ICMPv6 avoids broadcasts. The use of a whole range of solicited node multicast addresses means that nodes will usually only have to process Neighbor Solicitation packets that are actually of interest to them. This means that the interrupt load on IPv6 hosts should be much lower than on the equivalent IPv4 network.

---

* Solicited node multicast addresses are explained in "Multicast addressing in IPv6" earlier in this chapter.

DAD

Duplicate Address Detection (DAD) is a feature which is useful for network operation. It is used when an address is assigned to an interface and is a way of checking that no node on the link is already using that address. It can be used for any address type (e.g., Unicast or link-local) but can only detect duplicates that share a link with you. DAD is defined in RFC 2462.

When an interface is manually or automatically configured, the address is marked as *tentative*. The Duplicate Address Detection procedure then sends a Neighbor Solicitation message to the address that has just been configured. The idea is simple: you wait a certain amount of time, and if you have not received a reply, then you conclude the address is not in use and proceed merrily on your way. If you *do* receive a reply, it is in the form of a Neighbor Advertisement, so you mark the tentative address unusable and operator intervention is required.[*]

The Neighbor Solicitation message is addressed to the appropriate solicited-node multicast address, and the address that is being checked as unique is sent as the target. Since we do not want to use the tentative address yet, the source address is set to the all-zeros unspecified address ::. If a node replies to such a solicitation, the advertisement must be sent to the all-nodes link-local address ff02::1 because the host doing DAD may not yet have any addresses. If a duplicate address is discovered then the tentative address must not be used.

Unfortunately DAD is not a completely reliable mechanism; you might wait a long time but not long enough, or the reply could be lost or discarded for a variety of reasons. Compared to IPv4, DAD is a better approach to minimizing the chaos that ensues when addresses are unwillingly shared. If nothing else, mandatory DAD helps you as an innocent bystander and hinders you as a malicious attacker!

Who Stole My Address?

A University that one of the authors is familiar with had a new breed of extra-smart, network-addressable printer plugged in by someone on the far side of campus. This printer, although undeniably smart, was arrogant about its address management, and would occasionally decide that because it hadn't seen address X on the wire for a few minutes, it could be safely used (when all you have is Appletalk, everything looks like a nail). The printer proceeded to intermittently rob various important IP addresses, including the desktop machine of the network manager, which resulted in much running around and shouting. Eventually the culprit was tracked down, but it was a memorable lesson in the problems attendant on large broadcast networks.

---

[*] The security implications of this are not unlike the security implications of duplicate addresses in IPv4 networks, with the key difference being that machines won't "fight it out" between themselves for the address.

NUD

A host can fall off a network at any time, with reasons ranging from sudden power loss to malicious intent. Neighbor Unreachability Detection is a way of checking that we are still in *bidirectional* contact with a neighbor. Usually this can be inferred by what RFC 2461 refers to as "forward progress" of a high level protocol, such as TCP. However, if a neighbor seems to have gone missing, a Neighbor Solicitation can be sent to them to see if they are still available.

What good is determining if a neighbor has become unreachable? Well, in the case where the neighbor has become unreachable because of a change of layer 2 address (perhaps because of some hot-standby system), the Neighbor Solicitation will then discover the new layer 2 address corresponding to the original IPv6 address. If the system that has become unavailable is a router, then we may be able to choose another router. In cases where the unreachable neighbor was an end-host that has been powered off, then there probably isn't much we can do to restore useful communication.

Redirection

As in IPv4, sometimes a node makes a bad decision about the best router to receive a particular packet. Again, as with IPv4, a router can signal to a host and indicate a better choice of next hop. IPv6 does add some extra features to ICMPv4 redirection; it can indicate the link-layer address of the next hop and can let a node know that an address thought to be remote is actually local. One quirk of IPv6 redirection is that redirection uses link-local addresses, which means that routers need to know one another's link-local addresses.

Router/prefix advertisement

The remaining two packet types in the neighbor discovery suite are the Router Solicitation and Router Advertisement packets. Router solicitations are like neighbor solicitations, but rather than asking about other nodes, they are seeking information from local routers. Consequently, these are sent to the all-routers multicast address ff02::2.

Router solicitations are not strictly necessary, as router advertisements are sent automatically every so often. For example, a laptop that awakes from hibernation might not send a router solicitation, but it could refresh the prefix information after a few minutes when the router next sends an advertisement. The time between these announcements is configurable, but is usually randomized to prevent undesirable synchronization effects.

Router advertisements contain all sort of useful goodies that a host may want to know about: prefixes, link MTUs, and so on. Unless you are anxious to preserve the practice of manual configuration in your network, the router discovery mechanism will be the primary mechanism by which default gateways are learned for hosts. Essentially a host has to do very little other than listen to quasi-periodic announcements to configure itself. The announcements are issued per router per link. Each announcement contains information about the specific address prefixes that the host can contact on this link. Some of these prefixes may be marked as suitable for use in autoconfiguration. Router advertisements also indicate that the router is available as a default router to hosts on the link, and may even carry information about what routers are close to specific prefixes.

How does a host resolve the problem of hearing about multiple routers? In the absence of the routers advertising specific routing preferences, a host can pick any suitable router. Redirection and Neighbor Unreachability Detection will ensure that the traffic is directed in the correct way.

There are a number of parameters that enable the router administrator to influence the behavior of hosts who receive the messages. They can:

1. Specify that hosts must do stateful autoconfiguration (e.g., DHCPv6)
2. Specify that hosts must do stateless autoconfiguration
3. Specify the link MTU
4. Specify the default hop limit
5. Specify the length of time for which hosts are considered reachable

From the network managers' point of view, it is very useful to be able to control parameters like this centrally and with so little effort. This is part of why IPv6, when properly deployed, should save us money and time.

Of course there are security tradeoffs—if you were a host on a network, and able to fake router advertisements, the fun things you could do range from nasty but traceable (advertising the prefix for some important web site) to nasty and impossible to guess (changing the hop limit to two or three so that connecting to local servers would succeed, but long range connections would fail mysteriously). Again, because all this takes place at the IP layer, in principle it can be secured with IPsec, however key distribution issues make this tricky. In light of this, a secure neighbor discovery protocol called SEND has been proposed for networks where untrusted nodes are connected. In IPv4 there are simply no complete solutions to this kind of problem.

Stateless autoconfiguration

Stateless autoconfiguration is a long name for an extremely desirable thing: being able to get devices working—hence, configuration—without any manual intervention—hence, auto—and without requiring server infrastructure to support it—hence, stateless.

This is to contrast it with state*ful* autoconfiguration, exemplified by protocols such as DHCP. DHCP is extremely useful and is very flexible about delivering information that a host requires to use network resources, but it requires a server and someone to maintain it, and these are not things that every deployment of computers can expect to have—or indeed should need to have.

In stateless autoconfiguration on Ethernet, a host uses the following pieces of information:

1. MAC addresses

2. Network prefixes

in order to generate valid addresses.

To form the complete set of addresses, a host first applies a rule, which we describe below, to the MAC address of each of the network interfaces it has. MAC addresses are of course, unique, and it is this property which makes autoconfiguration as practical as it is. (If the uniqueness of the addresses were in question, then a host could just randomly formulate an address, but the lack of a tight coupling between node and address would create havoc for network managers. In fact, the use of the MAC address, which may be tied to a removable Ethernet card rather than the node itself, is one of the downsides of the scheme.)

The rule that is applied transforms the MAC address into an interface ID is shown in Figure 3-4. It works in the following way. Suppose you have a MAC address on your Ethernet card of 00:50:8B:C8:E6:76. First, the seventh bit of the address (which is defined by the Ethernet standard to be the "universal/local" bit), is set giving 02:50: 8B:C8:E6:76. Then this is split into two halves, 02:50:8B and C8:E6:76. Finally, FF:FE is inserted between them. In this case it would form 02:50:8B:FF:FE:C8:E6:76.

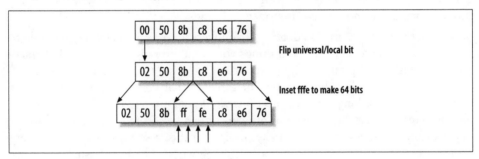

Figure 3-4. Automatic generation of host identifiers

These 64 bits are called an EUI-64 identifier, after the globally unique IEEE identifier, and are used as the interface identifier in stateless autoconfiguration. Initially, the link-local prefix fe80:: will have these 64 bits appended to form a tentative link-local address.

These newly-formed addresses, once they are tested for duplication via DAD, can thereafter be used for network communication with the node's neighbors. When router advertisements are received, the host can perform the process of concatenating the advertised prefixes with the interface identifier to produce other addresses. Thus link-local addresses can be generated without any connection to the outside world—perfect for an accountant's office, or other small-office/home-office scenario where internal network resources are more important. In this situation, name resolution can be done via broadcasts or similar mechanisms that do not require Internet access or a server. (Addressing in networks containing more than one link is more complex and really requires either global addresses or unique local addressing.)

The advertisements of prefixes also include information to say how long the prefix is valid for. As long as the router continues to re-advertise the prefix, then the address will remain valid. If a router stops advertising a prefix then the address can become *deprecated* after the prefix's valid lifetime elapses. Deprecated addresses can still be used, but other addresses are preferred for new communication. For this reason, addresses that have not been deprecated are sometimes called *preferred* addresses.

It is important to understand that the address generation ability of stateless autoconfiguration does *not* have to be invoked unless the administrator, should there be one, decides so. Some people, upon hearing of the mechanism, imagine it being applied to their servers and firewalls and so on, and the thought of them changing addresses arbitrarily if a network card fails and has to be replaced is unsettling. Thankfully, addresses in IPv6 can be statically defined just as IPv4 addresses are today, and neighbor discovery will take care of everything.

Privacy is another concern raised by autoconfiguration. If a laptop moves from network to network, using autoconfigured addresses, it will use the same interface ID on each network. This could allow the tracking of that laptop as its owner moves from work, to home, to the airport and so on. RFC 3041 proposes a extension to autoconfiguration where extra temporary addresses are generated, which can be used for outgoing connections to preserve the users privacy. These addresses are generated using MD5 and some random data associated with the node, and are disposed of periodically to make tracking impractical.

ICMP name resolution

There is a proposed mechanism for doing discovery of node names and addresses using ICMPv6. The usual mechanism for this is, of course, DNS. However, the IPv6 mechanism provides for name translation in serverless networks and also allows the querying of all of a node's addresses without having to hope that DNS is up to date or, indeed, in use at all.

The mechanism involves a Node Information Query packet, which can ask for the names or IP addresses of a node and a Node Information Reply packet, which is the corresponding response. These queries can be directed to any node, not just your neighbors, but a node can choose not to provide information if it wishes.

It also defines a new set of link-local multicast groups ff02::2:0:0/96, known as the node information groups. This allows a node to efficiently query the names and addresses of all nodes with a particular name without sending a broadcast, by calculating the correct multicast group based on a hash of that name.

The standardization of node information queries isn't in the near future, however a number of stacks implement it and it seems to be working well on KAME-derived implementations.

Router Renumbering

Autoconfiguration of IPv6 addresses makes it relatively simple to change the addresses assigned to groups of machines, by changing the prefixes advertised by routers. This reassignment of address is commonly referred to as *renumbering*. Hosts are easy, but what about routers themselves? An automatic way to renumber these also is required, since otherwise large networks* would require significant manual intervention to renumber anyway. Thankfully RFC 2894 provides a solution to the problem.

RFC 2894 defines a router renumbering ICMP message. These messages act like a search-and-replace operation on the existing prefixes used by the router, and can also change parameters like the prefix lifetime. The three operations that can be performed are ADD (adds new prefixes based on matching existing prefixes), CHANGE (adds new prefixes, but also deletes existing matching prefixes) and SET-GLOBAL (like change, but removes all global scope addresses, rather than just matching ones). Each of these operations can match a single prefix and produce several new prefixes from it.

To take an example, suppose we are moving a customer from the prefix 2001:db8:dead:/48 to 2001:db8:babe:/48, but otherwise want to leave the structure of their network intact. We first send a message to all routers, telling them that if the router has a prefix 2001:db8:dead:XXXX/64, then to add a new prefix 2001:db8:babe:XXXX/64, where the XXXX bits are copied from the old prefix to the new one. Then we can send a message to shrink the lifetime associated with prefixes under 2001:db8:dead:/48, so deprecation will occur more quickly. Finally, we can send out another change request to remove all prefixes under 2001:db8:dead:/48.

Router renumbering has serious implications for security, so updates need to be authenticated with IPsec. Furthermore, for ease of operation it would be desirable to have the site-local all-routers address listening for updates. Of course, while router renumbering provides a good way to renumber the routing infrastructure, it doesn't obviously extend to renumbering servers that may have manually configured IPv6 addresses on interfaces or stored in configuration files. These factors mean that renumbering is not as simple as one would like in the IPv6 world.

Multicast Listener Discovery

Most of the aspects of multicast that we have discussed in this section relate to link-local multicast, which doesn't involve the forwarding of packets across networks.

---

* Large being defined as having enough routers to make it worthwhile doing automatically.

When multicast groupings organizations, or the whole Internet, routers need to be involved. One of the basic things a router needs to know is the list of multicast groups in which the nodes it routes for are interested. This is where Multicast Listener Discovery (MLD) is used.

MLD (RFC 2710) has three message types. The first, Multicast Listener Query, allows a router to find a specific multicast address or all that nodes have joined. The second, Multicast Listener Report, announces that someone is listening on a specific group. The final, Multicast Listener Done, lets a router know that all the listeners on an address may be finished and it should send a query to make sure. The specifics of the protocol ensure that only a small number of these messages need to be sent to keep the local routers up to date.

Routers will usually use multicast promiscuous mode for MLD (see the "Multicast" section earlier in this chapter). The routing of multicast traffic between routers is a more complex issue, addressed by protocols such as PIM. There are two types of PIM, sparse mode and dense mode. Sparse mode was described in RFC 2362, but *http://www.ietf.org/internet-drafts/draft-ietf-pim-sm-v2-new-11.txt* is the draft that describes the current state of sparse mode PIM. Likewise, *http://www.ietf.org/internet-drafts/draft-ietf-pim-dm-new-v2-05.txt* describes dense mode PIM.

Summary of ICMPv6 Types

Table 3-4 shows the ICMPv6 message types that have been formalized by IANA. We've ordered these messages by the value of the ICMPv6 type field, and grouped them by function.

Table 3-4. Summary of IANA assigned ICMPv6 types

Type	Description/subtype	RFC
Error messages		
1	Destination Unreachable	RFC 2463 (rfc section 3.1)
	0—no route	
	1—administratively prohibited	
	2—(not assigned)	
	3—address unreachable	
	4—port unreachable	
2	Packet Too Big	RFC 2463 (rfc section 3.2)
3	Time Exceeded	RFC 2463 (rfc section 3.3)
	0—hop limit exceeded	
	1—fragment reassembly time exceeded	
4	Parameter Problem	RFC 2463 (rfc section 3.4)
	0—erroneous header field	
	1—unrecognized Next Header type	
	2—unrecognized IPv6 option	

Table 3-4. Summary of IANA assigned ICMPv6 types (continued)

Type	Description/subtype	RFC
Information messages:		
128	Echo Request	RTC 2463 (rfc section 4.1)
129	Echo Reply	RTC 2463 (rfc section 4.2)
MLD:		
130	Multicast Listener Query	RFC 2710
131	Multicast Listener Report	RFC 2710
132	Multicast Listener Done	RFC 2710
Neighbor discovery:		
133	Router Solicitation	RFC 2461 (rfc section 4.1)
134	Router Advertisement	RFC 2461 (rfc section 4.2)
135	Neighbor Solicitation	RFC 2461 (rfc section 4.3)
136	Neighbor Advertisement	RFC 2461 (rfc section 4.4)
137	Redirect	RFC 2461 (rfc section 4.5)
Router renumbering:		
138	Router Renumbering	RFC 2894 (rfc 2894 (rfc section 3.1)
	0—Router Renumbering Command	
	1—Router Renumbering Result	
	255—Sequence Number Reset	
Node information:		
139	Node Information Query	(ICMP name lookup draft)
140	Node Information Reply	(ICMP name lookup draft)
Inverse neighbor discovery:		
141	Inverse Neighbor Solicitation	RFC 3122 (rfc section 2.1)
142	Inverse Neighbor Advertisement	RFC 3122 (rfc section 2.2
MLDv6:		
143	Multicast Listener Report v2	RFC 3810 (rfc section 5.2)
Mobile IPv6:		
144	Home Agent Request	RFC 3775 (rfc section 6.5)
145	Home Agent Reply	RFC 3775 (rfc section 6.6)
146	Mobile Prefix Solicitation	RFC 3775 (rfc section 6.7)
147	Mobile Prefix Advertisement	RFC 3775 (rfc section 6.8)
Secure neighbor discovery		
148	Cert Path Solicitation	(SEND draft)
149	Cert Path Advertisement	(SEND draft)

Address Selection

At this stage, it's clear the typical IPv6 node can, and very probably will, have many addresses. Some may be manually configured, others may be automatically configured via router announcements; some may be link-local and others may be global; some may be permanent and others temporary. From this plethora of addresses, a node must make a choice of which address to use. Depending on the criteria used, the choice could change many times over the course of the uptime of a host. In some cases addresses will be explicitly chosen by users or applications, say where a user types telnet ::1, or where a server is bound to a single IP address. For other situations, there needs to be some predictable mechanism for guiding the selection of addresses by a host; these are the default address selection rules, dealt with in RFC 3484.

In any given two-ended communication, there are obviously two addresses that would potentially have to be decided on; the source, and the destination. Source address selection determines which of a node's addresses will be used to originate a connection to a given destination address. Destination address selection would be typically applied to a list of addresses returned by DNS, sorting them in order of preference.

The selection process is given in terms of a sequence of rules that compare two addresses. You start with rule 1, and if it doesn't tell you which address to prefer then you move on to rule 2, and so on. The rules for source address selection are shown in Table 3-5 and the rules for destination address selection are shown in Table 3-6. Curiously, the rules for destination address selection depend on the source address selection rules, because they involve calculating what the preferred source address would be, given that a particular destination address was chosen! Once a destination address has been chosen, a suitable source address can be selected.

Table 3-5. Source address selection rules

Priority	Description
1	Prefer if source matches destination.
2	Prefer if appropriate scope.
3	Avoid if addresses are deprecated.
4a	Prefer addresses that are simultaneously home and care-of.
4b	Prefer home addresses over care-of (may have sense reversed by configurable setting).
5	Prefer address on interface closest to destination.
6	Prefer if policy label of source matches destination.
7	Prefer public addresses (may have sense reversed by configurable setting).
8	Use longest matching prefix.

Table 3-6. Destination address selection rules (dependent on corresponding source address)

Priority	Description
1	Avoid destination addresses known to be unreachable.
2	Prefer if scope of destination and corresponding source match.
3	Avoid if corresponding source is deprecated.
4a	Prefer if corresponding source is simultaneously home and care-of.
4b	Prefer if corresponding source is home rather than care-of.
5	Prefer if policy label of destination and corresponding source match.
6	Prefer higher policy precedence of destination address.
7	Prefer native transport.
8	Prefer destination address with smaller scope.
9	Use longest matching prefix.
10	Prefer higher preference indicated by name service (e.g., DNS).

Let's take a moment to clarify some of the terms used in the rules. *Scope* refers to whether an address is a link-local/.../global address. *Home* and *care-of address* are to do with IPv6's mobility features, covered in "Introduction to Mobile IPv6," later in this chapter. We'll discuss policy label and policy precedence in a moment.

Most interesting from an ISP perspective is the "longest matching prefix" rule. Very simply, the longest matching prefix of a source and destination pair is the number of bits that the addresses have in common, if you start counting from the left-hand end. The reasoning behind this is the hierarchical routing model[*] pursued by IPv6; an address that has lots of bits in common with your address is likely to be close to you in the network.

Address selection optionally includes a way to express some user or administrator defined policies. These include "labels" on addresses (a source and destination pair will be preferred if their labels match) and precedence (a destination with higher precedence is preferred).

Not a lot of operational experience exists yet with address selection and with the associated policies. The full implementation of address selection, not only according to the specification but also in a usable form, could actually be rather tricky, so only time will tell what aspects of address selection will have a practical impact on the configuration of IPv6.

---

[*] The hierarchical routing model stems from the policy of only assigning provider aggregate addressing in IPv6. The IPv4 address space is assigned discontiguously, and machines that are close within a network often have radically different IPv4 addresses.

In IPv4, we often assume that the order DNS returns addresses in is important; for example, it often determines the order in which clients will go to hosts to access services. This changes in IPv6, and is a potential "gotcha." The ordering of addresses returned by the DNS is the *weakest* tie-breaker for the address selection rules. This means that the way that certain load-balancing services work may have to change.

More About Headers

Let's consider some of the implications of the design of the IPv6 header. There is no field equivalent to the IPv4 options field, so the equivalent facilities are now provided by *extension headers*. These headers, and the fact that the IPv6 header has no checksum, have some influence on how upper level checksums are calculated. Also, the larger addresses used mean that more of a packet is taken up with headers, so header compression is correspondingly more important.

Extension Headers

In the "Basic Header Structure" section earlier in this chapter, we observed that the IPv4 notion of including options directly within the main header had been abandoned. However, IP options did serve a purpose, and that purpose is now achieved in IPv6 using *extension headers*. These headers are chained together. Within the IPv6 header the Next Header field tells you the type of the next extension header, which in turn has a Next Header and so on. The basic types of header discussed in RFC 2460 are the Hop-by-Hop Options header (type 0), the Routing header (type 43), the Fragment header (type 44), and the Destination Options header (type 60).

To make sure this process of chaining headers together terminates, there are a few special types of Next Header that do not themselves have a Next Header field. These include 6 = TCP, 17 = UDP, 58 = ICMPv6 and the rather odd 59, which means "there is no next header."

For example, Figure 3-5 shows an IPv6 packet containing an IPv6 header, followed by a routing header, followed by TCP header and data.

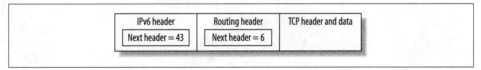

Figure 3-5. Use of the Next Header field

Aside from the Hop-by-Hop header, none of these headers are processed by a node simply forwarding a packet. If there is a Hop-by-Hop Options header, it must be immediately after the IPv6 header. This means that in the usual case a router won't have to look beyond the IPv6 header and doesn't have to go far to analyze the Hop-by-Hop header.

Another feature of extension headers is that although they can be variable sized, they must be a multiple of eight bytes in length, and fields within them must be suitably aligned for efficient access.

All IPv6 nodes should understand the extension headers discussed in *RFC* 2460, and also the authentication and ESP headers related to IPsec. If a node comes across a header it does not understand, then the packet will be dropped and an ICMPv6 parameter problem message will be generated. Note that since intermediate routers do not look beyond the Hop-by-Hop header they don't have to understand all the headers that they forward.

What happens if you want to send some option, and it doesn't matter if the node processing it understands it? This is provided for in the Hop-by-Hop and Destination *Options* headers. The options included within these headers fall into different four classes, according to what happens if they are not understood. The actions corresponding to these classes are "skip me and keep processing," "drop the packet," "drop the packet and send a ICMPv6 parameter problem message," and "drop the packet and send a ICMPv6 parameter problem message providing the packet is not a multicast packet." This provides enough flexibility to allow options to be either hints that can be ignored or made essential to the correct processing of the packet. In the latter case you can test if the option is supported by sending it and waiting for an ICMP response.

So, what can we actually do with these extension headers and the options they may contain? Table 3-7 shows a summary, but let us run through them briefly.

Table 3-7. IPv6 extension header summary

Header type	Subtype	RFC
Hop-by-Hop options		
	Padding	RFC 2460
	Router alert	RFC 2711
	Jumbo payload	RFC 2675
Destination options		
	Padding	RFC 2460
	Binding update	RFC 3775
	Binding acknowledgement	RFC 3775
	Binding request	RFC 3775
	Home address	RFC 3775
Routing header		
	Type 0	RFC 2460
Fragment header		RFC 2460
Authentication header		RFC 2402
ESP header		RFC 2406

Probably the most exciting of the Hop-by-Hop options is the Jumbo Payload option defined in RFC 2675. This implements one of the oft-hailed improvements of IPv6 over IPv4; to wit, more efficient handling of high-speed data. Usually IP packets are limited in size to 64KB, but this option permits the sending of IP packets of potentially up to 4GB in size! By sending larger packets, you reduce the fraction of the time sending header information. Naturally, this option will be most useful in networks where the maximum physical packet size is bigger than the old limit of 64KB.*

The other important Hop-by-Hop option is the Router alert option, which means a router should process this packet as well as forwarding it, and might be used in a multicast packet. The least interesting of the Hop-by-Hop and Destination options are the padding options, which allow the options header to be padded to the right size and the options therein to be aligned correctly. The other destination options relate to IPv6 mobility, which we describe in the "Introduction to Mobile IPv6" section later in this chapter.

The IPv6 routing header can specify variants of the usual routing procedure. The *type 0* variant of this implements source routing, in the sense that the packets must go via a number of prescribed intermediate routers. In the IPv4 world, this would be described as *loose source routing*.†

The Fragmentation header allows a source node to fragment packets, fulfilling much the same role as, and containing similar fields to the IPv4 header. This means it is still possible to send IP packets larger than the MTU of a link, but that the hard work must be done by end-nodes rather than the routers.

The authentication and ESP headers relate to IPsec, which we discuss in the "Security" section later in this chapter.

Checksums

With no checksum in the IPv6 header, catching errors in transit is left to upper layer checksums in IPv6. Also, extension headers mean that between the IPv6 header and the TCP/UDP/ICMPv6 header there may be arbitrary data. Consequently, upper layer checksums, that would have traditionally included the IP header, are instead defined to be calculated using a *pseudo-header*, which includes the source address, final destination address, the length of the upper-layer packet and the type of upper-layer packet. This is to avoid any confusion that might arise from Routing headers or Hop-by-Hop options which might change in transit.

---

* As an example, the MTU on Myrinet is, in theory, unlimited. In practice, you'd probably want to think twice about making the MTU unusually large.

† This used to be a security hot button in IPv4, when authentication based on source IPv4 address was common and packet filtering was not.

Header Compression

The basic IPv6 header is quite a bit larger than the IPv4 header,[*] and with extension headers could add up to a significant portion of the MTU. Header compression is a technique already in use in the IPv4 world and has been extended to cover IPv6. In fact, header compression in IPv6 can actually reduce headers to an overall proportion of packet size *smaller* than IPv4, thanks to the removal of frequently changing fields such as the IPv4 header checksum. Hence this is an ideal mechanism for link-expensive hosts to use, such as dial-up hosts and cellular devices.

The basic idea in header compression is that the non-payload data in a given data flow generally don't change very much. In other words, if you are downloading a large file using ftp for example, the packets that flow back and forth are mostly composed of application data (the contents of the file) and the bits of the headers that describe how much data must be acknowledged, and so on. Most of the header bits don't change at all in a given communication, and hence we can optimize for the common case by sending full length headers at the start of packet exchanges, with periodic updates, and only send "the differences" in between.[†]

There are two proposals on how to do header compression worth noting. First, there is a scheme defined in RFC 2507, published in February 1999, which has been around for a long time. Unfortunately it appears that this scheme does not deal tremendously well with high-loss links (as used by cellular/3Gdevices) so it, together with its supporting materials, are being reworked by the ROHC (RObust Header Compression) working group of the IETF. This work is taking place in a long series of RFCs, the most immediately relevant ones being RFC 3096 and RFC 3095. ROHC is not just addressing standard IP/TCP headers, they are also working on compressing headers for higher level application protocols like RTP[‡] that will find themselves running over wireless links more and more.

Introduction to Mobile IPv6

In these days of cellphones and wireless networking of all kinds, mobility for equipment now carries the expectation that you can take your laptop and use it for email, web, and so on more or less anywhere. By default, full mobility is not catered for—in other words, you cannot be on a wireless LAN in one office, put a machine to sleep, take it to another office, and wake it, and expect all existing connections to be preserved and everything to "just work." Furthermore, there are roaming issues with multiple points of access to a given network, address assignment issues and so on.

---

[*] The smallest IPv4 header is 20 bytes, compared to a fixed size of 40 bytes for IPv6.

[†] In fact this is only one of many ways of doing it. The complexity comes in attempting to compensate for protocols that do not retransmit in the case of error.

[‡] RFC 3242 reports they can get these headers down to one (!) octet in certain circumstances.

The mobility problems that Mobile IPv6 attempts to solve are a very well-defined subset of these, and have to do specifically with your layer 3 point of attachment to the network, and hence to your address, routing table, and other network infrastructure resources.

So how do we solve the problem of using a laptop in another person's network but still being able to get to your usual, within-home-network resources, as well as maintaining existing connections? The usual mechanisms invoked by the IPv6 stack on a link change, like stateless autoconfiguration, effectively kill existing TCP connections because TCP connections have a fixed address at either end of the connection. Furthermore, RAs in managed networks will have the same effect, and it would be inappropriate to suppress these mechanisms simply for this purpose.

The approach that Mobile IPv6 takes is as follows. Nodes are said to have a *home network*, which is the network to which they belong to in a logical or organizational sense. This could be a corporate network, in the case of a business laptop, a residential network, in the case of a personal laptop or a particular mobile phone network, in the case of a phone/PDA.

On this home network you will have a *home address*. While attached directly to the home network, you use this address normally. However, with Mobile IPv6 you can continue to use this address if you move to another network. This requires some infrastructural support.

In order to support this, another router is placed on this home network. Its job is to maintain a list of all known mobile nodes; it's called a *Home Agent*. The mobile nodes, when they move out of home network, register their changing addresses with the Home Agent. The address that a mobile node gets when it is on a different ("foreign") link is called a *care-of* address. The mobile node establishes a binding between the care-of address and the home address by communicating with the Home Agent.

This is fine for *correspondent nodes* who want to send packets to the mobile host, but what about for communication in the other direction? The mobile node can't just send packets with its home address, as these are likely to be blocked by ingress or egress filtering. Tunnelling back to the home agent might be possible, but could introduce significant latency or be prevented by firewalls. Thus, the approach taken is to send the packet from the care-of address, with a Destination option header saying what the source address should have been. This Destination header option is called the Home Address option.

Consequently, this means that the correspondent nodes must understand the Home Address option, and if they receive a packet with the home address option, the source address of that packet must be replaced with the home address when it is processed. A correspondent node can also support the same sort of binding between home-address and care-of address that Home Agents support, which allows them to send replies directly to the mobile node, without the intermediate step of sending them to the Home Agent.

So, the steps for sending a packet when mobile IP is in operation are:

1. Am I a mobile node replying to another node? If so, create reply packet with care-of address as the source address and add home address options header.

2. Am I a node replying to a mobile node and is its current care-of address in my binding cache? If so, create reply packet to care-of address as destination and add in home address as a part of routing extensions header.

Figure 3-6 shows the path that packets take from a mobile node to a correspondent node in various situations. Note that the packets always take a direct route. Figure 3-7 shows the path going in the opposite direction. Keep in mind that it is possible for the correspondent node to also be mobile. Before a mobile node uses any of these route optimizations, it will perform tests to ensure that they work correctly from the foreign network it is connected to.

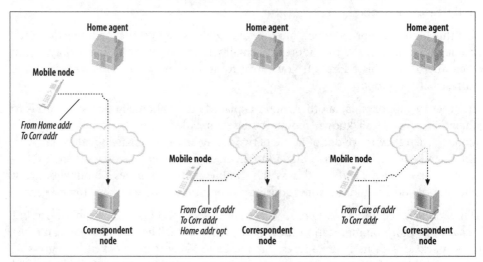

Figure 3-6. Packet path from mobile to correspondent node when it is at home, on a foreign network using its home address and on a foreign network using its care-of address

In addition Mobile IPv6 defines additional ICMPv6 messages and options for home agent discovery and Destination options for maintenance of home address and care-of address binding. Like Router Renumbering, Mobile IPv6 also has serious security implications and must be used in combination with IPsec. Mobile IPv6 is described in considerable detail in RFC 3775.

Surprisingly, mobile phone networks do not plan to use Mobile IP at least in their first incarnations. This is because GPRS and 3G networks behave like a gigantic seamless layer 2 network. That is, there are no intermediate layer 3 nodes; every

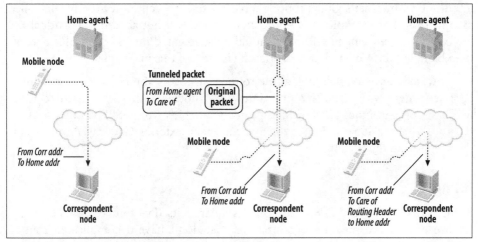

Figure 3-7. Packet path from correspondent to mobile node is at home, on a foreign network using its home address, and when its care-of address is known

node is connected via tunnels back to the main router, the GGSN. Thus, there's no real need for Mobile IP in this scenario.

At the time of writing IPv6 stacks have various degrees of support for Mobile IPv6. Support is not generally very complete, especially in release versions of software, though many vendors are monitoring the standard closely as has been finalized. For this reason we won't say much about mobile IPv6 in the rest of this book, as it is just a little early to deploy on the platforms we consider. However, for those of you who are interested in playing around, various stacks are available; in particular, Microsoft have one available, but you currently have to sign an NDA to gain access to it. Contact Microsoft at *mipv6-fb@microsoft.com* or through your usual support channel. Similarly Cisco mobile IPv6 is currently available as a technology preview; contact your Cisco representative for details.

Routing

Routing protocols are clearly very important to the operation of the Internet, but in a sense they are a separate issue from the problems of how low-level IP should operate.

So, how has IPv6 changed routing protocols? Well, the most obvious change you need to make is to allow IPv6 prefixes to be included, rather than IPv4 addresses. In fact, this is generally the only significant change between the IPv4 and IPv6 versions of well-known routing protocols.

Perhaps the most interesting changes in routing caused by IPv6 are in routing *policy*—in other words, not affecting the prefix processing per se, but affecting the administrative acquisition and control of prefixes. The routes that can be advertised into the IPv6 Internet's global routing table are to be much more strictly controlled than in IPv4. For example, it is hoped that people will not advertise individual /48 prefixes, because (remember!) these should be aggregated into a bigger block advertised by their ISP. We'll talk more about the impact of this in Chapter 4.

For now, let's have a quick look at the routing protocols you're likely to encounter. First we'll deal with IGPs (Interior Gateway Protocols). An IGP is used to route within an organization. IGPs include protocols such as RIP, OSPF, and IS-IS. After IGPs we'll take a look at BGP, which is the main Exterior Gateway Protocol currently in use on the IPv6 Internet.

RIPng

RIPng is defined in RFC 2080 and is very similar to its IPv4 forebear. It is designed for use in small to medium organizations that don't have a complicated routing setup. How does it work?

Well, each router sends messages (in UDP packets, port 521) that tell its neighbors what prefixes it knows how to reach and the *metric* associated with each prefix. A router may see a prefix advertised with several different metrics, so to choose the best one it adds a link related cost to each and then chooses the smallest. The cost assigned to each link is usually 1, so that the metric is actually a count of the number of links you must cross to reach that prefix.

Once a router has calculated the best available prefix and metric, it then advertises these new metrics and on to its neighbors. It also advertises prefixes that it can reach directly.

To stop routes hanging around forever, RIP expires routes that it hasn't seen advertised recently and also considers a metric of 16 to be so big that the route isn't worth considering.

Furthermore, it includes mechanisms for reducing the chance of routing loops, to only advertise changes and to avoid flooding the network in the case of frequent updates.

So, other than allowing IPv6 addresses in the protocol, what are the IPv6 specific details in RIPng? Well, RIPng uses the link-scope multicast address FF02::9 when it wants to send a message to all its neighbors. Also, routers are expected to specify their addresses as link-local addresses in RIP packets. Link-local addresses are good (in this case) for routing because you know they won't change if the network is renumbered.

OSPF

With RIP, all you learn about a prefix is its metric, which tells you how many hops away it is. For this reason RIP is sometimes called a *distance vector* protocol. Sometimes the distance to a prefix isn't enough to make a good routing decision.

OSPF has a different take on the problem. Rather than transmitting a prefix and a metric, each router transmits the information about the links attached to it, making it a *link state* protocol. This information is propagated through the network (in other words, routers pass this information on) and means that all routers have a full picture of the network. Then each router can make a decision based on the *global* situation about what routes it should use. The rule used is to choose the shortest path, where shortest is defined in terms of a combination of *weights* associated with each link.

Since OSPF routers have a full picture of the network, they don't have the same problems with loops or maximum hop counts that RIP has. However, there is a significant amount of complexity required to make OSPF practical and stable, and much of the OSPF protocol deals with this. To understand the details of OSPF takes more space than we have here, and for more details we refer you to John Moy's books on the protocol: *OSPF: Anatomy of an Internet Routing Protocol* and *OSPF Complete Implementation* (both published by Addison-Wesley).

OSPF for IPv6 is defined in *RFC* 2740, and it basically operates like a fully-featured IPv4 OSPF that understands IPv6 addresses instead of IPv4 addresses. Section 2 of the RFC is dedicated to describing the differences between OSPFv2 (*RFC* 2328) and and OSPF for IPv6. Perhaps the most interesting of these from an operational point of view are:

- IPv6 interfaces typically have several addresses belonging to different IPv6 subnets. OSPF used to work on a per-subnet basis, but to fit in better with the idea of multiple subnets per link, it now works on a per-link basis.

- Router IDs remain 32 bits wide and are written like IPv4 addresses. As your router may not actually have an IPv4 address, these can be assigned independently of IPv4 addressing. Router IDs are now always used to identify neighbors, rather than using IP addresses.

- Like RIP, OSPF uses link-local addresses for the next routing hop. The FF02::5 and FF02::6 multicast addresses are also used. Unlike RIP, OSPF isn't run over TCP or UDP, but is a protocol of its own (using a Next Header value of 89).

- Authentication, if required, must now be done with IPsec. This means no more md5.

Integrated IS-IS

IS-IS is a routing protocol very similar in idea to OSPF: it is also a link-state protocol and uses shortest-path routing, again based on metrics assigned to links. The main difference between IS-IS and OSPF is that IS-IS is part of the OSI protocol suite and turns out to be slightly more protocol agnostic than OSPF. The original additions to IS-IS for routing IPv4 are described in RFC 1195 and the minor extras for IPv6 are now being finalized at the IETF.

IS-IS, when used to route IP, is sometimes referred to as *integrated* IS-IS. Here "integrated" refers to the fact that you could run a single IS-IS instance on a router to route IP *and* ISO protocols. The advantages of this include reduced processing overhead on routers, and also a single routing protocol for network management staff to worry about.

With the appearance of IPv6, a single IS-IS instance can now route IPv4, IPv6 and ISO protocols. This has appeal for some network operators, and they have moved to IS-IS so that they can route their IPv4 and IPv6 traffic with a single protocol. Others have chosen IS-IS just for IPv6, so that they have a degree of protocol redundancy within their network (or maybe just to get a feel for a different IGP). Possibly for these reasons, it seems that IS-IS may end up being the most popular IGP for IPv6.

Interestingly, from a protocol point of view, IS-IS doesn't use TCP, UDP, IPv4 or IPv6, but instead uses its own ISO protocol for the exchange of routing information. This means that configuring IS-IS involves assigning ISO addresses to the routers in your network that will speak IS-IS.

BGP-4+

The BGP protocol is different from the previous routing protocols we've discussed for a few reasons. First, it is designed for routing between many independent networks, rather than routing within an organization. It is the protocol that determines the routes between all the networks in the Internet. To make things manageable, each network is treated as a black box: BGP can see where the networks connect to each other, but it can't see inside the networks. These black boxes are called autonomous systems (ASs).

Even still, the number of networks that BGP has to deal with is large and the number of links even larger. For this reason, using a link-state protocol isn't feasible. A distance-vector protocol isn't practical either because there are just too many hops and loops in the Internet.

BGP operates in a hybrid area between distance-vector and link-state. As in distance-vector, a router only tells its neighbors about the best route it has to a network, but rather than just telling them the metric of this route, it also communicates other information, including the list of ASs the best route goes through. This means that BGP may not know the state of all the links in the Internet, but it does at least know the hops along the routes it wants to use. This information can be used to avoid routing loops by discarding routes that would go through an AS twice.

As well as this AS path information, a BGP router also communicates a selection of information about how desirable various routes are. There are a dizzying array of rules and configuration knobs that can be used to get BGP to route traffic in particular ways. A lot of the operational complexity of BGP arises from these parameters.

In terms of low-level details, BGP-4 (RFC 1771) has a set of extensions to deal routing information for arbitrary protocols (RFC 2858). The details for IPv6 are made explicit in RFC 2545.

BGP actually runs over TCP (port 179), which means it can use IPv4 or IPv6 for transport. However, the address of the remote router can be important for calculating next hops, so if you are transporting IPv6 routing information over an IPv4 TCP session you may need to explicitly configure information about the next hop. (Typically, one would bring up two BGP sessions in parallel—one over IPv4, one over IPv6—and over each session one would exchange only the routing information specific to that protocol.)

Like OSPF, BGP also uses a router ID in the protocol, which remains a 32-bit number. For routers with IPv4 addresses, this ID is usually one of those addresses. If you have an IPv6-only router, the Router ID has to be configured manually.

BGP does have limitations that may become a problem as time progresses. For example, ASs are identified by 16 bit numbers, so some day we'll run out of AS numbers, just like IPv4 addresses. A protocol called IDRPv2 was supposed to address these, and other more complex issues. Today, however, BGP remains the routing protocol of the IPv6 backbone.

Security

IPv6 enhances network security considerably. Probably the most important contribution it makes is not a technical contribution, but rather a matter of policy—the standard mandates that an IPv6 stack must *not* be implemented without supporting some form of encryption. It's important to note that this encryption is not at an application layer; that is, it's not a separate ad-hoc mechanism which is differently configured in mail programs than in web browsers than in video streaming applets—it is at a lower layer and can also secure things like neighbor discovery.

This was quite an achievement by the IETF. There are certainly very many jurisdictions in the world that use computers; many of them have severe anti-encryption laws; some of them prohibit its use entirely.

The form of security, IPsec, is already familiar to many as it is the basis of many VPN (virtual private network) systems that are already deployed. IPsec is quite a complicated architecture; see RFC 2401 for more details. In IPv6 it is implemented using extension headers that say that the remainder of the packer is encrypted (the ESP header of RFC 2406) or cryptographically signed (the AH header of RFC 2402). These are basically the same techniques as used in IPv4.

IPsec does, however, come with some downsides. For example, if traffic is regularly encrypted within your network, then debugging or security-related packet-content sniffing is impossible, unless you have the key. For that reason alone, some network administrators insist on configuring a static key for intra-site communication between machines, for ease of debugging. There have been efforts made, however, to ensure that header encryption (as opposed to content encryption) is not mandatory under all circumstances.

Quality of Service

Quality of service, henceforth referred to as QoS, is a complicated area. The core concept is quite simple: we, both as network administrators and as users, want to ensure that a certain application can have guaranteed performance on a certain network. When desired by a user, this often translates to statements such as "I wish I could download that ISO before I've got to catch my bus..." and, when desired by a network administrator, generally translates as "How can I stop those ISO downloaders killing the rest of the network?"

Generally, the kind of application we want to guarantee performance for is a multimedia application, not the standard HTTP or SMTP transactions that take place billions of times a day (although in some cases we may want to guarantee that a certain portion of the network will be set aside for critical services). This is because multimedia applications are amongst the most sensitive to packet loss and jitter, given the necessity to have data arrive at the right time for reassembly and display. There are various theories regarding how this should be done:

1. Smart network, stupid end hosts
2. Stupid network, smart end hosts
3. Overdimensioning

The first two schemes differ over where to place the intelligence involved in making QoS decisions, while the last attempts to avoid the problem entirely. Exactly what scheme will provide the best QoS under all circumstances is unclear. Different schemes require different facilities to be available. Rather than make a call on how QoS should work, IPv6 provides some generic facilities that should help QoS designers. These include some fields in the IPv6 header and, of course, extension headers.

There are two ways in which the IPv6 header provides for manipulable QoS. One is the traffic class field, the other is the 20 bit flow label in the IPv6 header. Note, that these fields are available in the base IPv6 header, and so are immediately available to routers, regardless of the Extension Headers that may follow.

The traffic class field is discussed in RFC 2460, but leaves the classes to be defined after future research. Differentiated Services, one of the existing mechanisms used to provide QoS, provides its interpretation of the traffic class field in RFC 2474. In a network providing QoS via DiffServ routers would decide to give packets preferential treatment based on RFC 2474's interpretation of the traffic class field.

To explain what a flow label is, we must say what a flow is. A flow is some specified subset of the traffic making its way from one part of a network to another. Usually the flow is defined in terms of all the traffic from a particular running application, host or network to another.

In IPv6, a flow is envisaged as a one way association between an application on one host and another application, usually elsewhere in the network. A packet is identified as belonging to a particular flow by its source and destination IPv6 addresses and the flow label. The only special value for the flow label is zero, which indicates that the packet doesn't belong to any flow in particular.

The flow label mechanism makes flows easily identifiable, so an application or the OS can request particular handling of packets within a flow by the intervening routers and the end host(s).[*] The request for special treatment could be made using a protocol like RSVP. The idea of RSVP is that a message can be sent to the routers a flow passes through describing the special treatment that the flow requires.

Flow labels will usually be selected randomly to allow for efficient usage of hash tables, though routers aren't supposed to depend on this. There are even proposals to allow routers to rewrite flow labels to allow their use for MPLS-like routing. The description of the flow label's usage is described in RFC 3697.

Because of the general flexibility of IPv6, there are also other ways that QoS could be provided for, say by using the Routing header or Hop-by-hop options header. However, all these techniques are still areas of active research and deployment is still limited to relatively special situations. Whatever QoS system prevails, IPv6 should have the features to support it.

Today, in the real world™, the most common and perhaps the simplest approach has been to overdimension. In other words, making the capacity of links substantially more than your total projected traffic volume, so that you never experience the congestion and network performance deterioration that QoS is supposed to help you manage. It may not be cheap, but it does tend to work. Unfortunately if there are any low capacity links in your organization at all, chances are someone will want to do something exotic with them sooner or later.

The Promise of IPv6

Let's finish off this chapter with a quick review of what the features offered by the design of IPv6 are.

---

[*] Yep—the destination address can be a multicast address.

Simplicity and Flexibility

IPv6's scalability, the darling of many press releases, is perhaps best broken into two capabilities. First, the capability of the protocol to rise to the task of addressing and routing both the existing and the future Internet. We think everyone can agree that IPv6 has been engineered with this in mind, by allowing lots of address space for hosts and countering the routing problems with a more hierarchical address space, while being flexible enough for future developments. Second, the ability of the protocol to be extended naturally to meet future, as yet unknown, requirements. A very important component of this is the Extension Headers facility.

Mobility and Security

IPv6 offers significant mobility and security features which, unfortunately, by their nature, are not as simple as might be desired. While support for IPsec is widely available, configuring for interoperability can be tricky. Mobility is at an earlier stage of development, and while implementations are available, full implementations are not yet widely shipped.

PART II
Deploying IPv6

## CHAPTER 4

Planning

When in trouble or in doubt
Run in circles, scream and shout.
—*Anonymous*

At this stage, we've already looked at a good deal of the theory behind IPv6. It's now a good time to start thinking about the issues around deploying IPv6 in a wider environment, such as your company, college, or ISP network. In this chapter, we provide recommendations for what to think about and what to do when planning an IPv6 deployment; how to introduce IPv6 to your network, how to interoperate with IPv4, and planning for the growth of IPv6, all with an eye to maintaining stability and manageability on your network. We provide worked examples of IPv6 deployment for networks which are hopefully quite similar to yours, and also highlight under exactly what circumstances our recommendations are applicable. By the end of this chapter you should hopefully have a toolbox of techniques for implementing IPv6, and also the right mental framework for using that toolbox.

Since we will be talking in some detail about the planning process, it's incumbent upon us to outline the important building-blocks and techniques of IPv6 network design before we talk about how we actually put them together. So, ahead of outlining step-by-step plans, we need to tell you about getting connectivity, getting address space, and the intricacies of selecting transition mechanisms, amongst other things. With those under your belt, you'll be in a position to get the most out of the worked examples.

Note that a significant portion of this chapter is about network planning, and planning for larger networks at that. If you are more of a Systems Administrator, rather than a Network Administrator, then you still may want to skim this chapter before moving on to the latter chapters. For those of you staying on, let's get stuck right in to the detail.

Transition Mechanisms

Transition mechanisms are so called because they are ostensibly ways you can move your network to IPv6. In reality, IPv4 and IPv6 are likely to be co-operating on most networks for a long while, so they might better be called inter-operating techniques or IPv6 introduction mechanisms. In any event, there are quite a few of them, and they have a wide variety of capabilities. Some allow you to connect to the IPv6 Internet, even if intervening equipment only speaks IPv4 (tunnels, 6to4, Teredo). Some are suitable for providing internal IPv6 connectivity until your infrastructure supports IPv6 (tunnels, 6to4, ISATAP). Others are to help IPv4-only hosts communicate with IPv6-only (NAT-PT, TRT, Proxies). There are even some to help IPv4-only applications (Bump in the Stack/API).

 While there is a plethora of mechanisms available, you will in all probability only need to understand and use a small fraction of them. (We provide a table that gives an overview later.) At a minimum, you'll want to know about dual-stack, configured tunnels and proxies. You may want to browse through the others to see if they'll be useful in your network.

Dual Stack

The dual-stack transition mechanism is perhaps not so elegant as others we will discuss, but is common, useful and many of the other mechanisms we'll talk about require at least one dual-stacked host. We expect that dual-stacking a network will be the way most people choose to deploy IPv6, unless they have unusual requirements.

As the name implies, dual stacking involves installing both an IPv4 and an IPv6 stack on a host. This means the host can make decisions about when connections should be made using IPv4 or IPv6; generally this is done based on the availability of IPv6 connectivity and DNS records. The IPv4 and IPv6 stacks can and often are completely independent: logical interfaces may be numbered separately, brought up and down separately and essentially treated as being separate machines.

One problem with the dual-stack method is that the shortage of IPv4 addresses means that you may not have enough to give to every host. There is a proposal called DSTM (Dual Stack Transition Mechanism) that allows for the temporary assignment of IPv4 addresses to nodes while they need them, so a large group of dual-stacked hosts can share a small number of IPv4 addresses, akin to dialup hosts sharing addresses out of a pool.

The fact that these dual-stacked hosts can originate and receive IPv6 *and* IPv4 packets is extremely powerful, allowing them to form a connection between IPv4 and IPv6 networks. We'll look at ways in which this is possible next.

Configured Tunnelling

This is, in many ways, the simplest of transition mechanisms, although it is not as easily maintainable as others because it involves manually configuring some addresses.

The principle behind tunnelling is the encapsulation of IPv6 packets in IPv4 packets. If you haven't encountered this notion before, it might sound rather peculiar at first—wrap packets in other packets? But it's actually a very powerful technique.

The central idea to understand is that just like Ethernet headers surround IP packets, which surround TCP and UDP headers, which surround protocols such as SMTP, you can just as easily insert another packet where a TCP packet would go and rely on the routing system to get it to the right place. As long as the receiving and transmitting ends have an agreed convention for how to treat these packets, everything can be decoded correctly and life is easy.

Static tunnelling is meant to link isolated islands of IPv6 connectivity, where the networks are well-known and unlikely to change without notice. One example would obviously be branch offices—the Galway division of X Corp. has a dial-on-demand link to the Dublin branch with both IPv6 and IPv4 connectivity, say. The way it works is as follows: the egress points of the linked networks are configured to encapsulate IPv6 packets to specified IPv6 destinations through statically configured IPv4 gateways. The packets proceed over the normal IPv4 routing system and are decapsulated at the other end, with the IPv6 packet then being forwarded to the correct host by the IPv6 routing system. If a packet is lost or dropped in the IPv4 part of the forwarding system, the usual TCP or application retransmission mechanisms come into play, just as if the packet had been lost due to, e.g., an Ethernet glitch. The intention is that the IPv4 section of the journey happens in as transparent a fashion as possible to the IPv6 stacks and applications.

It's important to note that this IPv4 forwarding is not happening over any kind of TCP or UDP "port"—it's another protocol commonly referred to as IPv6 over IPv4.

So, where are you likely to see configured tunnels in practice? There seem to be three common situations, all used to work around pieces of IPv4-only infrastructure.

ISP to customer
> Here, possibly because a border router does not support IPv6, an ISP provides IPv6 connectivity to a customer by providing a tunnel to some dual-stacked host or router within the customer network.

Tunnel broker
> Here your ISP may not be providing IPv6 support and instead you get an IPv6 connection via a third party, who are known as *tunnel brokers*.* There are many

---

* Actually, a tunnel broker is someone who finds a tunnel for you and the tunnel may in turn be provided by a fourth party!

people who provide tunnels as a public service such as *http://www.freenet6.net/* and *http://www.sixxs.net/*.

Linking internal sites

In some cases, sites within an organization may be joined by sections of network that aren't IPv6 capable, and until they are upgraded tunnels are necessary to join up the sites. In these cases you have the option of putting the tunnel endpoints on either side of the IPv4-only blockage, or bringing all the tunnels back to a central point. Deciding which is appropriate probably depends on if you have centralized or autonomous IT management.

Example 4-1 shows an example of how a configured tunnel is set up on a Cisco router. We'll leave the ins and outs of this until the "Configured Tunnelling" section later in this chapter, but you can see that it isn't a complex configuration and only involves specifying the IPv4 and IPv6 addresses of the tunnel end points.

Example 4-1. Example static tunnel configuration on a Cisco

```
!
interface Loopback0
 ip address 192.0.2.1 255.255.255.255
!
interface Tunnel1
 description Tunnel for customer BIGCUST
 no ip address
 ipv6 address 2001:db8:8:6::1/64
 tunnel source Loopback0
 tunnel destination 192.168.200.2
 tunnel mode ipv6ip
!
ipv6 route 2001:db8:70::/48 Tunnel1
!
```

Automatic Tunnelling

RFC 2893 describes the encapsulation used for IPv6-in-IPv4 tunnels, and the notion of configured tunnels. It also describes the notion of an automatic tunnelling. In this situation, the prefix ::/96 is set aside for things called *IPv4 compatible addresses*, where the rightmost 32 bits of the IPv6 address is considered to be an IPv4 address. IPv6 packets addressed to these addresses could be automatically encapsulated in an IPv4 packet addressed to the corresponding IPv4 address and tunnelled to its destination.

This means that two hosts that both speak IPv4 and IPv6 could talk IPv6 to one another, even if neither had a connection to the IPv6 Internet. While initially this might seem useful, the real question is why wouldn't they just speak IPv4? In fact, automatic tunnelling has some security implications; for example, a host that replies to a compatible address may generate IPv4 packets, which may not be expected on the network. As a result compatible addresses are not usually assigned to interfaces, but are used as a way of indicating that IPv6 should be tunnelled. For example, setting the default IPv6 route to the IPv4 compatible address of a dual-stacked router would result in packets being tunnelled to that router.[*]

In general, automatic tunnelling isn't something that you will need to consider at a planning stage as anything more than a configuration device. Its close relative, 6to4, is something considerably more relevant, as we will see.

6to4

6to4 is a mechanism allowing organizations to experiment with IPv6 without:

1. An upstream ISP(s) supporting IPv6.
2. Applying for IPv6 address space.
3. Arranging a "tunnel" with another IPv6 user.

The only thing a 6to4 user needs is a global IPv4 address, reachable on protocol 41.[†] Again note that this is a *protocol* number, not a port number.

Here's an example of how it works. Suppose that a 6to4 machine is using IPv4 address 192.0.2.4 from a public allocation. By virtue of the fact that the machine has this IPv4 address, by definition, it can also use the entire IPv6 network 2002:c000: 0204::/48! You get this address by taking the 6to4 prefix 2002::/16 and replacing bits 17 to 49 with the 32 bits of the IPv4 address. Usually, the machine configures a "6to4" pseudo-interface which has a selected address from the 6to4 range of its IPv4 address. Other machines within the organization can then be assigned addresses from the 6to4 range, and outgoing packets should be routed to the host with the 6to4 pseudo-interface.

So, 6to4 automatically assigns you a range of addresses, but how can we get packets to and from the IPv6 Internet and your network?

Packets from the IPv6 Internet sent to an address in the range 2002:c000:0204::/48 will be routed to the nearest 6to4 *Relay Router*. Relay routers are routers which advertise routes to 2002::/16, into the local or global routing table, and they're connected to both the IPv4 and IPv6 Internet. The router looks at the 6to4 address, extracts the embedded IPv4 address, and so encapsulates the IPv6 packet in an IPv4 packet addressed to 192.0.2.4. When the packet arrives at 192.0.2.4 it will be decapsulated and routed as a normal IPv6 packet according to the normal IPv6 routing rules within your organization. (The whole strategy might remind you of the tunnelling mechanism described in the "Automatic Tunnelling" section earlier in this chapter.)

---

[*] More explicitly, if the router had address 10.0.0.1 this might be achieved by running a command such as route add -inet6 default ::10.0.0.1. Not all operating systems support this, but you can see examples of this in Table 5-13.

[†] The protocol number for encapsulated IPv6.

To get packets back to the IPv6 Internet from your 6to4 network, we need a relay router for the opposite direction. An IPv4 anycast address, 192.88.99.1, has been assigned for this job, so the default IPv6 route on 192.0.2.4 can be set to point to 2002:c058:6301::. This means that packets going to the IPv6 Internet will be encapsulated and sent to 192.88.99.1, which will be routed by the normal IPv4 routing system to the nearest 6to4 relay router with this anycast address. The relay router, which is again connected to both the IPv4 and IPv6 Internet, will forward the packet to the IPv6 Internet and the packet will then make its way to its destination.

Figures 4-1 and 4-2 illustrate how packets get from a 6to4 network to the IPv6 Internet and back again. 6to4 also allows for a short-cut for packets between 6to4 networks, where they can be sent directly to the appropriate IPv4 address.

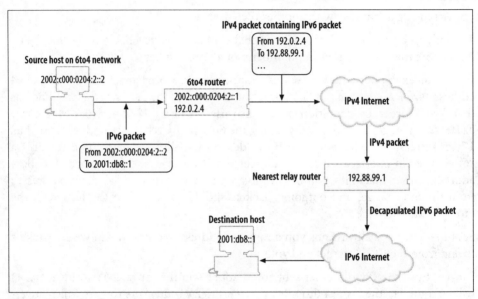

Figure 4-1. Packet flow from 6to4 to IPv6 Internet

The details of 6to4 are explained in RFC 3056, but it was written before the allocation of the IPv4 anycast address, so RFC 3068 covers the allocation and use of the anycast address. We'll cover the configuration of 6to4 in the "6to4 configuration" section in Chapter 5.

So, when is it a good idea to use 6to4? Well, 6to4 has advantages over configured tunnels for people who don't have a fixed IP address. Specifically, your tunnel broker or ISP needs to know your IPv4 address if they are to route packets for a fixed IPv6 address space to you. If your IPv4 address keeps changing, then you need to keep updating their configuration. With 6to4, when your IPv4 address changes, so do your IPv6 addresses, and they implicitly have your new IPv4 address embedded in them. This makes them good for most kinds of dial-up and certain kinds of DSL user.

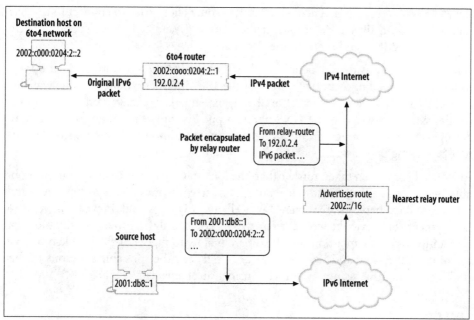

Figure 4-2. Packet flow from IPv6 Internet to 6to4

6to4 could also be used by an organization with fixed IPv4 addresses in the absence of an IPv6-capable ISP or nearby tunnel broker. Unfortunately, there are two disadvantages to using the technique here. First, you don't know where the nearest relay router will be, and second, you may find it tricky to get reverse DNS for your 6to4 prefix. However, it does mean you don't have to depend on a single tunnel broker.

An organization with a large IPv4 infrastructure might consider deploying separate 6to4 prefixes internally and using it to provide islands of IPv6 connectivity internally. They could also provide their own relay router to control the egress of IPv6 from the organization. See the "6to4 Relay Routers" section in Chapter 6 for some advice on running a 6to4 relay router.

DJB's AutoIPv6

One peculiarity of IPv6 is that it is neither forward nor backward-compatible. In other words, IPv4-only hosts cannot communicate with IPv6-only hosts, and vice versa. Even on a globally reachable IPv4 host with a working IPv6 stack, the machine still cannot communicate with IPv6-only hosts unless you configure one of the transition mechanisms or provide native connectivity.

Various people are eager to fix this problem, and 6to4 and Teredo go a long way to provide IPv6 client hosts with automatic connectivity to the IPv6 Internet. Dan Bernstein suggested a mechanism to try to extend this to servers. The idea is that each IPv4 server with an IPv6 stack automatically configures a well-known 6to4 address, say 2002:WWXX:YYZZ::c0de. Then when an IPv6-only client tries to connect to a server that only had an IPv4 DNS record, it then could generate the corresponding well-known 6to4 address and try to connect to that.

Dan's argument was that as people gradually upgraded the software on their servers to a version including AutoIPv6, more of the IPv4 Internet would become available over IPv6 without any further effort being expended. To make AutoIPv6 happen would require a tweak in the DNS libraries on IPv6-only hosts and for vendors to arrange automatic configuration of 6to4 and the well-known address: a simple matter of tweaking boot-up scripts.

AutoIPv6 hasn't been taken further than the idea stage yet. Some consideration probably needs to be given to how it would interact with firewalls, load balancers and other complex network hardware, as well as how it would impact native IPv6 deployment. However, it would seem that it could only improve the situation for IPv6-only hosts. We mention AutoIPv6 here mainly to highlight the problem of how to connect IPv6-only and IPv4-only hosts. We'll see other possible solutions to this problem later in this section when we consider mechanisms like SIIT.

Teredo

We know that there are many hosts that are stuck behind NAT devices, which can usually only deal with TCP, UDP and limited kinds of ICMP. As we have noted, configured tunnels and 6to4 make use of IPv4's protocol 41, which is neither TCP nor UDP. This means that it may not be possible for NATed hosts to use tunnels, 6to4 or indeed any other mechanisms using odd protocol numbers.

Teredo is a mechanism that tunnels IPv6 through UDP in a way that should allow it to pass through most NAT devices. It is a remarkably cunning design, intended as a "last-ditch" attempt to allow IPv6 connectivity from within an organization where end hosts may not have any other suitable networking available.

The operation of Teredo is somewhat similar to 6to4 as it requires a certain amount of infrastructure, namely Teredo servers and Teredo relays. Servers are stateless and are not usually required to forward data packets. The main function of Teredo servers is facilitate the addressing of and communication between Teredo clients and Teredo relays, so they must be on the public IPv4 Internet. They also occasionally have to send packets to the IPv6 Internet, and so need to be connected to it.

Relays are the gateways between the IPv6 Internet and the Teredo clients. They forward the data packets, contacting the Teredo servers if necessary. They must be on the IPv4 and the IPv6 Internet.

Much of the complication of Teredo involves sending packets to create state on the NAT device. These packets are given the name *Teredo bubbles*. Clients initially contact the Teredo server, allowing two way conversation with it. The client forms an address that is a combination of the server's IPv4 address and the IPv4 and port number allocated to the NAT device by this initial communication.

From then on, if a Teredo relay wants to forward packets to a Teredo client, it can contact the server to ask it to *ask the client* to send a packet to the relay. This packet will establish the necessary state on the NAT device to allow direct communication between the relay and the client.

Provision is also made for direct client-to-client operation and other optimizations, depending on the specifics of the NAT device you are behind. (There is a process a Teredo client can go through to determine what kind of NAT it is behind.)

Teredo uses the prefix 3FFE:831F::/32 and UDP port 3544. Since the IPv6 address assigned to a client depends on the server's address and the NAT's address, there is a possibility that it will change frequently, especially if the NAT's IPv4 address is dynamically assigned.

Christian Huitema from Microsoft is an important driving force behind Teredo. His draft describing the current state of Teredo's development is available at *http:// www.ietf.org/internet-drafts/draft-huitema-v6ops-teredo-03.txt*. Microsoft is very interested in technology like Teredo because many Windows machines are stuck behind NAT devices and Microsoft would like to be able to offer new technology and services to these machines and their users. Teredo is available as part of the peer-to-peer update for Windows XP, and though other vendors have not yet implemented it, it looks likely to become widely used. You can also get access to a preview of the server-relay technology component of Teredo—email *ipv6-fb@microsoft.com* for more details. (Although Teredo is currently at a somewhat experimental stage. some code is already shipping.)

While Teredo is likely to become widely used in unmanaged networks as a way for a computer to connect itself to the IPv6 network, Teredo is the sort of technology that you don't want to include in a deployment plan. Teredo is intended to be a last resort, used before any IPv6 infrastructure is available and when you have no access to a public IPv4 address. Your deployment should put infrastructure in place that eliminates the need for Teredo. However, if you are just trying to deploy IPv6 on your desktop and you're stuck behind a NAT, then Teredo may be your only choice.

6over4

In the same way as you can have "IPv6 over Ethernet" or "IPv6 over token ring," there is a mechanism to run an IPv6 network using IPv4 as the layer 2 transport, and this mechanism is called 6over4. This is different from tunnels and 6to4, because it aims to allow full neighbor discovery with the IPv4 network acting as a LAN. Remember, IPv6 makes use of layer 2 multicast, so 6over4 achieves this by using IPv4 multicast.

In the same way that Ethernet uses the EUI-64 interface IDs, 6over4 needs a way to form interface IDs so it uses the IPv4 address: a node with address 10.0.0.1 will end up with link-local address fe80::0a00:0001. Similarly, there is a mapping between IPv6 multicast addresses and IPv4 multicast addresses, so FF02::1 becomes 239.192.0.1. All this is explained in detail in RFC 2529.

In a way, 6over4 is a little like carrying IPv6 over MPLS, in that MPLS encapsulates IPv6 such that the internal details of the routing become invisible to the IPv6 layer 3 devices.

Since 6over4 is just another medium type that you can run IPv6 over, it doesn't have any special prefix associated with it. (If you want to use 6over4 you have to get your address space and external connectivity from some other source.)

6over4 doesn't really seem to have a lot of momentum, probably as a result of it requiring working IPv4 multicast infrastructure and the work on ISATAP, which provides many of the features 6over4 would have provided. It is also not widely implemented, so you probably do not need to consider it while planning your use of IPv6.

ISATAP

ISATAP is a rather funky acronym standing for Intra-Site Automatic Tunnel Addressing Protocol. The idea is very similar to 6over4, in that it aims to use an IPv4 network as a virtual link layer for IPv6. Probably the most important difference is that it avoids the use of IPv4 multicast.

To get this to work, ISATAP needs to specify a way to avoid the link-local multicast used by neighbor solicitation and router solicitation. To avoid the need for neighbor solicitation, ISATAP uses addresses with an interface ID of ::0:5EFE:a.b.c.d which are assumed to correspond to an IPv4 "link-layer" address of a.b.c.d. Thus link-layer addresses on ISATAP interfaces are calculated as opposed to solicited.

Avoiding multicast for router solicitations requires some sort of jump-start process that provides you with the IPv4 addresses of potential routers. It is suggested that these might be got from a DHCPv4 request or by looking up a hostname like isatap. example.com using IPv4 connectivity. Once the node has the IPv4 addresses of potential ISATAP routers it can then send router solicitations to each, encapsulated in an IPv4 packet. The routers can reply and the nodes can configure addresses based on the advertised prefixes and their ISATAP interface IDs.

So, what does ISATAP buy us? Without an ISATAP router, it acts like automatic tunnelling, but using link-local ISATAP addresses[*] of the form fe80::5EFE:a.b.c.d rather than IPv4 compatible addresses like ::a.b.c.d, allowing communication

---

[*] In case you are wondering where 5EFE comes from, it is the Organizationally-Unique Identifier (OUI) assigned by IANA that can be used for forming EUI-64 addresses.

between a group of hosts that can speak IPv4 protocol 41 to one another. This could be a group of hosts behind a NAT, or a group of hosts on the public Internet.

With an ISATAP router you can assign a prefix to this group of hosts and the router can provide connectivity to the IPv6 Internet via some other means (either a native connection, a tunnel, 6to4 or whatever). So, the thing that defines which group of hosts are on the same virtual subnet is the ISATAP router they have been configured to use.

ISATAP has some nice features, especially if you are doing a sparse IPv6 deployment in a large IPv4 network. You may not want to manually configure tunnels or deploy IPv6 routers for each subnet that you are deploying an IPv6 node on. ISATAP lets you deploy a number of centrally located ISATAP routers which can then be accessed from anywhere in the IPv4 network without further configuration.

Note that you can achieve something quite similar to this with 6to4, where 192.88.99.1 takes the place of the ISATAP router. However, with 6to4 the prefixes you use are derived from the IPv4 addresses, so if you are stuck behind a NAT you get bad 6to4 addresses. With ISATAP the interface ID is derived from the IPv4 address and the prefix comes from the ISATAP router, so you can give out real addresses IPv6 inside the NATed network.

The draft describing ISATAP can be found at *http://www.ietf.org/internet-drafts/draft-ietf-ngtrans-isatap-22.txt*. Unfortunately, ISATAP implementations are a bit thin on the ground at the moment: Windows XP supports ISATAP, and KAME and USAGI snapshots used to include ISATAP support, but its development is being hindered by intellectual property concerns.

SIIT

The previous techniques we have discussed allow us to use IPv4 infrastructure to enable IPv6 hosts to talk to one another, or to the IPv6 Internet at large. SIIT is the first technique we'll mention that's intended to allow IPv4-only hosts to talk to IPv6-only hosts.

SIIT is Stateless IP/ICMP Translation. The idea is that it allows you to take an IPv4 packet and rewrite the headers to form an IPv6 packet and vice versa. The IP level translations are relatively simple: TTL is copied to Hop Limit, ToS bits to traffic class, payload lengths are recalculated and fragmentation fields can be copied to a fragmentation header if needed.

Since TCP and UDP haven't really changed, they can be passed through relatively unscathed. However the differences between ICMPv4 and ICMPv6 are more significant, so SIIT specifies how to do these translations too.

There is one other tricky issue, which is how to translate addresses between IPv4 and IPv6. Getting an IPv4 address into an IPv6 address is straightforward, just embed it in the low 32 bits. Since IPv6 addresses are much larger, there's not a lot of point trying to encode them in an IPv4 address, so some mapping must be done. NAT-PT and NAPT-PT are ways of doing this, which we'll discuss in a moment.

So Many to Choose from...

Of course, since we have such wonderful transition mechanisms at our disposal, there is no doubt a great temptation to rely on them completely. After all, 6to4 gives us more address space than any reasonable organization could possibly use, for free—why bother one's upstream ISP when they're clearly not interested?

6to4 and its relatives are great as far as they go, but they have their limitations. Tightly bound with obtaining address space is the question of connectivity: in IPv6, the two almost always come together. This does not seem to be obvious; one national ISP tells us that the first question a customer always asks is how to get address space, without considering the more fundamental question of how they might use it.

Performance of an IPv6 connection is obviously important, especially since potential adopters might be put off by an under-performing tunnel. Ordinary configured tunnels are a repeat offender—Murphy's Law* states that the tunnels that are easy to get—that is, automated by means of a tunnel broker—will have an endpoint that's far away, and any that are nearby are likely to be more difficult to get. (You'll have to contact the operator, and possibly bribe him or her with alcohol).

6to4 has the potential to improve on this thanks to its clever use of anycast, but so far there isn't much evidence of this on the wider Internet. Some enlightened ISPs are advertising the anycast address internally to their IGPs, which is great for outbound traffic. Unless you're communicating with another 6to4 host, though, you need an efficiently placed relay in both directions, and those can be hard to come by. The ISP can't even make life better for its own customers by advertising its subset of 2002:: into the IPv6 routing table, because that would just be rude—we're trying to avoid the routing table swamp of IPv4!

The best answer, obviously, is to ask your ISP to provide a tunnel or, even better, native connectivity. But not everyone's ISP is so forward thinking, and some of us will need some other method to transition. A neat workaround is SixXS, *http://www.sixxs.net/*. It's a tunnel broker, but with more than one tunnel endpoint; if you register from a particular place on the Internet, you will be directed to use the endpoint that's "nearest" to you, as chosen by the network operator. It solves some of the problems we've discussed, because its users benefit from good connectivity, in both directions—and what's more, the operator remains sober.

---

* No relation.

Note that while SIIT involves copying lots of header fields around it doesn't actually require any state to be kept on the translating box, other than the rule to map IPv4 address back to IPv6 addresses.

If you want to know the details of SIIT see RFC 2765. Remember that SIIT is very definitely a translation technology: it takes IPv6 packets and removes all the IPv6 headers and replaces them with IPv4 headers. This is very different to tunnels, Toredo or ISATAP; they encapsulate IPv6 packets, retaining all their IPv6 headers. As we have all seen with IPv4 NAT, translation can cause problems with applications like FTP that transmit addresses internally. Also remember that if remote addresses of connections are logged by applications, then they will be translated addresses.

NAT46/64-PT

NAT-PT is an application of SIIT that allows the mapping of a group of IPv6 hosts to a group of IPv4 addresses, in much the same way that IPv4 NAT allows a group of IPv4 hosts using private addresses to use a group of public addresses. The extra PT in NAT-PT stands for *protocol translation*.

RFC 2766, which describes NAT-PT, also describes a "DNSALG" system for IPv6. DNSALG is a way of rewriting DNS requests and responses as they pass through the NAT system. This, in principle, means that DNS query for an IPv6 host inside the NATed network can be translated to one of the IPv4 addresses in use on the NAT automatically.

We have to admit that we haven't seen any NAT-PT devices in action, though there are both commercial and free implementations available.

TRT

TRT, Transport Relay Translation, is described in RFC 3142. It is similar in idea to SIIT, but rather than translate between IPv4 and IPv6 at the IP and ICMP levels, instead we translate at the transport level, i.e., TCP and UDP. A machine doing TRT will have some range of IPv6 addresses that it translates to a range of IPv4 addresses. When a TCP connection is made to one of these addresses the TRT machine will make a TCP connection to the corresponding IPv4 address on the same port. Then as TCP data packets are received the data is forwarded on, and similarly for UDP.

TRT has the disadvantages of translation, mentioned in the previous section; however, it avoids certain issues related to fragmentation. It does also require the storage of state associated with the ongoing TCP and UDP sessions that SIIT does not. It also tends to be deployed on an application-specific basis; in other words, it doesn't try to translate every possible protocol. This may be an advantage or a disadvantage, depending on your setup!

We give an example of a TRT setup in the "Faith" section of Chapter 6, using the KAME *faith* mechanism.

Bump in the Stack/API

Bump in the stack (BIS) is basically another SIIT variant, but the motivation is slightly different. Suppose you have some piece of software that you want to use over IPv6, but you can't get an IPv6-capable version of it. Even if you have great IPv6 connectivity, this software is pretty useless to you. BIS is a trick to make software like this usable.

Say the software makes tries to make a connection to www.example.com, with address 2001:db8::abcd. When the software looks up www.example.com the *address mapper* component of BIS picks an IPv4 address from a pool configured for BIS, say 192.168.1.1, to represent this host and returns this IPv4 address to the software. The software then uses this address normally.

Meanwhile, BIS intercepts packets coming out of the IPv4 stack that are destined to 192.168.1.1 and uses SIIT to rewrite them as IPv6 packets destined to 2001:db8:: abcd. Packets going in the opposite direction are similarly translated.

There is a variant of BIS called Bump in the API (BIA). It operates in a similar way: an address mapper intercepts name lookup calls and returns a fake IPv4 address for IPv6 hosts. The application uses the address as usual. However, library functions such as connect, bind and getpeername know about these fake addresses and actually translate these to/from IPv6 addresses before proceeding (otherwise) as normal.

Bump in the stack is described in RFC 2767 and Bump in the API is described in RFC 3338.

Both BIS and BIA have the usual drawbacks associated with translation: embedded addresses cause problems and logging of addresses may be inaccurate. They do have some advantages over NAT and TRT though because they distribute the translation task to the end hosts and consequently may scale better.

Proxies

Proxies are another way to connect IPv6-only networks to IPv4-only networks. Many people are already familiar with web proxies, where a web browser can be configured to make all requests to the proxy rather than directly to the appropriate web server. The web proxy then fetches the web page on behalf of the browser.

A web proxy running on a dual-stacked host can potentially accept requests over both IPv4 and IPv6 from web browsers and then fetch pages from both IPv4 and IPv6 servers, as required.

Proxying is not limited to HTTP either. A dual-stacked recursive DNS server behaves very similarly, accepting requests over IPv4 and IPv6 and answering those requests by making a sequence of requests to other DNS servers as necessary. Likewise, a dual-stacked SMTP server can receive mail for an IPv6-only domain and forwarded it as needed.

The main advantage of proxying is that it is a technology that is relatively familiar and it does not require any complex translation. The down side is that it can require some application support. Proxies are likely to be an important bridge between IPv4 and IPv6 for the foreseeable future.

We cover HTTP proxying in some detail in Chapter 7 ("HTTP Proxies and Caches"), and the issue of dual-stack DNS servers in Chapter 6, in the "Recursive DNS Servers" section. We also give an example of port forwarding, a form of proxying that can be used to get IPv4-only applications to talk over IPv6, in the "If All Else Fails..." section of Chapter 7.

Summary of Transition Mechanisms

Since there are such a large number of transition mechanisms that have been identified as being useful for IPv6 deployment, we offer you Table 4-1. It provides a one sentence description of each. Table 4-2 gives a one-sentence "serving suggestion" for each of the mechanisms.

Table 4-1. One-line summary of IPv6 transition mechanisms

Method	Summary
Dual-stack	Run IPv4 and IPv6 on nodes.
DSTM	Dual-stack, but dynamically allocate IPv4 addresses as needed.
Configured tunnel	Virtual point-to-point IPv6 link between two IPv4 addresses.
Automatic tunnel	Automatic encapsulation of IPv6 packets using "compatible addresses."
6to4	Automatic assignment of /48 network to each public IPv4 address.
Teredo	IPv6 in UDP through a NAT.
6over4	Using IPv4 as a link layer for IPv6, using IPv4 multicast.
ISATAP	Using IPv4 as a link layer for IPv6, using a known router.
SIIT	Rules for translating IPv6 packets straight into IPv4.
NAT-PT	Using SIIT to do NAT with IPv4 on one side and IPv6 on the other.
TRT	Translating IPv6 to IPv4 at the UDP/TCP layer.
BIS	Using SIIT to make IPv4 applications speak IPv6.
BIA	Using a special library to make IPv4 applications speak IPv6.
Proxies	Using application level trickery to join IPv4 to IPv6 networks.

Table 4-2. Possible deployment scenario for IPv6 transition mechanisms

Method	Deployment scenario
Dual-stack	Dual stack everything, if you have enough IPv4 addresses.
	Otherwise dual stack a few border devices.
DSTM	Can be used instead of dual stacking border devices.
	Not that widely available.

Method	Deployment scenario
Configured tunnel	Use to hop over IPv4-only equipment.
Automatic tunnel	Only used as a configuration device.
6to4	Good for isolated IPv6 networks (e.g., home/departmental networks).
Teredo	A last resort for people stuck behind NAT.
6over4	Not widely deployed because of IPv4 multicast requirement.
ISATAP	Useful for sparse IPv6 deployments within IPv4 networks.
SIIT	Not deployed by itself.
NAT-PT	Proxies are probably a cleaner solution, where available.
TRT	Ditto.
BIS	Getting software that supports IPv6 would be better.
BIA	Ditto.
Proxies	Dual-stack proxies for SMTP, HTTP and DNS will be important for some time.

Obtaining IPv6 Address Space and Connectivity

Obtaining address space and connectivity are generally so closely linked we deal with them in the one section here.

Getting IPv6 connectivity is in theory extremely easy. If you already have an existing IPv4 service, some of the tunnelling transition mechanisms discussed previously will suffice in the short term to get you connected to the greater IPv6 Internet. If you have no existing connection, or are looking to get an "IPv6-native" connection, you will have to talk to the ISPs serving your area. We will discuss the options here in greater detail later. Suffice it to say for the moment that getting IPv6 connectivity is approximately as hard as getting IPv4 connectivity.

Obtaining address space in IPv6 is also, in theory, extremely easy for the vast majority of the organizations who might want it. The hard and fast rule is: go to your upstream provider* and they will provide you with address space. This address space will be from the allocation of the provider, and is known as PA, or Provider Aggregate space. In this case your upstream provider is determined by who you get your IPv6 connectivity from, so this may be your ISP, a tunnel provider elsewhere in the Internet, or even the 6to4 mechanism.

If your upstream provider is your ISP or a tunnel broker, they should tell you which prefixes to use. In the case of an ISP you'll probably have to ask them to allocate you

---

* This simple phrase means the ISP at the other end of your leased line(s), DSL connection(s), or wireless link(s).

a prefix, in the case of a tunnel broker you'll probably be allocated a prefix when the tunnel is initially configured.

If you have no upstream providers, you are either the kind of organization that should be looking at getting an allocation by talking to the RIRs* directly, or the kind of organization that will *never* be using globally routable address space—a small office with specialist needs perhaps, or an organization for which security is paramount. (Having said that, it's difficult to imagine an organization that would not want to connect to the Internet these days.).

Another source of addresses is the 6bone, the original IPv6 test network, though as 6bone addressing is being phased out, we could only recommend it in an emergency.

Finally, you can receive address space via a tunnel, which is a special case of simply getting it from an upstream provider, or a tunnel broker, a kind of a middleman for providing automatically generated tunnels. (We'll talk more about that later.)

Let's have a look at each of these mechanisms for getting addresses now.

Upstream Providers

Of course, the place of first resort for most organizations will be their upstream provider. Usually these providers will have some kind of form for you to fill in; this may even greatly resemble your RIR's documentation, or reference it, so it might be useful for you to look at the RIR information in the "RIRs" section later in this chapter.

If you have multiple upstream providers, and are worried about which you should pick, well, just get a prefix from each of them! IPv6 is designed for this.

6to4

Congratulations! You already have an IPv6 address space of your very own, by virtue of having addresses in the IPv4 Internet. We explained the mechanics of 6to4 in the "6to4" section earlier in this chapter and looked at how to configure it in the "6to4 configuration" section in Chapter 5, but all you really need to know here is that if you have a public IP address 192.0.2.4, then the prefix 2002:c000:0204::/48 is yours, because 192.0.2.4 in hexadecimal is c0000204. For something small and quick, like making a particular web site reachable over IPv6 in a hurry, 6to4 can't be beat.

The main downside of 6to4 from an operations point of view is that the procedures for delegating reverse DNS for 6to4 addresses aren't well-defined yet.† This means

---

* We'll say what the RIRs are shortly, but for now you just need to know that they are the people who allocate addresses to ISPs.

† This has actually been resolved for ip6.int, but not for ip6.arpa. Currently *hostmaster@ep.net* manages ip6.int delegations.

that if you choose to use 6to4 addressing people won't be able to translate your IPv6 addresses into hostnames easily. Furthermore, the routing required to make these addresses work is not entirely within your control. These factors would combine to make it unsuitable for serious production use.

6Bone

6bone addresses are in the range 3FFE::/16 and were the original blocks of addresses assigned for testing IPv6 in the real world. These addresses are not so relevant these days, given the availability of "real" addresses from the RIRs. The current plan for 6bone addresses is that no new addresses will be assigned by the 6bone testbed after 1 January 2004, but existing addresses will remain valid until 06/06/2006 (full details of the phaseout are in RFC 3701). After this date it is anticipated that 3FFE::/16 addresses will no longer be routed in the Internet at large. (Note the long transition period—we can take from this that renumbering is not quite as easy as we would all like it to be.)

If you are starting from scratch, we couldn't recommend using 6bone addresses today. If you already have 6bone addresses you are safe enough for now, but probably want to start thinking about obtaining addresses from your upstream or the local RIR.

Details of the 6bone are available at *http://www.6bone.net/*.

Only Intermittently Connected

What do you do if you have a sizable internal network, but you are only occasionally connected to the Internet, possibly using different upstream providers? You might be in this situation if you were in a country where Internet access was very expensive, or if you were running a wireless community network. One of the fundamental questions is, how do you number your machines internally in order to maintain internal connectivity when your externally allocated prefix goes away? Until recently, the answer was to use IPv6 site-local addressing, perhaps in combination with an internal dynamically updated DNS. Unfortunately, since the deprecation of site-local addressing by RFC 3879 you are probably on your own if you want to use this method.

Your realistic options for addressing occasionally connected networks at this point are the same as for the always-connected case: going to your RIR for an allocation, or going to a nominated upstream provider. If you are thinking of using address space without explicitly informing either an RIR or an ISP that you are doing this, don't. This kind of behavior in IPv4 caused lots of trouble, and we'd like to forestall you even considering it.

In the case where going to your RIR isn't really practical (for one thing, it can cost significant amounts of money to obtain address space from an RIR) and going to an ISP isn't viable, then you are basically stuck. It is for these "corner cases" that we feel some kind of site-locals scheme will be created. We speculate about what might happen in the "Site-Local Addresses" section in Chapter 9.

I Want to Be Independent!

For those of you who are looking for an analogue to PI, or Provider Independent space, there is, in essence, no such beastie if you are an "ordinary" end network. If you are part of the default-free routing zone (e.g., a large ISP), then the RIR can allocate address space to you. There are ways to achieve more-or-less the same things as PI space allows you to achieve; we will look at this in more detail in the "Multihoming" section later in this chapter.

In the case of large global organizations who run their own networks, it seems likely they could be considered as providers and have address space assigned directly to them.

RIRs

The acronym RIR stands for Regional Internet Registry, and currently there are only a handful of them in the world. They are the bodies collectively responsible for the administration and allocation of IP addresses to ISPs, enterprises, and end-users of the Internet. Their jurisdiction is roughly geographical, with RIPE serving the European region, ARIN the North Americas, LACNIC for Latin American and Caribbean, and APNIC the Asia-Pacific region, although there are overlaps and occasional inconsistencies that should be corrected as more RIRs are created. ARIN has traditionally absorbed the greater part of the issuance of addresses, not only in North America but also internationally in the regions not covered by the RIRs, because of North America's role in creating the early Internet.

Politically speaking, RIRs are bottom-up organizations—the policies and plans flow from the members of the organization, and these policies are debated in as fair and as open a manner as one could hope for. In theory, this gives the ability to create or influence policy to any member, provided their arguments are lucid and well-phrased. In practice it is of course more difficult, but no superior mechanism has been developed, and there are some quarters in which the idea of democratic policy-making is viewed with dread; so bear this in mind while attempting to make sense of the paragraphs below.*

---

* Not everything is "perfect" yet, in other words.

Relevance to IPv6

As you may have guessed, since the RIRs have jurisdiction over IPv4 Internet address space, they have both *de facto* and *de jure* jurisdiction over IPv6 address space.

Throughout the lifetime of IPv6, the RIRs have evolved in their attitude towards it. Initially each RIR had a different and inconsistent policy; for example, ARIN used to charge for IPv6 address space as well as IPv4, a hurdle that has since been removed. Some commentators have remarked that a great abundance of address space, allocated in the main from the ISPs rather than the RIRs gives the RIRs much less to do, and effectively puts them out of a job. This, in combination with the traditional conservatism of network operators, may or may not go some way towards explaining the nature of IPv6 policies in the past. Thankfully, due to the efforts of various concerned people, more consistent IPv6 allocation policies have been approved and passed by the membership of the main RIRs. At the moment, that consistency seems to have been a useful intermediate stage rather than something the RIR communities were really insistent upon, since the RIRs are currently diverging in policy again. However, for this book, we are going to look at the current RIPE policy as it stands. Bear in mind that this may and probably will change over time—check your RIR site for details!

RIR operations background

First, you are only going to be talking to RIRs if you are the RIR responsible entity within an organization. End users do not have to talk to the RIRs in IPv6—they just go to their upstream ISP. In all likelihood, if you are in that position you already have an existing relationship with an RIR. You may however need to fill out an application for some IPv6 space, so we will deal with some of that detail here.

RIRs hand out *allocations*, and then *assignments* are made out of those allocations. Assignments are to end customers, including the requester itself.

RIPE

We deal with RIPE as a representative example of how to obtain IPv6 address space, since the policies are roughly harmonized. (As we said above, this is subject to change, but the direction of change appears to be in the more liberal rather than less liberal direction.)

With respect to getting IPv6 address space in the region covered by RIPE (generally "Europe," for large values of Europe) there are a number of documents to read and digest. The first is RIPE-261, accessible via the URL *http://www.ripe.net/ripe/docs/ ipv6-sparse.html*.

This presents a nice overview of the address space allocation algorithm that RIPE are using to enable the maximization of aggregation, and better aggregation is one of the stated goals of IPv6. It is useful to have this out in the open, because it tells ISPs what their next allocation of addresses is likely to be. This makes planning for ISPs easier, even if other aspects of the policy change.

The current IPv6 policy in force is RIPE-267, which can be found at *http://www.ripe. net/ripe/docs/ipv6policy.html*. The policy states the conditions under which addresses are allocated, and also indicates which forms must be filled in with which information in order to actually apply. Since these things change very quickly we are not going to examine the specifics of these forms here.

Current policy

The bones of the current policy are very simple. You qualify for an RIR-allocated chunk of IPv6 address space providing the following conditions are met:

Be an LIR
> This is reasonably self-explanatory. Your organization must be a Local Internet Registry, and be a member of RIPE already.

Don't be an end site
> This is also self-explanatory. You must not be an end site—in other words, singly homed, proving no connectivity to anyone else; solely a leaf node.

Provide IPv6 connectivity by advertising aggregated prefix
> The requirement here is to *plan to provide IPv6 connectivity to organizations to which it will assign* /48s, by advertising that connectivity through its single aggregated address allocation. This is where it starts to get complicated. Disentangling this sentence provides us with three main components: you must plan to provide the connectivity (if someone asks, you can't refuse them out of hand)—you must assign /48s (which is to say, subnettable address space)—and you must advertise this via the supernet you will get, and not a separate route for each /48.

Plan to assign 200 /48s in two years
> You must have a plan for making at least 200 /48 assignments to other organizations within two years. This is perhaps the most controversial element of the current policy. The number 200 is intended as a line in the sand—a semi-arbitrary demarcation point to designate some applications worthwhile and others not, because the new philosophy of the routing table requires being fascist about who is allowed a top-level allocation and who is not. The point about /48s is that the organization in question can't just be an end-user who could fit everything in a /64—there has to be some detail to the network, some subnetting. However, it's no news to anyone that if 200 customers requiring /48s have to be found, they will be, so it's not entirely clear what benefit accrues by requiring that specific number. It's probably best not to think of this number as necessarily a problem; rather think of it as a motivation for finding something or somethings in your network to which 200 /48 assignments could be made, or will eventually have to be made.

The RIRs operate policy fora where elements of particular policies can be debated and hopefully changed. If you are looking to change anything you feel is unreasonable, you would be positively invited to take part in these. One such is the IPv6 working group in RIPE, findable at *http://www.ripe.net/ripe/wg/ipv6/*. The address policy working group is also important, and you can find that at *http://www.ripe.net/ripe/wg/address-policy/*.

Network Design

Just as in IPv4 network design, any engineer with responsibility for deploying, migrating or inter-operating with IPv6 will have to have a plan for answering the three main questions of networking:

1. How do we address things?
2. How do we route things?
3. How do we name things?

The topic of primary importance is obviously addressing, but we will also talk about intra-site communication, multihoming, and VLANs. DNS we talk about primarily in Chapter 6. (For the moment, suffice it to say that you can put IPv6 addresses in the DNS just as well as IPv4 ones.)

Addressing

Planning the addressing of networks in IPv6 is simpler than IPv4. The algorithm to use is to first identify which networks under your control require distinct prefixes. You might assign different prefixes in order to apply different security or QoS properties to groups of addresses. When you've decided on your subnets, you then need to decide on automatic or manual addressing. In the automatic configuration scenario envisaged by RFC 2462, the addressing within a prefix is taken care of by the usual EUI-64 procedure. Conversely, in a manually configured situation, the same procedures with respect to address allocation within a prefix will have to be undergone as with IPv4: recording which machines have which addresses, and so on.

As in IPv4, you can of course still manually assign addresses. However, manual address assignment is considered harmful for many common pieces of network equipment. For example, assigning static addresses to desktops may be pointless if all desktop machines reside on one subnet and so can be identified by a single prefix.

For other portions of the network, such as firewalls, routers and some servers, manual address assignment may make sense. In this case your organizations usual address management techniques should be followed. Of course, if you are using software to manage your address space, the software may have to be updated to understand IPv6. If you're looking for a free address management product that can use IPv6, you might like to look at FreeIPdb, available from *http://www.freeipdb.org/*.

Sadly, spreadsheets, which are unfortunately in widespread use as IP-address registration tools, usually do not have a uniqueness constraint applicable to rows, making them next to useless for the purpose.

Subnetting

Why subnet? It's commonly done when you are growing your network, either by having existing customers/users come along with more servers to number, or occasionally when merging networks or starting up. When more address space is available, it is often used to group machines by function, for example putting finance and engineering on different subnets. Being able to do this is a function of having enough address space, having planned correctly for growth, and being able to manipulate the netmask.

The netmask, or *subnet mask* to give it its family name, is always paired with the address of a host, and indicates the size of the network that it is directly connected to. It's specified in terms of the number of *bits* in your prefix that are common to every machine on that network.

For example, in the network starting at 192.0.2.0 and with a subnet mask of /24, the first three octets—that's 24 bits—are shared. In IPv4, the very first and very last addresses are reserved, so you may assign addresses from 192.0.2.1 all the way to 192.0.2.254.

In IPv4, you need to size your subnet masks just right. If you assign too much address space to a LAN, the space is wasted and you might have to renumber. If you assign too little, the LAN will outgrow it and you *will* have to renumber.

Another example in IPv4: if you have a /16 in the above-mentioned CIDR format, you also have 256 /24s, and 65536 /32s. If you were faced with a couple of server farms, a dialup network or two, and some hosting customers, the most appropriate way to subnet might be to divide your /16 into chunks depending on the current and anticipated future size of the subnetworks you need to number. So the servers might get /24s or /23s, the hosting customers /29s and so on. The biggest mistake you can make is to arrive at a situation where you have underestimated growth.* since that generally requires a non-contiguous allocation to be made from somewhere *else* in your address space, which adds another routing table entry to your internal routing protocol table, creates another address space disconnected from the first one with the same security requirements, and is generally regarded as Not a Good Thing. Similarly, over-estimating growth leads to inefficient allocation, wasted address space, problems with your RIRs, and so on. The optimal choice of subnetting effectively hedges bets of future growth against covering existing infrastructure efficiently.

---

* Historically, the most likely of the two to have happened.

However, in IPv6 the same problems do not occur. The RFC 3177 recommendation that a /48 be assigned to end sites in the general case means that pretty much everyone has 16 bits to work with when subnetting. This gives you much more flexibility to create subnets freely than in IPv4, where you were limited to just enough IP addresses to cover what you could justify two years in advance.

How come 16 bits? Because just as every site can have a /48, every subnet in a site can have a /64.

That's another IETF recommendation. It's appropriate, nay encouraged, to assign a /64 to every subnet in your network, regardless of size. This is pretty shocking to those of us coming from the IPv4 CIDR world—we're so used to rationing addresses among networks that it's almost absurd to imagine "wasting" address space like this.

On the other hand, this is where the advantages of IPv6 really start to shine: by assigning a /64 to each network, you assign more address space than any network could possibly ever need, and therefore have much more confidence in the stability of your addressing plan. By allowing for 64 bits in the host part of the address, it's safe to use stateless autoconfiguration to hand out persistent addresses to servers and clients alike. Even for such minimal subnets as point-to-point links, where one would assign a /30 in IPv4, it's best to use a /64 to ensure that you don't encounter problems in the future with some incorrect assumptions about subnet size being made by your equipment. You have 65,536 of them to assign—feel free to use them.

Your addressing plan does not necessarily need to be complex. It is perfectly valid to split your /48 allocation into a bunch of /64s and start assigning them in sequence as need arises. (There are certainly worse ways to use address space.)

Then again, you may wish to impose a certain amount of structure and aggregation on your plan. If you have four sites, you may split the /48 into four /50s, like Table 4-3. Then, if you like, you could simplify routing between your four sites by advertising each /50 as an aggregate instead of individual /64s. Of course, you would still only advertise the aggregate /48 to your upstream ISP.

Table 4-3. Sample high-level addressing plan

Range	Assigned
2001:db8:100:0000:: – 2001:db8:100:3fff::	Dublin region
2001:db8:100:4000:: – 2001:db8:100:7fff::	Galway region
2001:db8:100:8000:: – 2001:db8:100:bfff::	Limerick region
2001:db8:100:c000:: – 2001:db8:100:ffff::	Cork region

That said, scalability is a key advantage of IPv6, and it would be unwise to carve up *all* of your address space without leaving room to manoeuvre. One way around this would be to assign /52s or smaller to each of the four sites, which should still leave more than enough room to assign /64s to each LAN, but will leave space in your allocation to allow you to grow your network further, or change your addressing plan completely without overlapping with already-used space (which should avoid conflicts during any transition period.)

Very much the same approach can be taken by a high-end provider that has been assigned a /32 by their RIR. Again we have 16 bits of address space to carve up, and in this instance aggregation between PoPs may be even more important. It's a matter of striking a balance; making sure that each PoP has more space than it will ever need, but that you leave room to assign further PoPs or regions in the event of unexpected growth.

There are a couple of resources that are worth investigating if you wish to look deeper into this topic: RFC 3531 on managing the assignment of bits of an IPv6 address block, and "Sipcalc," an IP subnet calculator at *http://www.routemeister.net/projects/sipcalc/*.

DHCP

DHCP is a prerequisite in sufficiently large IPv4 networks because of two very important features: its ability to automatically assign an address to any machine requesting such and keep track of them, which is stateful address assignment, and its ability to supply other network-related configuration information (such as DNS servers).

The position in IPv6 networks is slightly different. DHCPv6 is not an absolute *necessity* in IPv6 networks, particularly small ones, because the address assignment problem is taken care of by autoconfiguration, which as we remember is stateless address assignment, a lá RFC 2462. However, for larger networks, and for when there is no other way to usefully configure certain kinds of information, DHCPv6 is a useful addition to the network manager's toolbelt.

The main point to consider is under what circumstances one would use DHCPv6. At the moment, router advertisements can give you prefix (that is to say, routing) information, and address autoconfiguration can (obviously) give you addresses. For most networks the key remaining piece is DNS information: nameservers to use, and default search domains. There are efforts underway to make DNS configuration information easier to obtain (for example, by creating specially scoped addresses for DNS servers within a site). You can read more about these in Chapter 9, but these ideas have not yet solidified. It's our expectation you will have to keep using DHCPv6 in your network for DNS configuration information in the short term at least, although you can have autoconfiguration running in parallel for address generation with no problems.

We'll have a quick look at the reality of running a DHCPv6 server in the "Running DHCPv6" section in Chapter 6.

Changes to DHCP for IPv6

After a long gestation period, DHCPv6 was finally born in RFC 3315. There are several changes from DHCPv4 worthy of note. Since broadcasts no longer exist in IPv6, the server receives messages on a well-known link-scoped multicast address instead: FF02::1:2, and uses new port numbers: UDP 546 and 547 instead of the old 67 and 68 "bootp" ports. The client also uses its link-local address to send queries initially, which illustrates a major conceptual difference; IPv6 nodes have addresses, valid, working addresses, by virtue of having a link. They can have communication on-link without DHCP, unlike IPv4 hosts. Furthermore, since it is necessary to support prefix deprecation, clients must *continue* to listen for server-originated reconfiguration messages, which can be used not only for prefix deprecation, but for changing anything there's a DHCP option for.* These communications can be secured by a variety of means, but RFC 3315 defines an MD5 authentication scheme between server and client, while IPsec is possible between relays† and servers. Finally, if you want your clients to obtain their addressing information via DHCPv6 you must configure the RAs in your network to define the Managed Autoconfiguration flag. You would do this on IOS by setting ipv6 nd managed-config-flag on a per-interface basis.

Some interesting developments are on the horizon, including the notion of securing DHCP transactions between client and server—not just relay and server—over IPsec, outlined in RFC 3118, and the notion of "local" DHCP options, which could be defined on the client to mean more or less anything the administrator wants. We advise you to keep track of the IETF DHC working group if you are interested in learning more.

Multihoming

Multihoming can, in fact, be done in IPv6 exactly the same way as it is done in IPv4, with network prefixes being advertised from multiple upstream providers, ensuring independent reachability in the event of link failure. There is nothing inherently "IPv4-esque" about multihoming, just as there is nothing inherent in IPv6 that makes that approach more or less difficult, apart from the increased size of addresses. In other words, this style of multihoming should be *protocol-independent*.

However, just because it *can* be done the way it was in IPv4 does not mean that it *should*. The designers of IPv6 have gone to some lengths to engineer the capability to move away from this model of multihoming, because although we know it works for a size of Internet up to the current one, it will certainly not scale greatly above that, and therefore something new is required. The concepts of multiple addresses and address selection introduced by IPv6 mean that new styles of multihoming are

---

* Which is almost everything, believe us.

† Entities that forward DHCP messages.

possible, and we examine them in more detail below. These new styles of multihoming fulfil the same set of goals as IPv4 multihoming, but they do require some extra effort to understand.

Unfortunately, we are not yet at a stage where these new methods of multihoming can be deployed on a production basis. In fact, there is a lot of momentum for rethinking the whole multihoming paradigm, and that kind of reworking is probably on the order of years before it is ready for implementation. We discuss contenders for the multihoming crown in Chapter 9, but we'll talk a little bit about how multihoming works in general below, since it may have to be taken into account in your network design.

Multiple upstream providers, no BGP

In IPv4, it is generally found that one host with a single physical network interface has only one single address. In IPv6 of course, any interface may have multiple addresses, perhaps provided by some combination of static configuration and router prefix advertisement. This allows for a form of host-based multihoming, where the host makes the decision about which network to originate requests from, rather than an egress router making decisions based on information provided to it via BGP. On the plus side, there is obviously less overhead and complexity on the network level since you do not have to maintain a routing table via BGP—and this can translate into savings in router hardware—but on the minus side, in-progress connections are no longer independent of link failure, and a host encounters problems when trying to assure optimal connection origination characteristics; either the host is participating in routing and has the best possible information about making connections, in which case the load that *was* centralized is now multiplied all over your server farm, or the host is making decisions on incomplete information, and the optimality of the routing can not be assured (indeed, perhaps far from it).

Nevertheless, it *is* a viable option for certain circumstances, particularly those where money is at a premium, and incoming connections can be managed carefully to make link failure unimportant. For server farms that are dominated by traffic where connections are created and torn down quickly, such as web servers primarily using HTTP, it might even be termed suitable.

Furthermore, if you have your server farm management outsourced or hosted elsewhere, and you are not in control of network configuration, but your servers are configured to "hear" router prefix advertisements from your hosting provider, you may find yourself effectively availing of this service with little effort required on your part.

Decisions governing source address selection are covered in the "Address selection" section in Chapter 3, but to reiterate, the authoritative document is RFC 3484.

If you are the kind of web farm that is a content provider, then in this model, your responsibility is to advertise as many AAAA records for your web sites as possible, thus ensuring as much reachability as possible. See the address selection section for more details.

Multiple Upstream Providers, BGP

If you are in a situation where you have multiple upstream providers, and have your own /35 or, these days, /32 to advertise (i.e., you're probably an ISP), then your situation is such that you can continue to speak BGP to your peers and upstream providers. If this is the case, then operationally things are quite similar to IPv4.

Multiattaching

Multiattaching is a term for connecting to the same ISP multiple times, and may be done with or without BGP. Multiattaching doesn't have a great reputation from the end-organization point of view, primarily because failure modes that take out your ISP still end up taking out your Internet connectivity, despite having spent the money for multiple connections. However, it has some benefits—primary amongst them being that the Internet at large does not suffer from the extra AS and path bloat required when doing multiple provider multihoming. For IPv6, it also has the possibility to allow you to take different chunks of PA space from your upstream, meaning that a small degree of address independence is possible. Multiattaching is only useful under limited circumstances, however.

Managing IPv4 and IPv6 Coexistence

IPv4 and IPv6 will no doubt continue to coexist in your network for some years. Taking on this additional management burden successfully involves considering some entirely new questions, but many problems turn out to have answers that are simple extensions of the IPv4 answer. For the others, we outline what the best current practice consensus is, inasmuch as that is known!

Bandwidth planning
> Bandwidth planning is probably the least important of the considerations, but worth having a strategy for nonetheless. It's our expectation that since traffic is essentially driven by user needs—whether those needs are fulfilled over IPv4 or IPv6—there's probably going to be little enough variation in the bandwidth used. However, there is the chance that a wildly popular IPv6 application, say peer-to-peer networking a lá Microsoft's *Three Degrees*, might appear, creating *new* demand for bandwidth. Also, if your IPv6 infrastructure is physically separate, you will obviously have to dimension that accordingly. If it is not separate, there may be the potential for IPv4 traffic to suffer at the hands of IPv6, or vice versa, if there is congestion.

Network management

Incorporating network management is, despite implementation difficulties, relatively easy from a decision-making point of view. Either your commercial software package supports it, or it doesn't, in which case you've to build a separate IPv6 management infrastructure (ouch) or get a new package. And if you've a home-grown set of tools, perhaps based on MRTG, Nagios, or the like, we're pleased to inform you that IPv6 support is already in many open source management tools, and will be incorporated in more as time goes on. For example, one of the most widely deployed ones, Nagios, has IPv6 support in the 1.4.x series, currently in beta, but can easily have IPv6 support "retrofitted" by simply making the ping command which is executed by Nagios to monitor hosts a ping6 command instead.* Similar techniques can be used elsewhere if necessary.

Security considerations

Security considerations arise when there are two different ways to talk to your network devices, routers, etc. Unfortunately this part of managing the coexistence of these two protocols is often either ignored or worried about too much. Fortunately, some useful work has already been done on this, and you will find some of these issues discussed in the "Firewalls" section of Chapter 6, as well as later on in this chapter.

Fudging Native Connectivity with Ethernet

Frequently during our deployment planning we might run into equipment that does not support IPv6, and cannot be upgraded quickly. The IETF-supplied transition mechanisms, using various types of tunnel, are good ways around this problem, but they are not the only solution.

Since there is nothing intrinsically wrong with having separate routers on a LAN for IPv4 and IPv6, there are a variety of creative design hacks that one can use to provide native connectivity around a difficult router, awkward firewall or unhelpful layer 3 switch. If one treats the IPv4 and IPv6 networks as separate layouts sharing a single infrastructure, then a variety of options open up for providing IPv6 connectivity alongside IPv4, as opposed to studiously and fastidiously coupled with IPv4.

This is a long-winded way of suggesting that you deploy a dedicated IPv6 router (or, as appropriate, IPv6 firewall) alongside your troublesome IPv4-only kit. We discuss this in greater detail in the "Hacking Native Connectivity Around Incompatible Equipment" section of Chapter 6.

---

* Together with defining an IPv6 service to monitor.

Deploying IPv6

At this stage, we have looked at a good deal of the background information and deployment techniques relevant to IPv6. With this knowledge under our belt, it's time to start thinking about applying it to your own situation. As with any process, deciding what to do is half the battle—and executing on those decisions is the other.

The first question to consider during the planning process is the motivation for the change. You're thinking about enabling IPv6 in your network—why? Perhaps you have been handed a business requirement to support it by a certain date. Perhaps the standards for your specific network mandate it. Is there a technology trial planned? Or maybe you are an ISP who needs to deliver native IPv6 routing services to its edge networks. Indeed, perhaps customers are even asking for it!

Whatever the motivation is, it will help to establish what the important parts of the implementation are by identifying which areas of the network need attention. (For example, if you are converting your desktop network, the important parts are the desktop network itself, its path to the outside world, and its path to internal services.) You may be required to be more or less formal, depending on your organizational environment, but we would strongly recommend the production of some kind of document listing the existing network elements, describing their ability to support IPv6, and identifying of which parts will need to run IPv6 in the future. This allows you to prioritize your rollout correctly. You will come back to this document many times during the deployment, so keep it safe.

With your network document in hand, you can then begin to construct a deployment schedule, keeping in mind your original motivation for the change. A deployment schedule is, at its simplest, a list of things to change and a time to change them. For organizations with change request procedures, the schedule should probably be submitted as one request, since while there may be many distinct changes in the plan, the motivation behind them all is the same. The change request system should hopefully take care of communicating what is being done and why within your organization.

For example, perhaps you have a requirement to IPv6-ify your desktop network. It might be that your desktop network is highly segregated—perhaps on it's own VLAN. Modulo operating system support, the more segregated the network, the easier it is to turn on IPv6 for that specific piece of it. Conversely, for large flat networks, enabling IPv6 is a much larger job, purely because it's much more of an all-or-nothing proposition, and incremental deploy-then-test methods are not applicable. An example deployment schedule for such a segregated VLAN might be as simple as "Switch over desktops to IPv6 capable stack on evening of 21st; allow one week to settle. Switch over main router to dual stack on evening of 28th; test outgoing and incoming IPv4 and IPv6 connectivity." It should also have a section for fall-back, or reverting to the previous state of affairs if there is some kind of catastrophic failure.

The above raises some important general points. Any sufficiently large organization will have more than one person affected by what you are going to do. It is your responsibility to communicate about these changes, either through the change management process when that is appropriate, but directly to the stakeholders where necessary. Communication is a key element of any deployment plan, and IPv6 is no different. Tell everyone you can about what you're doing, why you're doing it, and when you expect it to be finished. Furthermore, a deployment plan for any new service, not just IPv6, should also have an operational component to it. How does this new service interact with what the help desk does already? To whom should calls or emails about it be directed? And so on. This final component of the generic IPv6 rollout we call an Operational plan, and it should list who will have to look after what you've done, and support it. The deployer should try to plan for the indefinite period of IPv4-IPv6 coexistence!

So, to reiterate: Decide why you are doing an IPv6 deployment. Identify what you need to change, and make sure everyone who cares knows what you're doing, and when. Schedule, perform, and test those changes. Tell the operations folks what's been done, and if you have network development and security folks, they need to know too. If caution dictates, do this as an incremental process so you can fully absorb the impact on your network. Always have a reversion plan in the highly unlikely event something goes very wrong. Finally, note that all of the above implies an already existing organization and an already existing network. For "green-field" setups, things are slightly different—we talk about those later.

Of course, this is a sadly generic deployment plan; you could use it for almost any big change. But that doesn't make it any less valid as a framework; however, it is the details of each network, and the details of actually configuring a particular desktop or router to do IPv6 that would most readily cause a deployment to fail. We describe how to do the most common IPv6-relevant operations in Chapters 5, 6, and 7, which will hopefully be useful input into your plans. (But for those looking for more concrete details of individual configurations at this stage, we recommend skipping ahead to the "Worked Examples" section later in this chapter, where we present three important model deployments.)

Inputs to Deployment Plans

Now, however, we need to drill down into more specific analysis. Below we consider various influences on a deployment plan. We consider the most important case, existing IPv4 infrastructure, first, then talk about considerations around converting hosts and routers.

Existing IPv4 Infrastructure

This will be by far the most common starting point for IPv6 deployment, and will continue to be for years. The good thing is that IPv6 is, as designed, able to run in parallel on almost any kind of layer 2 media: Ethernet, ATM, and so on. This means that you can start with as minimal a deployment as you want, by connecting IPv6 capable hosts to your existing layer 2 infrastructure. Adding to or changing the IPv6 deployment is very easy, and as time goes on, the amount of administrator effort required for getting IPv6 up and running on new equipment will go down. The tricky element obviously, is managing the two in simultaneously.

As noted above, there are various transition mechanisms that can help with deploying IPv6. One of the most useful for low-overhead connectivity is the dual-stack approach, where the OS can communicate using each protocol (IPv4 and IPv6) separately. We find that in situations where performance is not absolutely paramount, having a dual stack means that experimenting with IPv6 becomes very easy, as we illustrate below. For situations where dual stack is not feasible, there are other mechanisms to deal with IPv6-only hosts, and we look at those too.

In summary, existing IPv4 infrastructure is in general no problem for a deployment plan. One very useful transition mechanism is running dual-stack, and we find it does not introduce interoperability problems.

Converting a host at a time: dual stack

At some point, you will want all of your equipment, where feasible, to be running IPv6. This is really just a matter of setting up the dual-stack system on each host. Obviously that's a certain amount of work per machine, and while ad-hoc deployments may be suitable for small networks, for large networks being systematic is necessary.

One sensible way to proceed for converting hosts is to create a standard patch distribution for such old machines and operating systems as require it. Apply the patches via your standard systems maintenance or scheduled outage* interface and then evaluate the change. (You may prefer to do this with a sacrificial machine or two first, if you run unusual applications or have a particularly different O.S. configuration.) Usually vendors will have extensively stress-tested their stacks before letting the public see them, but occasionally your situation may trigger an obscure problem, so it is wise to evaluate patches before rolling out. Having done that, you can, at your leisure, convert the rest of the hosts on the network. Another option is to allow IPv6 to be deployed as part of your normal upgrade cycle—once the operating system

---

* For advice on how to manage and plan maintenance properly see *The Practice of System and Network Administration* by Limoncelli and Hogan (Addison-Wesley), but be prepared to feel embarrassed at how disorganized you are.

versions you install supports IPv6, you can just deploy it with IPv6 enabled (again after appropriate testing).

The great benefit of this rolling dual-stacked deployment is that there is no *flag day*: in other words, a day where everything changes. Experienced network managers know that changes on massive scales quickly expose hidden dependencies that can make life highly exciting for hours or even days. Apart from standard scheduled outage management, the overhead of the gradual roll-out is really quite small. Obviously the more equipment converted in a single session, the more you can amortize the cost (in both time and money).

At the end of this process, you can have systems that can pick up addresses via IPv6 router solicitation and behave as if they were solid citizens of both the IPv4 and IPv6 Internet. This is an important stepping-stone on the way to implementing almost any deployment plan.

 Roy, Durand, and Paugh have a draft, *http://www.ietf.org/internet-drafts/draft-ietf-v6ops-v6onbydefault-03.txt*, about their experiences of turning dual-stack on by default within Sun. One key element they found was that dual-stack machines, numbered privately in IPv4, would experience problems when attempting to make IPv6 connections in networks with no on-link IPv6 routers.

From a network managers perspective, if you are rolling out dual-stack throughout a network, or if dual-stack is mandated for you, as much on-link IPv6 infrastructure as possible is one obvious way to short-circuit many classes of performance or reliability problems experienced by these machines. There are other transition mechanisms which may also help, some relying on existing IPv4 infrastructure; you will find them discussed in the "Transition Mechanisms" section earlier in this chapter.

In summary, we feel the rolling dual-stack method to be quite well understood. Deployment plans that involve converting networks of desktop machines could use it with relatively small risk.

Connectivity and routers

One thing that you'll want to consider before doing an organized large scale roll out of IPv6 is how to provide connectivity. Deploying one or two test hosts with their own tunnels or 6to4 connectivity is relatively easy and sensible. However, it is probably not a good idea to deploy a LAN of many hosts all with their own individual tunnels to the IPv6 Internet! As we saw in Chapter 3, IPv6 routers play an important part in the IPv6 configuration process, so if you are deploying more than a couple of hosts, consider configuring a router and using a tunnel or 6to4 on the router. If you don't have dedicated router hardware, that's fine: most operating systems that support IPv6 can be configured as a router.

Dedicated routers themselves raise different questions. Depending on your manufacturer, you may have to buy an OS upgrade in order to have an IPv6 capable machine. Before that upgrade is bought or borrowed you'll need to do some planning. There are two points to be aware of when doing this planning. First, IPv6 dual stack obviously uses more CPU and memory resources than a single stack and sometimes routers don't have much of either to spare. Check your vendor's specifications to make sure the upgrade will fit on the router in question. (Router memory upgrades in particular can have unpleasant step functions in the financial resources required.)

The second issue that applies particularly to dedicated routers is that, because IPv6 is a younger protocol, the IPv6 path in a router can be less well optimized than the IPv4 path.* For core networks that expect to process millions of packets per second, this can be catastrophic, and if your router has this issue, we advise you to look at other options such as using a separate router for IPv6 or using 6PE.† Chapter 5 goes into more detail on the level of support in Cisco and Juniper routers. We'll talk more later about network topologies and how to ship traffic around.

With all this in mind, the question arises as to whether to use one's existing IPv4 router(s) for IPv6 traffic. Like always, this decision comes down to a balance of tradeoffs. The two main cases to consider are WAN links and ingress/egress routing, and the issue with both is whether the safety and resilience of a separate infrastructure justifies the management and cost overhead of supporting that infrastructure, even if that infrastructure is a single PC with a tunnel.

If you use a separate router on your LAN for IPv6, then you can gain experience‡ without fear of impacting your production IPv4 systems. As time goes on, however, you may find that this flexibility actually works against providing a reliable IPv6 service. It duplicates the administration and maintenance work involved and can create an easily-ignored support "ghetto" that busy staff without spare time will, despite best intentions, find themselves unable to gain experience with. Face it, who has spare time in this day and age?

Most importantly, it will also prevent you of taking full advantage of any IPv6 support that might become available on your WAN link. Workarounds like IPv6-in-IPv4 tunnels, while great to start with, don't scale very well and are prone to failure in ways that a native network is not. Maintaining it, of course, invites all the same problems of support ghettos. Once you have confidence that you understand IPv6 and its potential impacts on your network, the ideal way to leverage your existing experience and its similarity with IPv4 is to deploy it exactly in parallel, and use all the same troubleshooting and monitoring mechanisms to maintain it.

---

* Possible examples include processing firewall rules or fast hardware forwarding.

† This is a way of tunnelling IPv6 over MPLS.

‡ A euphemism for "break it then learn how to fix it."

As a result of this, our observation is that sites that experiment with IPv6 will typically start with an entirely separate infrastructure and move toward integration as time goes on and experience grows. On the other hand, sites looking to save money and have a deployment period with a fixed timescale, generally re-use existing infrastructure where possible.

Converting a host at a time: single stack

As above, this is a conversion process allowing your systems to run IPv6. However, in this case, you turn off the IPv4 stack when you have completed IPv6 configuration.[*] This is a scenario that you would probably only contemplate when one part of a network that is already converted to IPv6 is working well or if you need to deploy a large number of hosts but don't have the IPv4 address space available. The most important thing to remember is that routers and infrastructure service systems need to be in place *first*. IPv6-only machines that do not receive RAs are limited to purely local communication,[†] so you need a working IPv6 router to communicate with the outside world. Even if you do have fully functional IPv6 connectivity, you may need to think about how you will reach IPv4-only sites (including most of the web and DNS servers currently on the Internet). Your conversion plan will therefore need to address these dependencies very carefully.

You will very probably encounter problems in the act of performing the conversion. You could expect the issues to broadly fall into the following categories:

The IPv4 stack that wouldn't die
> In some cases, particularly with the older commercial operating systems, removing IPv4 is actually not yet possible. More accurately, removing it while *retaining* IPv6 can be problematic. However with popular, more modern operating systems, we're glad to say it is in general possible—for example, Windows allows you to bind and unbind protocols from an interface, and there was some work done on modularization of IPv4 in Linux. If you can't actually remove IPv4 you can always choose not to configure any IPv4 addresses.[‡]

Too simple
> There may be devices within your network (one classic example being network-enabled printers) that only speak IPv4 and will only ever speak IPv4. In this case it will require certain servers to retain their IPv4 addresses to front-end these devices.

---

[*] Probably removing the very stack that allowed you to install IPv6 in the first place!

[†] Although they may be able to communicate with a proxy on the same link, and hence the outside world.

[‡] You may need to configure 127.0.0.1, as some software becomes distressed if you don't have a loopback address.

Another possibility in this category is software that only supports IPv4 and an IPv6 version will not be available in the near future. In some cases it is possible to work around these issues; have a look at Chapter 7.

Low service availability

The service that you thought was available over IPv6 turns out to be available in the approximately twenty minutes that it stays up without crashing. In this case it may be possible to isolate the users of the service such that they continue to use dual-stack hosts while the rest of the network moves toward IPv6 alone. Sometimes the crashing problem may be easy to fix: a programming or configuration error. Sometimes there is another daemon that effectively achieves the same thing: samba instead of NFS for file sharing for example.

We have to say that most of the IPv6 services we have deployed have a similar level of reliability to their IPv4 counterparts, which is not surprising given that the transport level is essentially the only thing which is changing.*

Your system management process here involves the same test and rollout phase as before, only the dangers of removing IPv4 are significant—you are not only adding extra capabilities, you are removing old capabilities, and any users that were using the machine via IPv4, or any services that the machine needed to talk to over IPv4, had better be running on IPv6 also or things will get messy. For that reason alone it is probably best to run such infrastructure servers as are necessary (DHCP, DNS, and so on) on dual-stack until everything is running safely on IPv6.

In summary, if your deployment plan has an IPv6-only network in it, and it must communicate with an existing IPv4-only network, proxies or other front-ending should be deployed and tested first. If the IPv6-only network is "green-field" and does not need to communicate with IPv4 services, life is easier. We highly recommend dual-stacking infrastructure servers that provide DNS and DHCP. Additional single-stacked IPv6 servers performing the above functions are acceptable if the management and money overheads are acceptable.

No Existing IPv4 Infrastructure

At the moment, and probably for quite some time to come, this is the least likely scenario unless you are setting up a research lab. In many ways, since you have one less transport protocol to worry about, your life becomes much easier: there's no need to have separate firewalling rules, separate routing or anything like that. However, until the time when significant parts of the Internet can be reached via IPv6, you are likely to want to communicate with IPv4 entities *somewhere*. There are a variety of ways to do this, some of which are covered in this chapter, Chapter 6, and Chapter 7. The

---

* If an application is re-engineered entirely to support IPv6 there is of course the danger of introducing bugs, security problems, etc.

most relevant question for this scenario is whether or not you can get IPv4 addresses on the edge of your network. If you can, then you have the option of using various dual-stacked proxy techniques or using a router to do some form of NAT or gate-waying. Otherwise, you may have to rely on an upstream proxy server or some other mechanism to gain access to the IPv4 Internet.

Topologies

An obvious influence on a deployment plan is the existing network topology. This will dictate where things can be changed, and how expensive and difficult it will be.

Generally, your choice will be whether to modify topology on layer 2 rather than layer 3. If things are routed in your existing network there is generally a good reason for that (WAN links, security) and those reasons will be invariant under the application of IPv6. Of course the routers are a particularly crucial aspect of networking under both IPv4 and IPv6, which means that it may not be possible to change them as easily as we might like. Topology on layer 2 is relevant to intra-site communication, and may require one of the transition mechanisms to properly enable same. In the base case, IPv6 communication can flow naturally over normal switches, and as long as multicast is supported, everything should "just work." If one wants to separate out IPv4 and IPv6 communication, choices begin to appear. You can do it at a VLAN level, in which case your hosts must support the 802.1q VLAN tagging protocol; rare, but not impossible. Examples of how you might do this may be found in the "Hacking Native Connectivity Around Incompatible Equipment" section in Chapter 6.

Edge to core or core to edge

Historically speaking, it was envisaged that IPv6 would begin to appear in networks in an edge-to-core direction. In other words, given that one of the main benefits of IPv6 was to number large networks natively, it was envisaged that it would be enabled where the maximum benefit accrued. In fact, our experience is that it is going mostly in the opposite direction: the core is only slowly being dual-stacked or otherwise enabled for IPv6, and the edges which previously had to make do with tunnels are switching over to native connections. Based on the realization that most managers are somewhat scared to switch over a well-functioning core, this has prompted a move toward entirely separate IPv4 and IPv6 infrastructure. If existing IPv4 infrastructure and applications *absolutely must not be disturbed*, this is a good approach. In practice it is very rarely the case that you can have *entirely* separate infrastructure, especially when the expense of purchasing additional hardware is made clear. (There are of course still cases when it makes sense to buy a limited set of desktops or servers additional network cards, and create a separate switch VLAN for them.)

Conversely, with an edge-to-core implementation, the key question is building support inwards. In the case of ISPs, for example, CPE can often be less flexible and upgrading it to support IPv6 may be problematic. DSL routers are perhaps the canonical example of this, but old equipment is a problem for everyone, not just ISPs. Allowing IPv6 to transit your core until it is natively enabled is a matter for transition mechanisms discussed elsewhere.

Router placement and advertisement

With respect to router placement in general or reconfiguration, there are three main cases to consider:

1. Same IPv4/IPv6 router, with same exit route (i.e., native onward connectivity).
2. Same IPv4/IPv6 router, with different exit route (e.g., via a tunnel).
3. Separate IPv4 and IPv6 router (e.g., Figure 6-1).

These differences are important when considering your onward connectivity, but they will be transparent to the end host. In a flat (broadcast) network, such as a single LAN, your router's announcements will ensure that every IPv6-capable host receives an address and connectivity. If you happen to have more than one router on your LAN, both will announce themselves; if they are advertising different prefixes then your hosts will receive separate addresses from each.

Also be aware that if your prefix changes from time to time—for example, if you use 6to4 with a dynamic IPv4 address as the endpoint—then the addresses of all your hosts will change as well. This should happen fairly transparently, but you will need to set the lifetime of the advertised prefixes just right; long enough to overcome network instabilities, but short enough to time out when they are no longer valid.

While we like to insist that IPv6 is just like IPv4 in all the best ways, there are some interesting consequences to router advertisement that can catch you out if you use VLANs extensively. When a router turns up on a network, it will typically announce itself and start assigning addresses. If the router is not on the network it is supposed to be on—for example, by being plugged into a switchport on the wrong VLAN—it will start handing out addresses that will, briefly, work (for small values of "work"— they're not likely to be in the DNS and might not match any access control lists you or others have defined).

When the operator notices the error and pulls out the patch cable, the addresses will suddenly stop working, but they will hang around until they time out, and chances are that the machines that have them will continue to try to use them. Since mistakes happen, you might want to consider configuring reasonably short timeouts for router advertisement; after all, if the router *does* go away for a bit, its addresses aren't going to be much use anyway. Note also that, even when correctly configured, leakage of packets across VLAN boundaries is a well-documented feature of network equipment.

It all gets even more interesting if your router or switch runs a trunking protocol such as VTP. Rather than simply not working if you plug it into a non-VTP port, it's likely that traffic to the default VLAN will still get through, and you'll start getting addresses from *somewhere*. Typically , it'll almost certainly be wrong somewhere.

In summary, we have shown a number of the possible influences on a deployment plan. You will need to consider at a minimum addressing, routing and naming in your deployment plan, as well as organizational concerns such as who will pay for it, and who will support it.

Worked Examples

In this section we present an overview of the deployment of IPv6 in some representative networks. We look at both the technical and organizational aspects of same. The first example we look at is that of an enterprise-class IPv4-connected network, the second a transit ISP, and the third—a special case—an Internet Exchange Point.

Enterprise-class IPv4-connected network

Step 1

XYZ Corp, a company owning its own network, decides to implement a pilot IPv6 program to provoke a thorough audit of their in-house applications, which recently demonstrated fragility in the face of network instability. The pilot IPv6 programme will establish the minimum necessary IPv6 connectivity to test the applications on the internal desktop and server networks. External IPv6 connectivity is not absolutely required but will be delivered if possible.

The development team are instructed that when they are going through the code-base for the company applications, they should alter the code to be address independent and to be more resilient to failures. The implementation team have to deliver a working IPv6 platform not for the development team, who are anticipated to take quite some time when reworking the code, but for the testing team, so there is ample time for the deployment to take place.

Step 2

The deployment team begin the communication process by running an internal IT staff course in IPv6; they might use this book, vendor materials, and so on. They set up a machine for the IT department which has a tunnel via a tunnel broker, enabling them to become familiar with addressing, routing, and new features like router solicitation in an environment where it doesn't particularly matter whether connectivity is up or down. (Attempting to deploy a new protocol where a sizable proportion of staff have never executed any IPv6 related command is not recommended.)

They begin the network analysis process, and arrive at the conclusion that three things need to change: desktop network, server network (which are both separately addressed and routed networks in IPv4, and should remain so in IPv6) and egress routing. The company has decided that fiddling with their single egress router is not something they want to do, and therefore elects to get external IPv6 connectivity via some spare commodity kit they have lying around. Neither do they want to dual-stack all the internal routers between the egress router and the desktop network in question, so they decide on tunnelling as a "quick fix."

Step 3

The network design process results in an addressing architecture and subnetting architecture that looks very similar to the existing IPv4 network, except that where an existing RFC 1918 /16 was used for the internal network, the company's upstream ISP agrees to supply them with a tunnel and a /48 from their PA space. From an addressing point of view, they assign a single /64 to each WAN link for their remote offices, who are not yet IPv6 enabled, and reserve /64s for their server and desktop networks. Any tunnels between routers will also be numbered out of consecutive /64s. While it may not be optimal, it should work. The formal deployment plan now consists of commissioning a tunnel-capable router, dual-stacking the internal router between the desktop and server networks, dual-stacking the desktop network, and then dual-stacking the server network, with approximately a week's worth of testing between each step. Internal IT staff are reluctant to push an IPv6 stack into the standard patching methodology, so a supervised manual install and reboot of approximately 300 workstations is done by ten volunteers, which goes slowly but without incident. Simultaneously with this, a spare Cisco 3600 series is found, and connected to the DMZ which hangs off the existing router. Tunnels are brought up to the outside world, and to the router of the internal desktop network, for which delicate holes are punched in the firewalls. Both are found to be working.

Step 4

Internal IT staff balk at the notion of a full conversion of the existing server farm, so only four servers are converted: the two on which the server-side of the application runs, and the DNS/DHCP servers. IPv6 addresses are kept in AAAA records in the same internal zone in the same internal DNS servers—no IPv6 is exposed to the outside world. The server upgrade exposes a bug in one of the being-rewritten applications where if it makes a quad-A DNS request and does not get an answer, it returns a strange error to the user instead of falling back to A requests.

Step 5

The development team has IPv6 service enough to test their reworked application, and solicits feedback. The project is declared closed until the issue is re-opened by a later management fiat.

Transit-providing medium-size ISP

Step 1

Management in the company decides that it is time to gain experience with IPv6. While there hasn't been much direct customer demand to date, there are a couple of large influential clients that have it on their long-term radar, and there is a need to gain understanding now so as to avoid buying new equipment that might impede IPv6 deployment over its lifetime in the network.

A single individual is tasked with the job of gaining familiarity with IPv6, setting up a small test network (one router, one server and connectivity to the IPv6 Internet) and beginning the process of educating the rest of the operations staff.

Step 2

The "IPv6 expert" procures a UNIX-based server and a spare Cisco 7200 router with Ethernet and ATM connectivity. An IPv6-in-IPv4 tunnel is configured to one of the ISP's peers who have already set up IPv6, and address space is obtained from them. At the same time, the ISP begins the process of requesting IPv6 address space from RIPE, which involves preparing a deployment plan.

After connectivity is successfully set up, a variety of IPv6-capable services are configured on the server, including a web server (Apache 2), an SMTP daemon (Exim), an IMAP server (Courier IMAP) and a DNS server (Bind 9). The server is placed in the domain ipv6.ISPNAME.net, and acts as the primary DNS server for that domain. The ISP asks its (IPv4-only) DNS secondaries to carry the forward and reverse DNS zones, thereby checking on an isolated subdomain whether the addition of IPv6 records causes any unexpected problems.

To begin the very first stages of integration, IPv6 connectivity is enabled on the local office LAN of the operations centre by means of VLAN trunking on the Cisco 7200. IPv6 is then enabled manually one machine at a time on the LAN, and any problems are noted and dealt with.

A policy is instituted that any new network equipment bought must either be IPv6 capable, or have a roadmap for native IPv6 connectivity in a short time-frame.

Step 3

Having gained experience with the initial deployment, it is time to begin expanding the network and taking the first steps to integration. Expertise begins to grow throughout the company.

The ISP receives its own address space from RIPE and, while the deployment is still small, renumbering begins. This involves developing an addressing plan that will scale into the future. The organization has been granted a /32 prefix from RIPE. In the addressing plan, one-quarter of this (a /34) is assigned for the deployment project, with the rest reserved for future use. This space is then divided into four chunks of size /36 each, one for each region in which the network operates.

In line with the rules of their Regional Internet Registry, the plan then allocates one /48 to each PoP in the network. Note that these are not configured yet and may not be for quite some time—they are reserved in the addressing plan for when that time comes. As infrastructure in any one PoP is dual stacked, addresses are assigned from the appropriate block for that PoP. Customers in each region will be given allocations from the corresponding /36, which will allow the routing protocol to aggregate announcements between PoPs.

With renumbering complete, the way is now open for the ISP to run BGP and arrange peering and transit in the usual manner from other networks.

The ISP has an infrastructure based on, among other technologies, ATM and wide-area Ethernet. An additional router is procured and a dedicated IPv6 wide-area link is set up over ATM to another PoP. Private peering is arranged with a willing ISP that is also located at the same data center. This is still separate from the existing IPv4 routed network, but shares some of the switch infrastructure that, as it was used in the previous step, has been shown to be agnostic of IPv6 traffic.

Meantime, a policy is instituted that any service upgrades and new services should be IPv6-capable. Managed services staff can use the experience gained from the IPv6 server set up in the previous phase, and can carry out further experiments there before deploying IPv6-capable services in production.

Now that the prerequisites for deploying an IPv6 routing infrastructure are understood, the ISP surveys its existing network with a view to supporting dual-stacked operation. The policy of purchasing IPv6-capable equipment initiated in step 1 begins to pay dividends as the impact of IPv4-only equipment is minimized.

Early-adopter customers who are willing to participate in the IPv6 rollout can now be facilitated by means of IPv6-in-IPv4 tunnels or dedicated virtual circuits or VLANs on their wide-area links.

Step 4

The time has come to integrate IPv6 support with the existing network, upgrading or deploying workarounds where necessary. Training is provided for all operations staff, conducted by those who have gained experience in previous phases. A deployment plan is drawn up by the IPv6 team and, after an initial run-through on a single router, is handed over to the operations team to implement (with support from the IPv6 team) so that they are happy that they have the expertise to deploy and support IPv6 on their infrastructure.

In the meantime, the remaining IPv4-only managed services are undergoing upgrades drawing on the experience of dual-stacking services in the previous step. IPv6 is now provided in the routing infrastructure and on managed services as a matter of course.

As necessary for a production deployment, the monitoring infrastructure is adjusted and upgraded to ensure that IPv6-specific faults are detected and dealt with.

Customers, who are dealing with internal requests for IPv6 connectivity, can be facilitated by means of transition mechanisms and, as the rollout proceeds, with native connectivity as and when they are ready to take advantage of it.

Step 5

IPv6 is now rolled out and supported network-wide. Ongoing upgrades maintain existing IPv6 connectivity, removing workarounds where they were necessary and improving performance where only software-based forwarding was available on hardware-based routers. The IPv6 routing policy is brought into line with IPv4 and native peering is preferred over tunnels with existing peers and transit providers.

Special case: Internet Exchange Point

Introduction

An *Internet Exchange Point* (IXP) is a facility that provides a place multiple for Internet Service Providers to meet and exchange traffic. Their aim is to save money for the ISPs and improve connectivity for their customers. Think of it as a switch into which multiple customers connect over WAN links; it's a way to get direct peer-to-peer connectivity in a scalable fashion.

There are two basic scenarios for how IPv6 might be used within the context of an IXP. First, an exchange itself might like to enable IPv6 services to offer to its members, and second, a member might like to participate in IPv6 peering across an exchange.

Step 1

The members of the IXP decide to implement IPv6 as fully as possible within the exchange as part of the goals for the next financial year. As part of the usual schedule of rolling switch upgrades they specify that vendors will be unable to respond to tenders without including details on their level of support for IPv6.

Step 2

IXP operations decides to do the easy bit first, and applies for special IXP address space from their nearest RIR. They examine the RIR Comparative Policy Overview,* which specifies that to qualify for this space, "the IXP must have a clear and open policy for others to join and must have at least three members." The IXP qualifies, so they continue with their application. The exchange point mesh is itself "neutral" and should not be seen to receive transit from any particular member.

The address space that is received is for the peering mesh *only*. While it's assumed that the direct peers of an IXP will route this /48, it's likely that other more remote networks will reject advertisements of such a small network. The operations team therefore assumes that this address space, while unique, is *not* globally routable and so can't be reached from all places on the internet. Services such as looking glasses and NTP servers that need to be globally reachable must still get their address space from one (or more) transit providers. Thankfully in

---

* Found at *http://lacnic.net/en/rir_comp.html*.

this case, one of the members is already providing IPv4 address space for the services LAN, and can persuaded to provide IPv6 address space for it too. There is little danger in this particular case of the members falling out and withdrawing address space, so it is viewed as an acceptable risk.

Step 3

Fully-capable IPv6 switches and operating system versions are obtained, and a scheduled upgrade is performed. This upgrade also dual-stacks the existing server in the services LAN, as well as its associated services. Testing reveals no problems.

Members now have the choice of presenting at the exchange with a second IPv6-only router, or simply dual-stacking their IXP router. Policies are rewritten to ensure members turn off RAs on their IXP present routers, and peering is negotiated between members as usual. The operations team extends its monitoring system to include member IPv6 addresses, implemented via a database. Successful peering happens within weeks of the upgrade, and the project is declared a success.

Summary

We have brought up some of the issues which you may have to consider when planning your IPv6 experience, including obtaining address space, obtaining connectivity, the possible transition mechanisms and managing the indefinite coexistence of IPv4 and IPv6, as well as detailing some clever (and not-so-clever) techniques to help you work around awkward equipment.

## CHAPTER 5

Installation and Configuration

Of a good beginning cometh a good end.
—*Proverbes, John Heywood*

We now want to look at actually configuring the IPv6 stacks on various operating platforms. First we'll describe the support present in each platform and say how to install and enable it. As the state of the art progresses, of course, the sort of instructions in this chapter should become less and less relevant, since hardly anyone needs to know how to install their IPv4 stack on their machine! Then we'll move on to the specifics of commands for testing the stack, displaying information about it and troubleshooting. This part of the chapter contains many tables showing the details of configuring the basic aspects of IPv6 on all the platforms. Tables of details rarely make exciting reading, but they are necessary because of variations between the platforms we cover. The overall aim is that, at the end of this chapter, you should have the requisite information to take a new machine from zero to hero on your IPv6 network.

We don't cover anything other than the simplest of transition mechanisms, however, so if your network relies on complicated ways to get an IPv6 connection, or if you are looking to understand how best to support IPv6 from a network manager's perspective, we advise you to look at Chapter 4, the planning chapter.

Finally, before we close the chapter we have a look at some common problems you might encounter as you take your first steps with IPv6.

Right—now it's on to the fine detail!

Workstations and Servers

In this section, we run through various workstation and server platforms, commenting on their IPv6 support and anything you may need to watch out for while enabling them. The operating systems we look at include versions of Windows, Mac OS X, and various Unix(-like) systems.

Windows

Microsoft's support for IPv6 is quite thorough, albeit relatively recent and unfortunately geared towards for their current and future products more than their past ones. Microsoft's plan for IPv6, and numerous useful articles are available at *http://www.microsoft.com/ipv6*.

Windows 2000

Windows 2000 requires the installation of the Microsoft IPv6 Technology Preview for Windows 2000, available from *http://msdn.microsoft.com/downloads/sdks/platform/tpipv6.asp*. This package creates a new protocol, unsurprisingly called IPv6, which can be manipulated and bound to various network adapters via the usual control panel interface.

The package is slightly tricky to install. Be sure to follow the instructions that are included in the FAQ referenced on the page mentioned above. Note that the procedure is service pack specific and may need to be manually reinstalled after a service pack upgrade. Also, Microsoft consider the patch a technology preview and do not recommend running it in a production environment. For these reasons, Windows XP or Windows 2003 are a better choice for running IPv6 on a Windows platform.

Windows XP

Windows XP comes with IPv6 support by default, though you do need to enable it manually. Easily done: you open a command prompt and issue the command ipv6 install. Windows XP Service Pack 1 also supports installing IPv6 via the Network Connections control panel. Officially, the stack shipped with Service Pack 1 is of production quality, and the earlier versions are developer previews. Despite this, the stack shipped with Service Pack 1 identifies itself as a developers edition. This is slightly confusing but not actually harmful. Service Pack 2 extends this support even further, including an IPv6 firewall by default and Toredo which allows IPv6 through NAT.

Microsoft has some useful information about the capabilities and configuration of the stack shipped with XP available from its IPv6 pages at *http://www.microsoft.com/ipv6* but most of the configuration can be done with the ipv6 command, with finer control over the stack available using netsh. Basic testing of IPv6 connectivity can be accomplished with ping6 and tracert6.

There is one peculiarity however: some versions of Windows will automatically configure routing via 6to4 if a global IPv4 address is found and no IPv6 router is present on the LAN. This has caught some people by surprise.

Windows Server 2003

Windows Server 2003 also has IPv6 support, but it goes beyond what's included in Windows XP—the IPv6 stack is a full stack nearly on a par with its IPv4 cousin. The ipv6 command is also being deprecated in Server 2003, and the equivalent netsh commands are now preferred. Microsoft provides a handy crib sheet of ipv6 and netsh equivalent commands at *http://www.microsoft.com/windowsserver2003/technologies/ipv6/ipv62netshtable.mspx*.

Again, IPv6 can be enabled via the command line by running netsh interface ipv6 install, or from the Network Connections control panel (right click on a LAN interface to edit its Properties → Install → Protocol → Add → Microsoft TCP/IP Version 6).

Support for IPv6 ping and traceroute are also available in the traditional ping and tracert commands without the "6" suffix.

Other versions of Windows

If you run any variety of Windows 98 or NT 4, then, at the moment, you are out of luck. Since these products have been end-of-lifed, it is unlikely that useful IPv6 support for them will be forthcoming from Microsoft. However, third party support is available via products such as Trumpet Winsock[*] and Hitachi's Toolnet6.[†]

A stack for Windows CE.NET is available. One interesting question is whether or not we will see IPv6 on the X-Box. You would expect that non-NATed peer-to-peer gaming would be a core attraction of IPv6, but we'll have to wait and see.

IPv6 applications on Windows

As mentioned, all versions of the Microsoft IPv6 stack come with the basic diagnostic tools like ping and traceroute. Some versions also ship with a tool called pathping, which is an interesting cross between traceroute and ping. It does an initial traceroute and then calculates statistics relating to round-trip-time and loss.

The old command-line tools, telnet and ftp, also support IPv6. For applications, such as Internet Explorer, that use wininet.dll. IPv6 support should be essentially transparent, particularly for those applications using DNS rather than endpoints specified by explicit IPv6 address.

Microsoft's P2P update for Windows XP[‡] is a platform for the development of peer-to-peer applications. It makes heavy use of IPv6 and even provides a personal IPv6-enabled firewall. There are also other sites that provide IPv6 enabled versions of Windows software, such as *http://win6.jp/*.

---

[*] *http://www.trumpet.com.au/ipv6.htm*

[†] *http://www.hitachi.co.jp/Prod/comp/network/pexv6-e.htm*

[‡] Currently a beta version is available for download from *http://msdn.microsoft.com/library/default.asp?url=/downloads/list/winxppeer.asp*, Windows XP Service Pack 2 includes some of the features of the P2P update.

Points of interest

IPsec on top of IPv6 within Windows XP and Windows 2003 is missing one or two features currently. ESP payload encryption is not available in general, though it *is* available for tunnels. Automatic key configuration with IKE is also not available, so IPsec policies must be configured manually with `ipsec6.exe`, using preshared keys.

At time of writing, Microsoft's IPv6 implementations do not support mapped IPv4 addresses.* While Internet Explorer will support both protocols simultaneously, it does mean that cross-platform applications, such as some versions of Mozilla, that use mapped addresses must disable IPv6 support or lose IPv4 compatibility. For services such as Apache this is not a problem, as they can listen for IPv4 and IPv6 connections independently.

Microsoft has moved the operation of CIFS (or to use another acronym, the SMB file-sharing service) to use port TCP port 445 exclusively over IPv6.† IPv6-based SMB requests from non–on-link addresses seem to be automatically refused; this must be applauded as a useful security measure for unmanaged networks.

Macintosh (OS X and Darwin)

The Unix-like layer, Darwin, that underlies Mac OS X supports IPv6 as of version 10.2 (Jaguar) and automatic configuration is enabled by default. While many of the lower level Darwin utilities support IPv6, this has not yet percolated upwards to most familiar Mac OS applications. In essence, this means that most of the command line tools support IPv6, including `ping6`, `traceroute6`, `telnet` and so on, but things like iSync, iPhoto, etc., don't necessarily. One thing that's missing in 10.2 is IPv6 support in `ssh`.‡ Naturally, OS X's IPv6 support derives from the KAME project, so resources and documentation for KAME will apply usefully to OS X. Version 10.3 of Mac OS X is based on FreeBSD 5.x and also supports IPv6.

Panther (OS X version 10.3) extends the IPv6 support introduced in Jaguar into the OS X network control panels and also into a number of subsystems, including allowing DNS lookups over IPv6, IPv6 personal firewalling and IPv6 support in `ssh`.

As far as we're aware, you're out of luck if you want to run IPv6 on Mac OS 9 or anything earlier.

---

* See the "Mapped IPv4 Addresses" section in Chapter 8 to find out more about mapped addresses.

† Prototype patches allowing Samba to speak SMB over IPv6 are available from *http://v6web.litech.org/samba*, although this work has yet to be brought into a mainstream Samba release.

‡ The authors just compile a version of OpenSSH and keep it handy for IPv6-only occasions.

Linux

IPv6 in the Linux kernel has a slightly uneven history. Initial support began in 1996, with contributions by Pedro Roque, who later went on to work for Cisco. Under-resourcing got the better of developer effort some while thereafter, and the stack quality suffered, with the result that a project called USAGI was started in Japan in late 2000, whose aim was to bring the kernel implementation up to spec with the reality of what the RFCs required. Thankfully things these days are a lot better; most of the Linux vendors have brought their stack into shape with the relevant USAGI patches, and if you are running a 2.4.x (or better) kernel, many of the more egregious faults with 2.2.x are no longer a problem. The USAGI patches provide things like ICMPv6 node information queries, IPsec support, and fix a number of bugs. If any of these are important to your network, you may want to investigate applying these patches.*

To get IPv6 working with Linux, you must first distinguish between the kernel and the distribution or userland that you happen to be running. All modern kernels (=>2.2, but you really want =>2.4) support IPv6—you can either compile it into the kernel statically, following the standard Linux kernel compilation instructions, or use a module. Most modern Linux software vendors will ship this as the module *ipv6.o*. The kernel module supplies the ability to actually speak the protocol; the userland tools supply the ability to work with it. It is unfortunately possible, although unlikely, to have kernel support but no userland support, and vice versa.

A lack of userland support is the easiest problem to remedy: simply download the relevant RPMs and install them.

If you are missing kernel support and the *ipv6.o* module is not provided then you will have to recompile your kernel.† Recompiling your kernel is something that your Linux distributor should provide documentation for. In general, it involves going to where your kernel sources are, generally */usr/src/linux*, typing make menuconfig, selecting IPv6 under Networking Options, saving your changes and then doing make bzImage, but the your vendor's documentation should be your guide here. One complication you might encounter is that IPv6 may be marked "Experimental" and hence might not be shown as a selectable option unless you indicate that you want to see experimental options under menuconfig's Code Maturity Level Options. Note that while you are adding IPv6 support, you may also want to enable the IPv6 firewalling support (a.k.a. netfilter/iptables) as well.

---

* Of course the state of the art will move on, and they may make their way into mainstream kernel deployment eventually.

† Another reason you might want to recompile your kernel is to apply some of the USAGI patches from *http://www.linux-ipv6.org/*. These are for the more expert user and aren't required for normal operation.

If you are wondering whether your current kernel has IPv6 support, there are two quick tests you can do. If you are using a software vendor's distribution, try the simple modprobe ipv6. That should load the module in question (lsmod | grep -w ^ipv6 should report the presence of the module if you want to be extra sure). If that doesn't work, perhaps because the kernel has it statically compiled in, then check out the contents of */proc/net/*—network protocols register their presence here when they are loaded, so *if_inet6* and *igmp6* will be present if the kernel had IPv6 compiled in.

 A good way to check for IPv6 support in a script is test -d /proc/sys/ net/ipv6.

Of course the kernel itself has some knobs allowing you to change its IPv6 behavior more to your satisfaction. Possibly the most useful of these is being able to turn off address autoconfiguration on a per-interface basis by running echo 0 > /proc/sys/ net/ipv6/conf/eth0/autoconf where eth0 can be replaced by the relevant interface name. This only disables address configuration, but other information like default routes can still be learned from router advertisement packets. You can more completely disable the processing router advertisements with echo 0 > /proc/sys/net/ ipv6/conf/eth0/accept_ra. Both of these commands have a system-wide equivalent, but we've found it simpler and more reliable to use the per-interface settings.

The first place to go to if you want to find out more is Peter Bieringer's wonderful IPv6 resources at *http://www.bieringer.de/linux/IPv6/*, which provide not only useful resources for IPv6 users under Linux, but also a wealth of information about IPv6 support in various applications and services on all Unix-like platforms.

We deal with the different distributions below.

Red Hat and derivatives

Enabling IPv6 on recent Red Hat-derived Linux systems is as easy as adding the line:

```
NETWORKING_IPV6="yes"
```

to */etc/sysconfig/network*. This should configure the boot-time scripts to load the IPv6 kernel module, *ipv6.o* if required, and enable autoconfiguration of network interfaces. Manual configuration of the interface address is covered in the "Enabling, Testing, and Troubleshooting" section later in this chapter.

Fedora Core, the community-maintained version of Red Hat, activates IPv6 in the very same way.

SuSE

Support for IPv6 varies widely across SuSE distributions. We will focus on the 8.x series here, since they were the most recent output from SuSE at time of writing.

In general, one drives the SuSE 8.0 distributions by editing */etc/sysconfig/network/ifcfg-eth0* (where one is attempting to configure interface eth0) and inserts the line

```
IP6ADDR="<IPv6 address>/<prefix length>"
```

For SuSE 8.1, use IPADDR instead of IP6ADDR.

Debian

The key configuration file for IPv6 support in Debian is */etc/network/interfaces*. We include some configuration file examples below that serve to illustrate how IPv6 is configured:

```
iface sit1 inet6 v4tunnel
        address <your end>
        netmask <tunnel netmask>
        endpoint <tunnel broker IPv4 address>
        up ip route add 2000::/3 via <their end>
```

This brings up a tunnel between the nominated places.

```
iface eth0 inet6 static
        pre-up modprobe ipv6
        address 2001:db8:1234:5::1:1
        netmask 64
```

This is a static configuration for your local Ethernet interface.

Note that many of the examples later in this chapter use the ip command, which is not installed on Debian by default. To get this command you can apt-get install iproute.

Userland/administration support for IPv6

Simple tools like ping6 are supplied with most modern distributions. Since they're useful for testing, if your distribution doesn't have them we would recommend that you install them from your OS vendor supplied material, or download them. Here's a list of common distributions and the names of the RPMs, together with where to get them:

Red Hat 8+

While Red Hat has shipped ping6since sometime around Red Hat 6.2, we'll consider version 8 onwards. The iputils RPM that is distributed with Red Hat 8 and newer contains ping6 and traceroute6. Iputils also has a tracepath command, which is similar to traceroute but also provides path MTU information. Unfortunately, the Kerberos version of telnet and ftp that ships with Red Hat 8 does not seem to support IPv6. One option here is to remove */usr/kerberos/bin* from your path.

Debian

Debian also includes good userland support for IPv6. ping6 and traceroute6 can be found in iputils-ping and iputils-tracepath respectively, and the normal version of telnet supports IPv6.

SuSE 8.x

The normal networking RPMs contain all the commands that you are likely to need.

Solaris

From Solaris 8 onwards, IPv6 is included in the normal Solaris installation process, and you are asked if you want to configure IPv6 during the install. There is good coverage of both IPsec and IPv6 in the networking sections of the Solaris Administration Guide, available online at *http://docs.sun.com/*.

Sun have always been advocates of NIS, and have extended the Solaris Name services to deal with IPv6. The traditional */etc/hosts* database, which is actually a symbolic link to */etc/inet/hosts*, is only used for IPv4 addresses in Solaris. A new database, */etc/inet/ipnodes*, can be used for *both* IPv4 and IPv6 name lookups: which of these is used can be controlled with settings in */etc/nsswitch*. If the hosts database is commented out, the ipnodes database will be used for all lookups.

People familiar with Solaris may remember that the IPv4 address for an interface is stored in the file */etc/hostname.ifname*. Similarly, the IPv6 configuration of an interface is controlled by */etc/hostname6.ifname*. As with IPv4, this file can contain a numerical address, or a hostname to be looked up using the Solaris name service. It is also possible to leave this file empty, which will cause the interface to use IPv6 autoconfiguration. Autoconfiguration is managed by the in.ndpd daemon, which sends Router Solicitation messages and acts on the Router Advertisements received.

The ping and traceroute commands both support IPv4 and IPv6. Specifying an IPv4 address causes these commands to use IPv4. Specifying an IPv6 address causes these commands to use IPv6. Specifying a hostname causes the commands to use IPv6, if the host has an IPv6 address and IPv4 otherwise. You can explicitly choose address family by using the flags -A inet4 and -A inet6 respectively.

There are IPv6 patches for some earlier versions of Solaris available from Sun, however these were considered "developer" quality.

AIX

IPv6 should be available in AIX from version 4.3.3 onwards. Autoconfiguration can be enabled from AIX's SMIT configuration tool under the following menus: Communications Applications and Services → TCP/IP → IPV6 Configuration → IPV6 Daemon/Process Configuration → Autoconf6 Process → Start Using the Autoconf6

Process. In addition, you will want to enable ndpd-host, also available under the IPV6 Daemon/Process Configuration menu.

AIX's version of ping and traceroute includes support for IPv6. Utilities such as telnet also include IPv6 support. The IPv6 support in AIX is based on work at INRIA.

Although not strictly related to AIX, IBM also offer a prototype IPv6 implementation for OS/390.

Tru64

Version 5.1 of Tru64 contains basic IPv6 support. The first step is to make sure your kernel supports IPv6; if you've built or installed a kernel with support for *all* optional features, then it will contain IPv6 support. Otherwise, you'll need to configure your kernel with doconfig -c KERNELNAME, choose to include the IPV6 option, install it with cp /sys/KERNELNAME/vmunix /vmunix and reboot.

A script, /usr/sbin/ip6_setup, is provided to make enabling IPv6 easier. It will ask you if you have network interfaces on which you want to enable IPv6, and if you want to configure tunnels for IPv6 connectivity. As a minimum, you can tell it to configure IPv6 on your Ethernet interface, probably tu0, then tell it to save the changes and start IPv6 networking.

The usual ping and traceroute commands support IPv6 in Tru64, with a flag -V 4 or -V 6 to determine the version of IP to use (IPv6 is the default for hostnames with both types of addresses). Other base utilities such as telnet and ftp support IPv6. The version of ssh shipped with Tru64 5.1 seems to support IPv6, but prefers IPv4 DNS records over IPv6, so you need to give explicit IPv6 addresses on the command line, or only have quad A records in your internal DNS for servers to which you want to ssh using IPv6.

The Tru64 Network Administration Manual contains both an introduction to IPv6 and details of how it can be configured under Tru64.

FreeBSD

The IPv6 support in FreeBSD is based on the work by the KAME group. Initially it was available as a set of patches to FreeBSD, but IPv6 has been a shipping feature of the FreeBSD distribution for some time, and is included in the standard 'GENERIC' kernel. In fact, it is possible to install FreeBSD over IPv6 if you choose an IPv6 enabled FTP server during the setup process.

If, for some reason, IPv6 is not present in your kernel you will need to recompile it after adding the options INET6 line to your kernel configuration (full details of how to recompile your kernel are in the FreeBSD handbook at *http://www.freebsd.org/handbook/*).

IPsec is also incorporated into FreeBSD and more recent releases include support for hardware acceleration of IPsec. However, IPsec is not part of the GENERIC kernel, and may require a kernel recompilation after the addition of options IPSEC and options IPSEC_ESP to your kernel's configuration file.

Most of the FreeBSD base applications support IPv6 including ssh, telnet, ftp, sendmail, and inetd. Where possible, additional software from the FreeBSD ports/packages system is compiled with IPv6 support; there's even a ports category specifically for IPv6 software!

To enable the boot-time configuration of IPv6 on FreeBSD, you must add a line ipv6_enable="YES" to your */etc/rc.conf* file. Other configuration options for the setting up of tunnels, routing and so on, are listed in */etc/defaults/rc.conf* under the "IPv6 options" heading.

Other Workstation/Server OSs

Naturally, the list of operating systems that now support IPv6 goes on and on. The list above is just a sample of the operating systems commonly associated with IP networking, biased by the authors' experience. Let's take a moment to glance at some of the other OSs in this area.

BSDi, NetBSD, and OpenBSD certainly warrant a mention, as they are other platforms based on the KAME IPv6 code and have supported IPv6 for several years. On these platforms, the command line utilities will be similar to those on FreeBSD and Mac OS X, though boot-time configuration knobs will differ slightly. It is also worth noting that if you require up-to-the-minute IPv6 features, KAME provide *snap kits* of their development work for various platforms. These are available from the KAME web site *http://www.kame.net/* but are strictly for the courageous expert.

IPv6 support for SGI's Irix has been available as a beta release for some time to people with support contracts. Since February 2003 it has been available in the normal releases of Irix 6.5.19 and above. Similarly, IPv6 is available for HP-UX 11i from the HP web site, *http://www.hp.com/products1/unix/operating/internet/ipv.html*. The IP stack shipped with VMS and Multinet both support IPv6.

Routers

In this section, we look at Cisco's and Juniper's support for IPv6. They are not the only vendors in the IPv6 market, but they are two vendors that many people will be familiar with.

Cisco

Cisco detail support for IPv6 across their various routers on their web site at *http://www.cisco.com/ipv6/*. However, IPv6 performance varies from platform to platform.

For software-based routers, such as the 2500, 2600 and 7200, it is possible to achieve respectable IPv6 performance at the current time with just an IOS upgrade. Maximum speeds are not yet on a par with IPv4, and many of the more complex features haven't been implemented for IPv6 yet, but this should improve as releases continue.

Cisco IOS support for IPv6 first appeared on the public radar with the 12.2T stream. As a "new technology" release, some readers may be familiar with the T streams if they are using other new features. Like all new technology releases, it has a rather large memory footprint, and may contain other new features that one may not wish to deploy in production yet.

The 12.3 stream is the first mainline IOS stream with support for IPv6. Cisco provides TAC support for the IPv6 features of 12.3. This is also a fairly hefty piece of code, and older equipment might require memory upgrades in order to support it.

An alternative is the 12.2S stream which appeared in 2004. It is aimed at service providers who wish to use IPv6 in a smaller package more tuned to their needs, or who are reluctant to make the leap to 12.3 mainline for a single feature. At the time of writing, this is also the stream on which IPv6 support for layer 3 switches, such as the Catalyst 6500/Cisco 7600, is based.

For hardware-based routers, such as the 12000 series, the situation is rather different. The 12.0S stream of code now supports IPv6 in its more recent incarnations, and a number of ISPs are using this in their backbones. However, performance of these routers is dependent on hardware support in the linecard, not the central routing processor, and this could mean expensive upgrades. Engine 3 linecards support IPv6 in hardware; Engine 0, 1, 2 and (perhaps surprisingly) 4+ linecards only support IPv6 with software forwarding, with a much lower throughput. Engine 5 linecards were promised but not yet available at the time of writing, so check with your equipment vendor for more details on those.

To discover the types of linecard already deployed in a 12000 series router, use the `show diag` command—it is listed for each slot on the line starting "L3 Engine:".

If you have a mix of cards, the throughput you may achieve depends on the input interface; if it's capable of native IPv6, you should achieve reasonable traffic rates, regardless of the output interface. If it's not, the packet will be forwarded in software, with a much lower maximum throughput. For those providers who use MPLS in their backbone, Cisco suggests 6PE, a method of transiting traffic from a dual-stacked provider edge (presumably based on 7200/7500 routers or similar) over an IPv4-only core, using MPLS tunnels. This might be an excellent workaround for an organization already familiar with MPLS, but those who aren't already using MPLS might think twice about deploying it solely for IPv6.

IPv6 configuration on Cisco is typically straightforward, especially if one is already familiar with the procedure in IPv4. IOS commands are generally derivable from the names of their predecessors by the simple expedient of replacing "ip" with "ipv6" (s/ip/ipv6/ for all you regexp fans). This works for commands like show ipv6 route and show ipv6 interface. However, there are ipv6 specific commands like show ipv6 neighbors and ipv6 unicast-routing.

 Don't forget to turn ipv6 unicast-routing on. Everyone forgets to turn this on. Everyone is then surprised when the routing protocols come up but traffic isn't forwarded or router advertisements aren't sent. Some people get quite a distance into a support call before realising that they forgot to turn this on. Remembering to turn on IPv6 forwarding applies not just to Cisco, but to any platform you choose to route on.

In BGP land, there have been some subtle changes; sh ip bgp becomes sh bgp ipv6. Also, when you configure your first BGP session over IPv6, you might get a bit of a shock when you look over your configuration; the IPv4-specific parts are moved automagically into their own section. We'll deal with this in more detail when we discuss routing in the "Routing Protocols" section in Chapter 6.

Juniper

Juniper have been offering IPv6 support in JUNOS for some time; most of the features arrived in JUNOS 5.1 or JUNOS 5.2. This support covers the core parts of IPv6: the protocol itself, forwarding, IPv6 over various media and the all routing protocols you'd expect. Hardware support extends to all Juniper's platforms and interface cards.

Again, the obvious commands are fairly similar to their IPv4 equivalents—or in many cases, show IPv6 information alongside IPv4. Like Cisco, ping on Juniper will attempt IPv6 if it is available. Unlike Cisco, show bgp summary lists IPv4 and IPv6 sessions in sequence.

To configure an IPv6 address on an interface, one substitutes family inet6 for family inet. Example 5-1 shows the configuration of a dual-stacked Fast Ethernet interface on a Juniper router.

Example 5-1. Configuring a Fast Ethernet interface on a Juniper

```
interfaces{
    fe-1/0/0 {
        description "HEAnet Cork PoP LAN";
        unit 0 {
```

Example 5-1. Configuring a Fast Ethernet interface on a Juniper (continued)

```
            family inet {
                address 193.1.199.75/26;
            }
            family inet6 {
                address 2001:0770:0800:0003::1/64;
            }
        }
    }
}
```

One important note about Juniper's IPv6 support is that if you plan to use IPv6 tunnelled over IPv4 (configured tunnels, 6to4 etc.), then you'll need to have a suitable processor to do the encapsulation and decapsulation. For example, the devolved architecture of M-series routers doesn't allow the router's CPU to get bogged down in intensive tasks like forwarding packets over tunnels. You may need an a *tunnel services PIC* or a *adaptive services PIC*. Some routers, such as the T-series, don't need extra hardware.

Enabling, Testing, and Troubleshooting

In this section we'll go through the particular steps required to enable and test IPv6 on a host, including showing tables of the relevant commands.

On some systems, IPv6-aware utilities are shipped with a suffix of "6," so ping becomes ping6 and so on. On others systems, IPv6 operation is selected based on the name/address given. If you give a name that has both IPv4 and IPv6 addresses associated with it then there is usually a flag to allow you to explicitly select which protocol you want to use. There are, unfortunately, degrees of variation between systems which merely begin with the naming of commands. Consequently, these tables should serve as a useful phrase-book.

In general, utilities also live in the same directory as their IPv4 counterparts, and hence would tend to be in your PATH (we only include the full path to a command if it is in some unusual location).

Turning on IPv6

Table 5-1 show a summary of how to enable IPv6 at boot on the various operating systems we are considering. Once IPv6 is enabled, the boot-time behavior of most platforms is to perform autoconfiguration, unless they are explicitly configured otherwise. As it may not be easy to restart the network subsystem to initialize IPv6, Table 5-2 shows how to configure IPv6 and enable autoconfiguration while the system is actually running. This may be useful during your initial experimentation. In fact, on some systems, squeezing variations on these commands into a user-editable part of the boot sequence is the only way to introduce persistent IPv6 configuration. *Caveat configurator.*

Table 5-1. Boot time enabling of IPv6 with autoconfig

OS	Enable IPv6 at boot (with autoconf where possible)
Solaris	Create an empty */etc/hostname6.ifname*
Red Hat	Add `NETWORKING_IPV6="yes"` to */etc/sysconfig/network*.
AIX	Use `smit` or `chrctcp` to enable `autoconf6` and `ndpd-host` under: Communications Applications and Services → TCP/IP → IPV6 Configuration → IPV6 Daemon/Process Configuration.
WinXP	`ipv6 install`
Win2003	`netsh interface ipv6 install`
FreeBSD	Add `ipv6_enable="YES"` to */etc/rc.conf*.
Mac OS X	Enabled by default (see */etc/hostconfig*).
Tru64	Use `ip6_setup` to start IPv6 on an interface or edit */etc/rc.config* directly.

IOS	`conf term`
	  `interface` *if number*
	  `ipv6 enable`
	You may also want `ipv6 unicast-routing`.

JUNOS	`set interfaces` *if*`unit`*no* `family inet6 address` *addr*

Table 5-2. Runtime enabling of IPv6 with autoconfig

OS	Runtime IPv6 enable (with autoconf where possible)
Solaris	`ifconfig` *ifname* `inet6 plumb up` and then run */usr/lib/inet/in.ndpd*.
Linux	Load kernel module with `insmod ipv6` then `sysctl net.ipv6.conf.`*ifname*`.accept_ra=1`.
AIX	`autoconf6 -a` followed by `ndpd-host`.
WinXP	`ipv6 install`
Win2003	`netsh interface ipv6 install`
FreeBSD	`sysctl net.inet6.ip6.accept_rtadv=1`
Mac OS X	`sysctl -w net.inet6.ip6.accept_rtadv=1`
Tru64	Ensure kernel contains IPv6, `ifconfig` *ifname* `ipv6 up` and then run `nd6hostd`.

IOS	`conf term`
	  `interface` *if number*
	  `ipv6 enable`
	You may also want `ipv6 unicast-routing`.

JUNOS	`set interfaces` *if*`unit`*no* `family inet6 address` *addr*

Of course, if you do not have an IPv6 router on your network, autoconfiguration isn't much use. You can do the initial testing with link-local addresses, but manually configuring addresses may be more satisfactory. Tables 5-3 and 5-4 show how to manually configure addresses on a variety of systems, at boot time and while they are running.

If you are manually configuring a system at runtime, remember that you may need to configure the loopback interface by assigning it address ::1. If you enable IPv6 at boot time, this will usually be taken care of for you.

Table 5-3. Manual IPv6 addressing at boot time

OS	Manual assignment of address at boot
Solaris	Add hostname and IPv6 address to */etc/inet/ipnodes* and then put hostname in */etc/hostname6.ifname*.

Red Hat	Add
	 `IPV6INIT="yes"`
	 `IPV6ADDR="2001:db8::1/64"`
	 to */etc/sysconfig/network-scripts/ifcfg-ifname*.

AIX	Use the Communications Applications and Services → TCP/IP → IPV6 Configuration → IPv6 Network Interfaces menu in `smit` to set the address, or use `chdev` to set the "netaddr6" attribute on the interface.
WinXP	`ipv6 adu` *ifindex*`/2001:db8::1`
Win2003	`netsh interface ipv6 add address interface=`*ifindex* `2001:db8::1`
FreeBSD	Add `ipv6_ifconfig_`*ifname*`="2001:db8::1 prefixlen 64"` to */etc/rc.conf*.
Mac OS X	No specific technique, but could use Startup Items.
Tru64	Can be set using `ip6_config` or using `IP6IFCONFIG_`, `NUM_IP6CONFIG`, and `IP6DEV_` in */etc/rc.config*.

IOS	`conf term`
	   `interface` *ifnumber*
	   `ipv6 address 2001:db8::1/64`

JUNOS	`set interfaces` *if* unit *no* `family inet6 address 2001:db8::1/64`

Table 5-4. Manual IPv6 addressing at runtime

OS	Manual assignment of address at runtime
Solaris	`ifconfig` *ifname* `inet6 addif 2001:db8::1/64 up`
Linux	`ip addr add 2001:db8::1/64 dev eth0`
AIX	`ifconfig` *ifname* `inet6 2001:db8::1/64`
WinXP	`ipv6 -p adu` *ifindex*`/2001:db8::1`
Win2003	`netsh interface ipv6 add address interface=`*ifindex* `2001:db8::1`
FreeBSD	`ifconfig` *ifname* `inet6 2001:db8::1 prefixlen 64 alias`
Mac OS X	`ifconfig` *ifname* `inet6 2001:db8::1 prefixlen 64 alias`
Tru64	`ifconfig` *ifname* `ipv6` `ifconfig` *ifname* `inet6 2001:db8::1`

IOS	`conf term`
	   `interface` *ifnumber*
	   `ipv6 address 2001:db8::1/64`

JUNOS	`set interfaces` *if* `unit` *no* `family inet6 address 2001:db8::1/64`

The first thing to check on a host is what IPv6 addresses are automatically configured. Either use the commands in Table 5-1 to enable IPv6 with autoconfiguration at boot, or the commands in Table 5-2 to enable IPv6 at runtime. Then display the configured addresses using the commands outlined in Table 5-5. The link-local addresses, beginning fe80::, should be available and the loopback address ::1 will also be available. If you see any 2001::, 3ffe:: or 2002:: addresses and you are surprised by their presence, then either a tunnel has been automatically configured, or someone has set up an IPv6 router on your network unbeknownst to you.

Table 5-5. Displaying IPv6 interface information

OS	Showing configured addresses
Solaris	ifconfig -a
Linux	ifconfig -a
AIX	ifconfig -a
WinXP	ipv6 if
Win2003	ipconfig
FreeBSD	ifconfig -a
Mac OS X	ifconfig -a
Tru64	ifconfig -a
IOS	show ipv6 interface
JUNOS	show interfaces

Example 5-2 shows the interface configuration on a FreeBSD host and Solaris host using the ifconfig command. They both have link-local addresses and autoconfigured 2001:: addresses provided by the local router. Note, FreeBSD assigns all the addresses to a single interface, while Solaris uses sub-interfaces and displays different families of addresses separately. These are cosmetic differences that have no real impact on the operation of IPv6. Note there are other minor differences such as how the prefix length or scope information is displayed.

Example 5-2. Displaying interface configuration

```
freebsdhost% ifconfig -a
dc0: flags=8843<UP,BROADCAST,RUNNING,SIMPLEX,MULTICAST> mtu 1500
        inet 10.0.0.1 netmask 0xffffff00 broadcast 10.0.0.255
        inet6 fe80::204:e2ff:fe33:e3ac%dc0 prefixlen 64 scopeid 0x1
        inet6 2001:db8:babe:1:204:e2ff:fe33:e3ac prefixlen 64 autoconf
        ether 00:04:e2:33:e3:ac
        media: Ethernet autoselect (100baseTX <full-duplex>)
        status: active
lo0: flags=8049<UP,LOOPBACK,RUNNING,MULTICAST> mtu 16384
        inet6 ::1 prefixlen 128
        inet6 fe80::1%lo0 prefixlen 64 scopeid 0x2
        inet 127.0.0.1 netmask 0xff000000
```

Example 5-2. Displaying interface configuration (continued)

```
solarishost% ifconfig -a
lo0: flags=1000849<UP,LOOPBACK,RUNNING,MULTICAST,IPv4> mtu 8232 index 1
        inet 127.0.0.1 netmask ff000000
le0: flags=1004843<UP,BROADCAST,RUNNING,MULTICAST,DHCP,IPv4> mtu 1500 index 2
        inet 10.0.0.15 netmask ffffff00 broadcast 10.0.0.255
        ether 8:0:20:72:74:9e
lo0: flags=2000849<UP,LOOPBACK,RUNNING,MULTICAST,IPv6> mtu 8252 index 1
        inet6 ::1/128
le0: flags=2000841<UP,RUNNING,MULTICAST,IPv6> mtu 1500 index 2
        ether 8:0:20:72:74:9e
        inet6 fe80::a00:20ff:fe72:749e/10
le0:1: flags=2080841<UP,RUNNING,MULTICAST,ADDRCONF,IPv6> mtu 1500 index 2
        inet6 2001:db8:babe:1:a00:20ff:fe72:749e/64
```

Testing with ping and telnet

Initially, the most useful test you can make is to check that you can ping localhost. Check the ping command in Table 5-6 and try pinging ::1 and any link-local addresses that are configured.

Table 5-6. Basic IPv6 diagnostic tools (including interface specifier flag for link-local addressing)

OS	ping	traceroute
Solaris	ping -A inet6 -i *if*	traceroute -A inet6
Linux	ping6 -I *if*	traceroute6
AIX	ping	traceroute
WinXP	ping6	tracert6
Win2003	ping	tracert
FreeBSD	ping6 -I *if*	traceroute6
Mac OS X	ping6 -I *if*	traceroute6
Tru64	ping -V 6 -I *if*	traceroute -V 6
IOS	ping ipv6	traceroute ipv6
JUNOS	ping inet6	traceroute inet6

To ping link-local addresses, you may need to specify the interface to use. This can usually be done with an option to ping or by giving a scope ID in the address (as supported by KAME and Microsoft stacks). See Example 5-3. Scope IDs are explained in the "Scope identifiers" section of Chapter 3.

Example 5-3. Output from pinging ::1

```
% ping6 ::1
PING6(56=40+8+8 bytes) ::1 --> ::1
16 bytes from ::1, icmp_seq=0 hlim=64 time=0.537 ms
16 bytes from ::1, icmp_seq=1 hlim=64 time=0.381 ms
16 bytes from ::1, icmp_seq=2 hlim=64 time=0.384 ms
```

Example 5-3. Output from pinging ::1 (continued)

```
16 bytes from ::1, icmp_seq=3 hlim=64 time=0.384 ms
^C
--- ::1 ping6 statistics ---
4 packets transmitted, 4 packets received, 0% packet loss
round-trip min/avg/max/std-dev = 0.381/0.421/0.537/0.067 ms
```

Of course, networking is moderately uninteresting unless there are multiple computers in the picture. If you have a second machine with IPv6 enabled, you should be able to ping that computer using its link-local IPv6 address. For example, if you have a Linux machine that has autoconfigured address fe80::2b0:d0ff:fed7:741d on eth0 and a FreeBSD machine that has configured address fe80::202:b3ff:fe65:604b on fxp1, then the Linux host should be able to ping the FreeBSD host with the command ping6 -I eth0 fe80::202:b3ff:fe65:604b and the FreeBSD machine should be able to ping the Linux machine with the command ping6 fe80::2b0:d0ff:fed7:741d%fxp1*. Note that we've used an explicit flag to ping to give the interface in the Linux case, but used the KAME scope ID in the FreeBSD case.

Naturally, if there are global addresses assigned to these hosts then you should also be able to ping these without specifying any scope ID.

There is a nice trick for finding the addresses of IPv6 nodes on your network using ping: we can do this by pinging the all-nodes multicast address, ff02::1. For example, on the Linux machine mentioned above, we can ping this address on eth0 via the command ping6 -I eth0 ff02::1. The output is shown in Example 5-4—here we received six responses to the ping (five of which are marked as duplicates) and the addresses of the nodes are shown.

Example 5-4. Output from pinging ff02::1

```
$ /usr/sbin/ping6 -I eth0 ff02::1
PING ff02::1(ff02::1) from fe80::2b0:d0ff:fed7:741d eth0: 56 data bytes
64 bytes from ::1: icmp_seq=1 ttl=64 time=0.062 ms
64 bytes from fe80::2b0:d0ff:fe05:fc06: icmp_seq=1 ttl=64 time=0.194 ms (DUP!)
64 bytes from fe80::206:5bff:fe68:249b: icmp_seq=1 ttl=64 time=0.224 ms (DUP!)
64 bytes from fe80::202:b3ff:fe65:604b: icmp_seq=1 ttl=64 time=0.256 ms (DUP!)
64 bytes from fe80::2b0:d0ff:fef4:c6c5: icmp_seq=1 ttl=64 time=0.334 ms (DUP!)
64 bytes from fe80::203:93ff:fe46:17a6: icmp_seq=1 ttl=64 time=0.384 ms (DUP!)

--- ff02::1 ping statistics ---
1 packets transmitted, 1 received, +5 duplicates, 0% loss, time 0ms
rtt min/avg/max/mdev = 0.062/0.242/0.384/0.103 ms
```

Unfortunately, this trick is not completely foolproof. Some versions of ping do not show duplicates and some nodes reply with an address other than their link-local

---

* This is of course all providing there is an appropriate communications medium between them! We cover debugging some aspects of how layer 2 things can go wrong later.

address. However, it will usually even work on manually configured tunnels, which can be very useful for testing if the host at the remote end is properly configured.

This trick isn't limited to pinging the all-nodes multicast address; so with very little effort, it can be used to perform small administration tasks on arbitrary multicast groups. This is useful for working with specific, generally functional, groups of servers.

Even we occasionally forget that ICMPv6 includes features that didn't exist in IPv4. For example, these days you can request a lot more than a simple ECHO_REPLY; using an ICMPv6 node information query you can request the addresses used by the responder, and hostnames of the destination endpoint. KAME's version of ping6 supports these queries nicely—you can ask remote nodes what they think their host name is with the -w flag. We can squeeze even more out of this technique by combining it with pinging multicast groups, as shown in Example 5-5. The figure shows a node information query being sent to the all-nodes multicast group with ping6, which then displays the address and name of each host that replied.

Example 5-5. Output from node info query to ff02::1

```
% ping6 -w -I en0 ff02::1
PING6(72=40+8+24 bytes) fe80::203:93ff:fe46:17a6%en0 --> ff02::1
39 bytes from fe80::206:5bff:fe68:249b%en0: adric
26 bytes from fe80::2b0:d0ff:fe05:fc06%en0: ace
37 bytes from fe80::202:b3ff:fe65:604b%en0: jo
40 bytes from fe80::2b0:d0ff:fef4:c6c5%en0: sarah-jane
^C
--- ff02::1 ping6 statistics ---
1 packets transmitted, 1 packets received, +3 duplicates, 0% packet loss
```

If we compare Example 5-4 and Example 5-5 we can see that not all nodes responded to the node information request. Unfortunately, these queries are not yet a full part of the standard.

If ping is working okay, then it should also be possible to telnet, even if you only get a "connection refused" message in response. Note that most versions of telnet do not have an explicit option to allow you to specify the interface to be used for a link-local address. To get around this, some platforms automatically use a default interface. On platforms that support scope IDs in addresses, these can be used instead. Example 5-6 shows some examples of these in use. The first example, on Linux, shows telnetting to a unscoped link-local address and the corresponding error. In the next example, on Windows XP, it is unclear why the unscoped connect failed, but adding a scope ID allows the connection to proceed. The final example is with a Solaris host, where the LAN interface is used by default for link-local addresses.

Example 5-6. Telnetting to link-local addresses

```
linuxhost% telnet fe80::204:e2ff:fe33:e3ac
Trying fe80::204:e2ff:fe33:e3ac...
telnet: connect to address fe80::204:e2ff:fe33:e3ac: Invalid argument
```

Example 5-6. Telnetting to link-local addresses (continued)

```
C:\Documents and Settings>telnet fe80::204:e2ff:fe33:e3ac
Connecting To fe80::204:e2ff:fe33:e3ac...Could not open connection to the host, on port
23: Connect failed
C:\Documents and Settings>telnet fe80::204:e2ff:fe33:e3ac%4
FreeBSD/i386 (gonzo) (ttypb)

login:


solarishost% telnet fe80::204:e2ff:fe33:e3ac
Trying fe80::204:e2ff:fe33:e3ac...
Connected to fe80::204:e2ff:fe33:e3ac.
Escape character is '^]'.

FreeBSD/i386 (gonzo) (ttypc)

login:
```

Know Thy Neighbor (Before Thyself)

Pinging a node on your local network only requires Neighbor Discovery to be working correctly. The commands in Table 5-7 show how to display the neighbor cache. After pinging a host, its link-layer address should show up in the neighbor cache. If it does not, there is probably some problem with multicast—see the "Gotchas" section later in this chapter for problems we've encountered in this area. Table 5-8 shows how to display IPv6 caches.

Table 5-7. Displaying IPv6 neighbors

OS	Showing neighbor cache
Solaris	netstat -p
Linux	ip -f inet6 neigh
AIX	ndp -a
WinXP	ipv6 nc
Win2003	netsh interface ipv6 show neighbors
FreeBSD	ndp -a
Mac OS X	ndp -a
Tru64	netstat -N
IOS	show ipv6 neighbors
JUNOS	show ipv6 neighbors

Table 5-8. Displaying IPv6 routes

OS	Showing routes
Solaris	netstat -rn
Linux	ip -f inet6 route

Table 5-8. Displaying IPv6 routes (continued)

OS	Showing routes
AIX	`netstat -rn`
WinXP	`ipv6 rt`
Win2003	`netsh interface ipv6 show routes`
FreeBSD	`netstat -rn`
Mac OS X	`netstat -rn`
Tru64	`netstat -rn`
IOS	`show ipv6 route`
JUNOS	`set route forwarding-table family inet6`

Example 5-7 shows the neighbor cache on a Red Hat Linux host. The first two entries are actually for two different addresses on the same node. The first is a global 2001:: address. It is marked as stale because no communication has recently taken place using this address; the cache entry would be renewed by neighbor discovery if the address needed to be used. The second is the link-local address for the same node—we can tell this because the link-layer addresses and interface IDs are the same for both addresses. Note that this address is marked as a router. Finally, there is a global address for another node on the same network. Note that the corresponding link-local address is not in the table, indicating that these two nodes have been communicating using only the global address.

Example 5-7. Displaying the neighbor cache on Linux

```
$ ip -f inet6 neigh
2001:db8::202:b3ff:fe65:604b dev eth0 lladdr 00:02:b3:65:60:4b nud stale
fe80::202:b3ff:fe65:604b dev eth0 lladdr 00:02:b3:65:60:4b router nud reachable
2001:db8::2b0:d0ff:fef4:c6c5 dev eth0 lladdr 00:b0:d0:f4:c6:c5 nud reachable
```

Configuring Name Resolution

Name resolution is the process of turning host names into addresses and back again. Usually, configuring name resolution amounts to telling the operating system the IP address of your nameserver. Of course, now you have a choice of telling it an IPv4 or an IPv6 address.[*]

The easy option is to use an IPv4 address. You probably either already know the IPv4 address of your nameserver, or you don't need to know it, because it's been automatically configured by DHCP or PPP. Configuring an IPv4 address for your nameserver is quite simple because it doesn't involve any configuration other than the usual

---

[*] You don't need to tell it both of the IP addresses of the nameserver because the DNS can resolve both IPv4 and IPv6 addresses, regardless of if you send it queries over IPv4 or IPv6.

procedure for setting up IPv4 on a host, and then editing */etc/resolv.conf* on Unix-like systems or using the network control panels on Windows and Mac OS.

Of course, in the long run we'll want to tell the operating system to be able to configure an IPv6 address as a nameserver. This is essential when we are configuring, say, an IPv6-only node. However, there are several obstacles to doing this from the start. First, we have to make sure our nameserver has an IPv6 address, which we discuss in the "IPv6 Transport" section of Chapter 6. Second, we need the operating system's resolver libraries to support the use of an IPv6 nameserver. Unfortunately, at the time of writing, many operating systems have a problem with this. Even on platforms such as Linux and FreeBSD, where this is supported, there can be unexpected problems: Chapter 5 gives an example of the sort of problem that might crop up.

Finally, most of us don't manually configure the DNS servers on every host, instead we use DHCP to manage this information centrally. In the IPv6 world the same effect can be achieved with DHCPv6, which we describe in "DHCP" in Chapter 4.

Old Dusty Libraries

A piece of commercial scientific software started misbehaving shortly after IPv6 DNS records were added for some Unix hosts. When run on some machines, its graphical interface wouldn't work if there was an IPv6 address associated with the name of the name of the X-Windows display. Strangely, the error given was "Permission Denied" or "Network Unreachable."

As a work around, the startup script for the software was changed to translate the display name into an IPv4 address and the problem was investigated further. After much system call and library call tracing, it emerged that the software used gethostbyname in an old version of the Linux C library. The C library then parsed */etc/hosts* using the inet_addr library function without checking the return value. When it encountered an IPv6 address, it returned INADDR_NONE to indicate an error, but this was erroneously converted to the address 255.255.255.255 and this value was returned to the application. The application then tried to make a TCP connection to this broadcast address, resulting in a "Permission Denied" or "Network Unreachable." This problem only occurred on hosts that consulted */etc/hosts* before DNS, because DNS knows how to parse both type of address correctly. The problem was resolved by having all hosts consult DNS first.

This shows why putting IPv6 addresses in files that may be parsed by old applications or libraries may not be such a good idea. Consequently, Solaris's strategy of using the *ipnodes* database may, in fact, be quite a good idea.

If you plan to do some small scale testing, you may want to add names for some of the IPv6 addresses you will be using. For small scale testing, setting up DNS records (as we describe in the "DNS" section of Chapter 6) may be too heavy-duty, especially if the DNS server is not under your direct control. For this type of situation, it may be sufficient to add addresses to the */etc/hosts* file, or its equivalent.

Table 5-9 shows how to configure DNS resolving over IPv6, if it is available.* In some cases, you may want to use hostnames without configuring DNS, and so you may want to use a mechanism equivalent to the hosts file. Table 5-10 shows how to do this on the platforms considered in this chapter.

Table 5-9. Configuring IPv6 Resolver

OS	Enabling IPv6 transport resolver
Solaris	No support.
Linux	Edit */etc/resolv.conf*
AIX	No support.
WinXP	Use `netsh interface ipv6 add dns` *ifnameserver IP*
Win2003	Use `netsh interface ipv6 add dns` *ifnameserver IP*
FreeBSD	Edit */etc/resolv.conf*
Mac OS X	Not supported in Jaguar.. Supported on Panther through network control panel or by editing */etc/resolv.conf*.
Tru64	No support.
IOS	The `ip nameserver` command accepts IPv6 addresses.
JUNOS	`set system name-server` *v6addr*

Table 5-10. Static IPv6 address to hostname mapping (/etc/hosts or equivalent)

OS	IPv6 hosts file
Solaris	*/etc/inet/ipnodes*
Linux	*/etc/hosts*
AIX	*/etc/hosts*
WinXP	*C:\WINDOWS\SYSTEM32\DRIVERS\ETC\HOSTS*
Win2003	*C:\WINDOWS\SYSTEM32\DRIVERS\ETC\HOSTS*
FreeBSD	*/etc/hosts*
Mac OS X	*/etc/hosts*
Tru64	*/etc/ipnodes*
IOS	The `ipv6 host` command adds static entries to the host name cache.
JUNOS	`set system static-host-mapping` *hostname* `inet6` *v6addr*

---

* Some versions of Windows come preconfigured to use DNS over IPv6, with the server addresses set to be fec0:0:0:ffff::1,2,3. These addresses are site-local addresses that may be assigned to DNS servers. See the "DNS" section of Chapter 9 for more details.

Testing Further Afield: ping, telnet, and traceroute

As we have outlined, there are several choices for how you can connect to the IPv6 Internet. Rather than go into the details of those right now, let us assume that someone has provided you with a working IPv6 router and that autoconfiguration has provided you with a global address. What tests might you now perform?

Well, the telnet and ping tests listed in the "Testing with ping and telnet" section earlier in this chapter should work, but using the global addresses of local machines instead of their link-local addresses.

If routing is in place, you should also be able to telnet and ping machines out on the Internet—www.kame.net is probably a good machine to test with. Try telnet www.kame.net 80 and then typing GET / HTTP/1.0 and then pressing return twice.* If everything works, you should be presented with the HTML for the KAME home page.†

What can go wrong here? Well, the first thing is that you'll need working DNS to get the IPv6 address for www.kame.net. The only situation where configuring DNS is tricky is if you have an IPv6-only host but have not yet set up an IPv6-capable nameserver. In this case you can always look up the address on an IPv4 host, using a command like nslookup -query=aaaa www.kame.net or dig aaaa www.kame.net, and then transfer it the old-fashioned way.‡

If the name is being translated to the address correctly, the next step is that the packets will need to get to your local router. Autoconfiguration should result in hosts learning the local default routers correctly, and you can check this by examining the routing table using the commands shown in Table 5-8. If the routing table is configured correctly a default route or a route for 2000::/3 should exist.

Note that the default router may advertise its link-local address, rather than a global address, so be prepared to see either as the gateway. Both router-discovery and neighbor-discovery are important here, because once a host has learned its default router's address, it may need to do neighbor discovery to learn the router's link-layer address.

If there is a routing problem, it should be possible to narrow it down using traceroute, as is done in IPv4. Table 5-6 shows the syntax of the IPv6 commands on our various platforms and Example 5-8 shows three traceroute examples. Each example shows tracerouting between two organizations under the same ISP. The first traceroute gets to its destination successfully; the times shown are the round trip times to each hop. The second example shows a situation where packets are being lost because a router had

---

* The Windows version of telnet does not display the characters you type here, so you will have to type blind. It is possible to enable local echoing of what you type using set localecho on the telnet command-line.

† Note that towards the bottom of the HTML the KAME home page tells you if you are using IPv4 or IPv6.

‡ Pen and paper, or cut and paste.

been powered off. Note that a "*" is shown instead of a time, to indicate a timeout. The final example shows a router returning ICMPv6 errors for an address that is not currently routable, indicated by the 'A!' after the time.

Example 5-8. Traceroute examples

```
freebsdhost% traceroute6 -n 2001:db8:10:300::86e2:5103
traceroute6 to 2001:db8:10:300::86e2:5103 (2001:db8:10:300::86e2:5103) from 2001:db8:68:
ff::1, 30 hops max, 12 byte packets
 1  2001:db8:68:ff::2  0.801 ms  0.691 ms  0.669 ms
 2  2001:db8:8:9::1  6.843 ms  3.472 ms  3.457 ms
 3  2001:db8:8:3::2  4.432 ms  4.1 ms  4.166 ms
 4  2001:db8:8:4::2  4.665 ms  4.417 ms  4.458 ms
 5  2001:db8:10:100::86e2:a33  5.306 ms  4.781 ms  4.798 ms
 6  2001:db8:10:300::86e2:5103  5.369 ms  5.228 ms  5.076 ms

freebsdhost% traceroute6 -n 2001:db8:10:200::86e2:5103
traceroute6 to 2001:db8:10:200::86e2:5103 (2001:db8:10:200::86e2:5103) from 2001:db8:68:
ff::1, 30 hops max, 12 byte packets
 1  2001:db8:68:ff::2  0.779 ms  0.721 ms  0.669 ms
 2  2001:db8:8:9::1  3.719 ms  3.409 ms  3.269 ms
 3  2001:db8:8:3::2  4.527 ms  4.606 ms  3.966 ms
 4  2001:db8:8:4::2  4.649 ms  4.294 ms  4.374 ms
 5  2001:db8:10:100::86e2:a33  4.997 ms  6.483 ms  5.125 ms
 6  * * *
 7  * * *
 8  * * *
 9  *^C

freebsdhost% traceroute6 -n 2001:db8:100:300::86e2:5103
traceroute6 to 2001:db8:100:300::86e2:5103 (2001:db8:100:300::86e2:5103) from 2001:db8:68:
ff::1, 30 hops max, 12 byte packets
 1  2001:db8:68:ff::2  0.786 ms  0.701 ms  0.647 ms
 2  2001:db8:8:9::1  9.608 ms  3.649 ms  3.298 ms
 3  2001:db8:18:2:201:3ff:fe2c:960c  4.142 ms !A  3.936 ms !A  4.167 ms !A
```

As we have mentioned, path MTU discovery is an important part of IPv6 because IPv6 routers are not permitted to fragment packets. If some firewall between you and the destination does not allow ICMPv6 Packet Too Big messages through, then Path MTU discovery may not work correctly. The usual symptom is that TCP connections involving interactive or slow transfers work OK, but large or fast transfers hang unexpectedly and then time out. Some versions of traceroute, or variants of it such as Linux's tracepath can display Path MTU information, which may help diagnose this sort of problem.

Static Routing

In this section we'll have a quick look at configuring static routes. Static routes are routes that are configured by hand and don't really change often, as opposed to those routes learned from the network, which do. In the world of IPv4 we are often used to configuring a static route for the default gateway.* An IPv6 host will usually learn its default route from the network, so in the usual case the job of configuring the default route is effectively the job of configuring the local router.

However, there are reasons why you might want to configure static routes. First, you may want to configure a static route on your router if you are not using IS-IS or OSPF to generate a routing table. Second, if you have a host connected to the IPv6 Internet via a tunnel (or some other transition mechanism) then you may not have a local router and you may need to configure your default route manually.

Table 5-11 and Table 5-12 show how a static route can be configured at boot time and at runtime. In this case, we show how to configure a route to the `2001:db8:beef::/48` network via a next hop of `2001:db8:babe::1`. Naturally, there are variants of these commands where you can add routes to a specific host or routes via a specific interface; to find out how to configure these permutations, consult your vendor's documentation.

Table 5-11. Boot time configuration of static routes: adding a route to 2001:db8:beef::/48 via 2001: db8:babe::1

OS	Configuring static routes at boot
Solaris	Create new script in */etc/init.d* and arrange for it to be run after *S*inet*, or add a command such as: `route add -inet6 2001:db8:beef::/48 2001:db8:babe::1` to the end of */etc/init.d/inetinit*.
Red Hat	Add entries of the form: `eth0 2001:db8:beef::/48 2001:db8:babe::1` to */etc/sysconfig/static-routes-ipv6*.
AIX	Use the Communications Applications and Services → TCP/IP → IPV6 Configuration → IPV6 Static Routes → Add an IPV6 Static Route menu in `smit` to add the route.
WinXP	`ipv6 rtu 2001:db8:beef::/48 ifindex/2001:db8:babe::1`
Win2003	`netsh interface ipv6 add route 2001:db8:beef::/48 ifindex 2001:db8:babe::1`

FreeBSD	In */etc/rc.conf* you can give the names of the static routes by setting:
	
	`ipv6_static_routes="name1 name2"`
	
	Then specify the routes themselves by setting:
	
	`ipv6_route_name1="2001:db8:beef::/48 2001:db8:babe::1"`
	
	and so on, also in */etc/rc.conf*.

Mac OS X	No specific technique, but could use Startup Items.
Tru64	Use `ip6_setup` or edit */etc/routes* and add a line like: `-inet6 2001:db8:beef::/48 2001:db8:babe::1`
IOS	`ipv6 route 2001:db8:beef::/48 2001:db8:babe::1`
JUNOS	`set routing-options rib inet6.0 static route 2001:db8:beef::/48 next-hop 2001:db8:babe::1`

---

* Though it's generally done for us if we use DHCP.

Table 5-12. Runtime configuration static routes: adding a route to 2001:db8:beef::/48 via 2001: db8:babe::1

OS	Configuring static routes at runtime
Solaris	`route add -inet6 2001:db8:beef::/48 2001:db8:babe::1`
Linux	`ip -6 route add 2001:db8:beef::/48 via 2001:db8:babe::1`
AIX	`route add -inet6 2001:db8:beef::/48 2001:db8:babe::1`
WinXP	`ipv6 rtu 2001:db8:beef::/48 ifindex/2001:db8:babe::1`
Win2003	`netsh interface ipv6 add route 2001:db8:beef::/48 ifindex 2001:db8:babe::1`
FreeBSD	`route add -inet6 2001:db8:beef::/48 2001:db8:babe::1`
Mac OS X	`route add -inet6 2001:db8:beef:: -prefixlen 48 2001:db8:babe::1`
Tru64	`route add -inet6 2001:db8:beef::/48 2001:db8:babe::1`
IOS	`ipv6 route 2001:db8:beef::/48 2001:db8:babe::1`
JUNOS	`set routing-options rib inet6.0 static route 2001:db8:beef::/48 next-hop 2001:db8:babe::1`

If you wanted to configure a default route, rather than one to a /48, then you can use one of three ways to express this. The first is to add a route to ::/0, which will catch any address that you don't have a better (i.e., more specific) route too. This may include unusual addresses, such as site-local addresses and the loopback address, so some people prefer to use 2000::/3 to configure their default route—this only covers the currently-used IPv6 global unicast space and doesn't catch unusual addresses. Finally, in the same way as you can say route add default in the IPv4 world, many IPv6 implementations allow you to use the keyword default also. This is the same as using ::/0.

Note that an IPv6 router can only send ICMP redirects if it knows the link-local address of the next hop. If, for example, you have multiple routes out of a LAN and you want hosts to learn the best route via ICMP redirects from default router, then you must specify the next hop using its link-local address. This problem should not arise if you are using a dynamic routing protocol because these protocols calculate the link-local address of the next hop automatically.

Configuring Transition Mechanisms

In this section we'll talk about configuring some of the transition mechanisms. We'll give more complete descriptions for the more common ones (configured tunnels and 6to4) that are widely used to provide connectivity before native IPv6 is available.

Configured Tunnels

Configured tunnels are normally used to encapsulate IPv6 in IPv4 and ship it from one point in the Internet to another. To configure a tunnel of this sort you usually need 4 pieces of information: the source and destination IPv4 addresses used for encapsulation, and the source and destination IPv6 addresses assigned to either end of the virtual, point-to-point link.

The exact mechanism used to create tunnels varies a bit from platform to platform. On some platforms, the tunnel is presented as a point-to-point interface, but on others, the tunnel is created by setting the next hop to be an IPv4 compatible IPv6 address. Table 5-13 and Table 5-14 show the steps for boot-time and run-time configuration of tunnels on our selected operating systems.

Table 5-13. Boot time configuration of IPv6 over IPv4 tunnel

OS	Enabling a configured tunnel at boot

Solaris	Create */etc/hostname6.ip.tun0* containing the following:
	<pre>tsrc localv4 tdst remotev4 up
	addif localv6 remotev6 up</pre>

Red Hat	Create a */etc/sysconfig/network-scripts/ifcfg-sitX* where X > 0 containing the following:
	<pre>DEVICE="sitX"
	BOOTPROTO="none"
	ONBOOT="yes"
	IPV6INIT="yes"
	IPV6TUNNELIPV4="remotev4"
	IPV6ADDR="localv6/prefixlen"</pre>

AIX	Use smit to set up a tunnel using Communications Applications and Services → TCP/IP → IPV6 Configuration → IPV6 Network Interfaces → Configure Tunnel Interface.

WinXP	Interface 2 is the automatic tunnelling interface. We route packets to 2000::/3 over the tunnel.
	<pre>ipv6 rtu 2000::/3 2/::remotev4
	ipv6 adu 2/localv6</pre>

Win2003	Interface 2 is the automatic tunnelling interface. We route packets to 2000::/3 over the tunnel.
	<pre>netsh interface ipv6 add route prefix=2000::/3 interface=2 nexthop=::remotev4
	netsh interface ipv6 add address interface=2 address=localv6</pre>

FreeBSD	Add the following to */etc/rc.conf*:
	<pre>gif_interfaces="gif0"
	gifconfig_gif0="localv4 remotev4"
	ipv6_ifconfig_gif0="localv6 remotev6 prefixlen 128"</pre>

Mac OS X	No specific technique, but could use Startup Items.
Tru64	Use ip6_setup to set up a tunnel edit */etc/rc.config* directly.

IOS	<pre>interface Tunnel0
	 ipv6 address localv6/64
	 tunnel source localv4
	 tunnel destination remotev4
	 tunnel mode ipv6ip</pre>

JUNOS	<pre>set interfaces ip-1/0/0 unit 0 tunnel source localv4
	set interfaces ip-1/0/0 unit 0 tunnel destination remotev4
	set interfaces ip-1/0/0 unit 0 tunnel family inet6 address localv6/64</pre>
	Note: the unit number should match the slot of the Tunnel/AS PIC.

Table 5-14. Runtime configuration of IPv6 over IPv4 tunnel

OS	Enabling a configured tunnel at runtime

Solaris	```ifconfig ip.tun0 inet6 plumb```
	```ifconfig ip.tun0 inet6 tsrc localv4 tdst remotev4 up```
	```ifconfig ip.tun0 inet6 addif localv6 remotev6 up```

Linux	```ip tunnel add sit1 mode sit ttl 64 remote remotev4 local localv4``` ```ip link set dev sit1 up```
AIX	The tunnel attributes srctunnel4, destunnel4, srctunnel6, and destunnel6 can be set using chdev.

WinXP	Interface 2 is the automatic tunnelling interface. We route packets to 2000::/3 over the tunnel.
	
	```ipv6 rtu ::/0 2/::remotev4```
	```ipv6 adu 2/localv6```

Win2003	Interface 2 is the automatic tunnelling interface. We route packets to 2000::/3 over the tunnel.
	
	```netsh interface ipv6 add route prefix=2000::/3 interface=2 nexthop=::remotev4```
	```netsh interface ipv6 add address interface=2 address=localv6```

FreeBSD	```ifconfig gif0 create```
	```ifconfig gif0 tunnel localv4 remotev4```
	```ifconfig gif0 inet6 localv6 remotev6 prefixlen 128 up```

Mac OS X	The "gif" interface on OS X is self cloning—when you use gif0, gif1 will automatically be created, and so on.
	
	```ifconfig gif0 tunnel localv4 remotev4```
	```ifconfig gif0 inet6 localv6 remotev6 prefixlen 128 up```

Tru64	```iptunnel create -I ipt0 remotev4 localv4```
	```ifconfig ipt0 ipv6```
	```ifconfig ipt0 inet6 localv6```
	```ifconfig ipt0 up```
	```route add -host -inet6 remotev6 localv6 -interface -dev ipt0```

IOS	```interface Tunnel0```
	``` ipv6 address localv6/64```
	``` tunnel source localv4```
	``` tunnel destination remotev4```
	``` tunnel mode ipv6ip```

JUNOS	```set interfaces ip-1/0/0 unit 0 tunnel source localv4```
	```set interfaces ip-1/0/0 unit 0 tunnel destination remotev4```
	```set interfaces ip-1/0/0 unit 0 tunnel family inet6 address localv6/64```
	Note: the unit number should match the slot of the Tunnel/AS PIC.

After you have configured your tunnel, testing configured tunnels is like testing any other link. First, you'll want to check that you can ping all the addresses of both ends of the link, from both ends of the link. If the link is represented as an interface on your platform, then you may even be able to ping the all-nodes multicast address and get a response from both ends!

Debugging configured tunnels is slightly more tricky. Using a tool such as tcpdump can be quite useful. Generally, tcpdump allows you to attach to a specified interface and watch the packets arriving. The first thing to check is that the encapsulated IPv6 packet is being transmitted and arrives as expected. We can do this by using tcpdump's -i flag to specify the actual interface we expect the IPv4 packet to pass through. If the IPv4 packet does not arrive, then some firewall may be filtering protocol 41. Remember also to check the hosts at both ends of the tunnel, as either of them might be running IPv4 or IPv6 firewall software.

On some platforms, we can actually run tcpdump on the tunnelling interface itself and see the IPv6 packet once it has been decapsulated. Seeing the decapsulated packet will confirm there is no problem with the encapsulation/decapsulation.[*] Example 5-9 shows an example of running tcpdump on both the PPP interface (tun0) and then on the tunnel interface (gif0) on a FreeBSD host. Some versions of tcpdump give a warning when run on an interface with no IPv4 address configured, but this is harmless. Note that when we see the packets on the PPP interface, we can see the IPv4 addresses used for the tunnel, but when the packet gets to the tunnel interface the IPv4 addresses are stripped off.

Example 5-9. Using tcpdump to view encapsulated and decapsulated IPv6

```
# tcpdump -i tun0 -n -s0 ip proto 41
tcpdump: listening on tun0
11:34:09.181300 192.0.2.151 > 192.0.2.1: 2001:db8:68:1ff:2b0:d0ff:fef4:c6c5 > 2001:db8:
ccc1:1::1: icmp6: echo request
11:34:09.181486 192.0.2.1 > 192.0.2.151: 2001:db8:ccc1:1::1 > 2001:db8:68:1ff:2b0:d0ff:
fef4:c6c5: icmp6: echo reply

# tcpdump -i gif0 -n -s0
tcpdump: WARNING: gif0: no IPv4 address assigned
tcpdump: listening on gif0
11:35:17.736014 2001:db8:68:1ff:2b0:d0ff:fef4:c6c5 > 2001:db8:ccc1:1::1: icmp6: echo
request
11:35:17.736093 2001:db8:ccc1:1::1 > 2001:db8:68:1ff:2b0:d0ff:fef4:c6c5: icmp6: echo reply
```

If the encapsulated packets are visible at both ends, but there still seem to be problems, then one possible occurrence is that the routing table is not directing all the desired IPv6 packets to the tunnel interface. Check that the routing table contains the correct routes using the commands shown in Table 5-8. The "Static Routing" section earlier in this chapter shows how to configure static routes.

Note, that some NAT systems will actually allow configured tunnels to function through NAT! In this case the NAT device will replace the destination/source IPv4 address of tunnelled packets on the way in/out of the NATed network. This complicates the configuration of the tunnel: the end of the tunnel inside the NATed network should use its private IP as the local IPv4 address and the end of the tunnel outside the NAT should use the NAT's public IP address as the remote end. To create the necessary NAT state and keep the connection alive, you may need to arrange for packets to be sent over the tunnel regularly (say, by running ping6 with an inter-packet time of a minute or so).

---

[*] Encapsulation/decapsulation problems should be rarer, as there are basically no configurable parameters. However, software or hardware bugs might lead to problems like this.

6to4 configuration

Setup of 6to4 is relatively straight-forward; in many ways it is like a configured tunnel, but you don't need to ask anyone for the local and remote IPv4 and IPv6 addresses. This makes things even simpler!

What you do need to know is your local IPv4 address and then a script like the one shown in Example 5-10 can do the rest. This script takes the IPv4 address of the host as its first argument, computes an IPv6 address for the host and configures the stf0, which is the 6to4 interface on KAME-derived systems. Table 5-15 and Table 5-16 show configuration details for various operating systems. The examples also show how to point the default route to the 6to4 interface, as this is a common configuration.

Note that not all the operating systems that we're considering can act as a 6to4 router. Solaris, for example, only supports it if you have the Solaris 9 4/03 Update installed. This shouldn't pose a problem though because you only need one 6to4 router to provide connectivity for a whole network.*

Example 5-10. Example 6to4 setup script

```
#!/bin/sh

IPV4=$1
PARTS=`echo $IPV4 | tr . ' '`
PREFIX48=`printf "2002:%02x%02x:%02x%02x" $PARTS`

STF_IF="stf0"
STF_NET6="$PREFIX48":0000
STF_IP6="$STF_NET6"::1

ifconfig $STF_IF inet6 $STF_IP6 prefixlen 16 alias
route add -inet6 default 2002:c058:6301::
```

Table 5-15. Boot time configuration of 6to4 as default route

OS	Enable 6to4 at boot
Solaris	Make */etc/hostname6.ip.6to4tun0* containing: `tsrc v4addr 6to4addr/64 up` then edit */etc/default/inetinit* and set ACCEPT6TO4RELAY to YES and check that RELAY6TO4ADDR is set to 192.88.99.1.

Red Hat	Add:
	    `IPV6TO4INIT=yes`
	to */etc/sysconfig/network-scripts/ifcfg-if* for the interface with the local IPv4 address and add:
	    `IPV6_DEFAULTDEV=tun6to4`
	to */etc/sysconfig/network*.

---

* In fact, for 65536 networks, each being a /64!

Table 5-15. Boot time configuration of 6to4 as default route (continued)

OS	Enable 6to4 at boot
WinXP	`netsh interface ipv6 6to4 set relay 192.88.99.1 enabled`
Win2003	`netsh interface ipv6 6to4 set relay 192.88.99.1 enabled`
FreeBSD	Set: ``` stf_interface_ipv4addr="v4addr" ipv6_defaultrouter="2002:c058:6301::" ``` in *etc/rc.conf*.
Mac OS X	No specific technique, but could use Startup Items and `ip6config`. Settings for `ip6config` are configurable in */etc/6to4.conf*.
Tru64	Use `ip6_setup` to setup 6to4 or edit */etc/rc.config* and */etc/routes* directly.
IOS	``` interface Tunnel2002 ipv6 address 6to4addr/16 tunnel source if tunnel mode ipv6ip 6to4 ipv6 route ::/0 2002:c058:6301::1 ```

Table 5-16. Runtime configuration of 6to4 as default route

OS	Enable 6to4 at runtime
Solaris	``` ifconfig ip.6to4tun0 inet6 plumb ifconfig ip6to4tun0 inet6 tsrc IPv4-address 6to4-address/64 up 6to4relay -e -a 192.88.99.1 ```
Linux	``` ip tunnel add tun6to4 mode sit ttl 64 remote any local v4addr ip link set dev tun6to4 up ip -6 addr add 6to4addr/16 dev tun6to4 ip -6 route add 2000::/3 via ::192.88.99.1 dev tun6to4 metric 1 ```
WinXP	`netsh interface ipv6 6to4 set relay 192.88.99.1 enabled`
Win2003	`netsh interface ipv6 6to4 set relay 192.88.99.1 enabled`
FreeBSD	``` ifconfig stf0 inet6 6to4addr prefixlen 16 route add -inet6 default 2002:c058:6301:: ```
Mac OS X	`ip6config start-stf if`
Tru64	``` ifconfig tun1 ip6interfaceid ::v4addr ipv6 up ifconfig tun1 inet6 ip6prefix 6to4addr/64 route add -inet6 2002::/16 fe80::v4addr -iface -dev tun1 route add -inet6 default 2002:c058:6301:: -dev tun1 ```
IOS	``` interface Tunnel2002 ipv6 address 6to4addr/128 tunnel source if tunnel mode ipv6ip 6to4 ipv6 route 2002::/16 Tunnel2002 ipv6 route ::/0 2002:c058:6301::1 ```

As 6to4 is another tunnelling technology, the techniques used to debug it are pretty similar to those we described for configured tunnels. One thing that you may want to do is find out where the nearest relay router is. You can do this by tracerouting to its anycast address 192.88.99.1, which will reveal its location within the IPv4 network.

Example 5-11 shows an example of this. If the relay is a long distance away, then you may want to talk to your ISP about a configured tunnel or ask them to provide a 6to4 relay for their customers.

Example 5-11. Locating your 6to4 relay

```
% traceroute 192.88.99.1
traceroute to 192.88.99.1 (192.88.99.1), 64 hops max, 44 byte packets
 1  gw-81 (134.226.81.1)  0.290 ms  0.171 ms  0.156 ms
 2  gswte1r1-vlan3.tcd.ie (134.226.1.104)  0.488 ms  0.440 ms  0.406 ms
 3  tcd.ge.link.hea.net (193.1.192.185)  0.738 ms  1.228 ms  0.615 ms
 4  Mantova-v101.Dublin.core.hea.net (193.1.196.149)  0.850 ms  0.892 ms  0.909 ms
 5  193.1.196.18 (193.1.196.18)  2.106 ms 2.960 ms  4.325 ms
```

Applications

So, you've now got your workstation talking IPv6. What's next? Well, it would be nice to be able to run some applications that use IPv6. We'll look at IPv6 support in the sort of applications many of us use regularly. We'll leave the configuration of the corresponding server-side software until Chapter 7.

Naturally, we can only survey the support available at the time of writing. As we'll see in Chapter 8, adding IPv6 support can be relatively straightforward, so if your favorite application is listed as not supporting IPv6 then you should contact your vendor as they may have added it since we checked their software.

Web Browsers

A growing number of web browsers now support IPv6. In some cases the support varies from platform to platform; for example, some browsers have restrictions on how IPv6 web servers can be specified.

There are various sites you can visit to check if your browser supports IPv6. The standard test is to visit *http://www.kame.net/*, where the turtle at the top of this page will dance if you requested the page by IPv6. The KAME page also shows your IPv4 or IPv6 address at the bottom of the page.

 Remember to hit reload or refresh on your browser if you have visited the page by IPv4 recently; otherwise, it may have the IPv4 version of the page cached.

Note that on all platforms it is possible to view IPv6 content on an IPv4-only browser by using a dual-stack proxy. We'll talk more about this in the "HTTP Proxies and Caches" section of Chapter 7.

Unix

Several browsers under Unix support IPv6. The best known is probably Mozilla, which has full IPv6 support on platforms with a working IPv6 stack. Similarly, browsers related to or competing with Mozilla, such as Netscape 7, Firefox, Konqueror and Galeon will also support IPv6. As of version 7.20 or so, Opera advertises experimental IPv6 support.

Nautilus, the Gnome file manager, can also be used as a browser, but in the versions of Nautilus we've tried, we've either found no IPv6 support or rather strange IPv6 support that only works for sites with both IPv6 and IPv4 DNS records.

For the console lovers amongst us, versions 2.8.4 and newer of the text based browser, lynx, also support IPv6.

Windows

Getting Internet Explorer to talk IPv6 is simple. First, it supports IPv6 only if the underlying core operating system also supports IPv6. In most cases, with modern editions of Windows (XP and later), the work has been done for you; Internet Explorer will initiate IPv6 connections once the IPv6 stack has been enabled. One annoying limitation of the XP version of Internet Explorer 6 is that it does not support literal IPv6 addresses in URLs (as described in the "When IPv6 Addresses Don't Fit" section of Chapter 8).

For Windows 2000, the procedure is somewhat more complicated. Some DLLs need to be replaced, and due to the way Windows Update (as well as System Protection) works, you have to be very careful about those DLLs getting wiped out by the system and removing your IPv6 capabilities.

Up to date versions of Opera, Mozilla, Firefox and Netscape also now seem to have good IPv6 support on Windows (some early versions had problems with things like IPv4 and IPv6 simultaneously, but these issues seem to have been resolved).

Mac OS

Safari, Apple's web browser, can visit IPv6 web sites. However, the API it uses under Jaguar does not currently support resolving IPv6 hostnames, so URLs have to include the address explicitly, i.e., using *http://[::1]/* rather than *http://localhost/*. Under Panther, Safari will use IPv6 to contact IPv6-only web sites and IPv4 to contact dual-stack or IPv4-only web sites, however it seems that it no longer understands IPv6 addresses in URLs. It is expected that the preference for IPv4 or IPv6 will become either user-configurable or dependent on the current network configuration. Safari can be downloaded from *http://www.apple.com/safari/* (it may come with your operating system distribution).

Mozilla on OS X will also supports IPv6, though it seems to have a similar restriction to Gnome's Nautilus in that it will not visit a server that advertises only an IPv6 address in the DNS. Servers with both IPv4 and IPv6 addresses can be contacted over IPv6. URLs with explicit IPv6 addresses also work. Firefox and Camino (formerly known as Chimera) have a similar level of support.

Internet Explorer on OS X does not currently support IPv6, and, given Microsoft's discontinuation of the product, is unlikely ever to support it.

Email Clients

Outlook Express, as shipped with Windows XP SP 1, doesn't seem to support IPv6 for POP, IMAP or SMTP. Apple's *Mail* client seems to be similarly constrained under Jaguar but has the beginnings of IPv6 support under Panther. Older Unix mail programs such as elm and mh do not yet support IPv6, though work is under way for some of the more recent ones like pine, kmail, and Evolution.

Lotus

Lotus Domino supports IMAP, POP, SMTP, LDAP and HTTP over IPv6 on AIX, Solaris and Linux. You should be able to add TCP_EnableIPV6=1 to *NOTES.INI*.

Mozilla

We mentioned Mozilla above as a browser, but it also includes a mail reader. Again, on any Unix platform that supports IPv6, the Mozilla mail client should support IPv6.

Mutt

Mutt has supported IPv6 for some time. The use of IPv6 addresses can be controlled by the use_ipv6 configuration variable in your *.muttrc*, but it defaults to yes, so no additional changes should be needed.

Sylpheed

As an example of a less well-known mailer that supports IPv6, we'll mention Sylpheed, a nippy GTK+ based mailer available from *http://sylpheed.good-day.net/*.

SSH

Now that telnet has been thoroughly discredited, SSH tends to be the remote access service of choice, especially for people who care about security. Many of the systems we talk about ship with the portable release of OpenSSH, from *http://www.openssh.com/*, which supports IPv6 if your system provides the standard IPv6 APIs. OpenSSH provides -4 and -6 flags for restricting operation to IPv4 or IPv6. It also accepts IPv6 addresses on the command line. The scp command uses a colon as a separator between hostname and filename, so if you want to use an IPv6 address with scp, it needs to be enclosed in square brackets, for example scp "user@[2001:db8::a00:2]:/etc/ipnodes" /tmp.

For Windows users, a version of Simon Tatham's popular PuTTY program, compiled with IPv6 support, is available from *http://unfix.org/projects/ipv6/*. Some versions of IPv6 PuTTY would *only* connect to hosts that have IPv6 DNS records, but up-to-date versions should also connect to hosts with IPv4-only DNS. Which protocol is preferred can be configured in PuTTY's connection panel. At some time in the future, IPv6 support should be rolled into the standard version of PuTTY.

Miscellaneous

Full support for IPv6 is currently in development by Wipro Technologies for the Gnome Desktop and Developer Platform, and should begin to appear in Gnome 2.4.

Naturally, a prerequisite for IPv6 on Unix desktops is IPv6 support in X11. This work is well underway and the first release of this code was in version X11R6.7. Details of the design of the IPv6 support can be found at *http://www.x.org/IPV6_Review.html*. Release 4.4.0 of XFree86 and X.org's 6.7.0 release both use this code on platforms that support IPv6. From an end user's point of view there should be no noticeable change, though you can now prefix a display name with inet/ or inet6/ to force a connection to be made over IPv4 or IPv6. Thus, you can say:

```
xclock -display desktop.example.com:0
xclock -display inet6/desktop.example.com:0
```

or even:

```
xclock -display ::1:0
```

Gotchas

Once a computer has IPv6 enabled it is likely to begin to find records relevant to IPv6 in the DNS. In an ideal world, this would cause no problems, even if the device was not connected to the IPv6 Internet. However, a bug in some DNS servers has caused then to respond with a "host does not exist" message, rather than a "no record of this type" message. The best known occurrence of this led to IPv6 users not being able to connect to news.bbc.co.uk unless they first looked up its IPv4 address, although this problem has since been resolved. Others have had problems with ad.doubleclick.net, where some of its servers do not respond to queries for IPv6 addresses.

Native IPv6 over Ethernet uses multicast at the link-level for a number of things, and thus is sensitive to the correct operation of multicast in Ethernet drivers. There have been several reports of vendors discovering that Ethernet multicast is broken only when users complain that IPv6 does not work correctly.

The usual manifestation of this is that Neighbor Discovery behaves oddly. One way to test this is to run a tool such as tcpdump that puts the Ethernet interface into *promiscuous* mode. This means that the Ethernet interface examines *all* packets, thus working around incorrect filtering of multicast packets. If IPv6 seems to work correctly while the interface is in promiscuous mode, there's probably a multicast problem. You will need to contact your vendor for a fix.

One other confusing thing that can happen is that router solicitation and advertisement do not properly occur, but ping6 appears to work fine if the host is already in the neighbor cache! This is of course because ping6 is unicast and the ND/RA protocols rely on multicast. Again, this is indicative of a underlying multicast problem.

We have also seen switches that have trouble forwarding IPv6 multicast packets if features such as IGMP snooping are enabled. In this case, while pinging the all nodes multicast address ff02::1 from one node, we saw no packets at all arriving at another node. Using the all nodes address here is useful because it does not require neighbor discovery, which depends on multicast anyway. In a similar way, some wireless access points do not forward Ethernet multicast or require special configuration to do so. They would exhibit similar symptoms to above.

We have also seen one strange problem where IPv6 would not operate correctly between a router and a switch using ISL encapsulation for a VLAN trunked port. Switching the encapsulation to 802.1Q resolved the issue. Don't ask us—we just work here.

Summary

We've gone into the details of how to do the basic configuration of IPv6 for a variety of devices you might encounter on an IP network, covering the basic details for each OS and the commands you'll need to use. We've covered the most common complications you're likely to face, but at the end of the day, complications can arise in almost any procedure. Probably the best approach, if you anticipate a tricky install, is to use this chapter as reference material for the install, and as a list of pointers of what to do if you have problems. Remember, the vendor documentation can be quite detailed and it is worth revising or keeping open beside you as you work.

Finally, if something isn't working, take heart, there is very probably a way to do what you want to do—it's often a case of lateral thinking, and using Google or similar search engines to look for the exact error you've been getting.

CHAPTER 6

Operations

Whenever I see the word Operation, especially Trifling
Operation, I at once write off the patient as dead.
—George Bernard Shaw

In this chapter, we deal with the issues involved in actually *operating* your network once you have it installed. We'll look at how to configure the necessary infrastructure services and network glue such as DNS and firewalls. Finally, we'll consider some examples of transition and interoperability—how to live peacefully with IPv6 and IPv4 into the foreseeable future.

DNS

DNS is the first service that needs to be configured while you are working with IPv6, since just about every network service of consequence involves converting hostnames to IP addresses and back again. (It's even more crucial than in IPv4, since the addresses are so much longer to type and harder to remember.)

When you add IPv6 addresses to your existing DNS records, it is worth emphasizing that you are *adding* them. Your usual IPv4 addresses remain in place and applications that know nothing about IPv6 will continue to use IPv4. Even applications that understand IPv6 but are not yet connected to the IPv6 Internet should work too, since they should "fall back" to the IPv4 addresses once it becomes apparent that IPv6 isn't connected.

A second important thing to keep in mind is your DNS server doesn't have to speak IPv6 itself to answer a request for an IPv6 address: any request, irrespective of whether it's for an IPv4 or IPv6 address, can itself be made over IPv4 or IPv6. In short, this means that you can start adding IPv6 addresses to the DNS without upgrading your nameserver. Answering DNS queries over IPv6 is referred to as using IPv6 *transport*.

In the following sections we will first look at the relevant record types for including IPv6 addresses in the DNS, and then look at how they fit into the various DNS zone files. Then we'll look at configuring nameservers to answer requests that arrive over an IPv6 network connection (i.e., IPv6 transport) and finally advertising your nameserver as being available over IPv6.

Once you have some IPv6 DNS records, other IPv6 enabled hosts automatically begin to speak IPv6 to your machines. We look at problems that can arise at this stage.

Record Types

During the design phase of IPv6, there were two competing schemes for how requests for IPv6 addresses would be satisfied: the first scheme was based on a simple generalization of the way that DNS works for IPv4; then later a more complicated scheme was proposed that was designed to allow changes of address prefix more easily, to aid network renumbering. After an epic struggle between the two, the scheme more closely resembling IPv4 has been selected as the standard, though some adjustments have been made to it along the way.

IPv4 DNS lookups

Let's begin by briefly reviewing how IPv4 DNS requests are conducted. The DNS provides two commonly used services relating to IPv4 addresses: converting hostnames to addresses and converting addresses to hostnames.

Suppose we want to know the IPv4 address for `www.example.com`. IPv4 addresses correspond to a DNS record of type "A," so we send a request to our local *recursive* nameserver looking for a type A record for `www.example.com`. If this recursive server does not have the answer cached, then it will send the request to one of the root servers.

The root server will send a reply that it doesn't know the A record for `www.example.com`, but will return NS records telling us the names of the `.com` nameservers and possibly A records for some of these names. These A records are referred to as *glue*.

Now our recursive server knows who to ask about `.com` domains and so picks one of the nameservers it was told about and asks one of them for the A records for `www.example.com`. The `.com` nameserver will say it doesn't know the A record for `www.example.com` but, as before, will return NS records with A record glue so our recursive server knows who the nameserver for `example.com` is.

Finally, the recursive server will ask an `example.com` nameserver for the A record for `www.example.com` and will receive a reply containing the IPv4 address. This response is forwarded to the client that originally made the request.

The process for converting IPv4 addresses to hostnames is similar but we look for a PTR record containing a hostname rather than an A record containing an IPv4 address. There is one twist—the `in-addr.arpa` domain. If we want to know the hostname for `192.0.2.4`, it is treated as a lookup for a PTR record for `4.2.0.192.in-addr.arpa`. Where does this come from? We reverse the order of the 4 parts of the IPv4 address and then stick `in-addr.arpa` on the end. This is because DNS stores the most specific information at the left hand end of an address, but IP addresses store the most specific information at the right hand end. Once we have this name our recursive nameserver asks the nameservers for arpa, in-addr.arpa, ... 4.2.0.192.in-addr.arpa until we find the PTR record telling us the name for 192.0.2.4.

In summary, IPv4 DNS is built on a mix of A, NS and PTR records containing IPv4 addresses, nameserver names and hostnames respectively, where 'reverse' lookups are done in the in-addr.arpa domain.

V6 lookups

The scheme that has been adopted for IPv6 lookups makes the minimum number of changes to the IPv4 method. Instead of A records containing an IPv4 address, a new record type called AAAA (pronounced "quad A") containing an IPv6 address was created. NS and PTR records remain unchanged and continue to contain host-names, which are, of course, address-type independent.

Reverse lookup for 2001:0DB8::3210 in this scheme were originally done by request-ing a PTR record for 0.1.2.3.0.0.0.0.0.0.0.0.0.0.0.0.0.0.0.0.0.0.0.0.0.0.8.b.d.0.1. 0.0.2.ip6.int. So we basically use the "reverse the digits" method from IPv4, but appending ip6.int rather than in-addr.arpa. As a matter of housekeeping this is being moved to looking up 0.1.2.3.0.0.0.0.0.0.0.0.0.0.0.0.0.0.0.0.0.0.0.0.0.0.8.b.d.0.1.0. 0.2.ip6.arpa, so the ip6.int domain is being deprecated in favor of ip6.arpa. This for-mat is referred to as the "reverse nibble" format.

A6, DNAME, and Bit Strings

The other, now deprecated, way of doing lookups involved using things called A6 and DNAME records.

An A6 record contains a portion of an IPv6 address and a pointer to a further A6 record where more of the address can be found. You begin by looking up an A6 record for the host in question, which gives you part of the address and then follow the chain of A6 records until you have the whole address. DNAME worked much like CNAME, but was intended to allow aliasing of whole domains, rather than individual hosts.

These were part of a mechanism to help make renumbering networks easier. With the hard boundary between host and network components of an IPv6 address, it was sug-gested that a DNS record for a host could be composed of a host part and a network part. Then it would be possible to update the network part as new prefixes were adver-tised by routers, or even to have multiple network parts if a organization had two ISPs and so two different prefixes. (You can find an example of its operation in RFC 2874).

A6 and DNAME met with significant opposition because although they simplify the writing of DNS records they also introduce a significant element of unpredictability into the DNS resolution process. Given that the DNS is a write-seldom, read-often database, introducing an optimization for writing at the expense of instability in read-ing did not seem to make much sense. After the IETF meeting in London in 2001, A6 and DNAME were consigned to Experimental status.

Setting up DNS

Adding an IPv6 address to the DNS is a straight-forward matter. Suppose we have the entries for example.com as shown in Example 6-1, and we want to let people know that www.example.com can be reached at IPv6 address 2001:0DB8::3210, then all we need to do is add an AAAA record to the zone, as shown in Example 6-2.

Example 6-1. Traditional V4 zone file

```
; Zone file for example.com
@          IN      SOA     ns.example.com. hostmaster.example.com. (
                           2002101900; Serial
                           28800        ; Refresh       8 hours
                           7200         ; Retry              2 hours
                           604800       ; Expire        7 days
                           86400 )      ; TTL                1 day
           IN      NS      ns.example.com.
           IN      NS      ns2.example.com.

ns         IN      A       10.11.12.13
ns2        IN      A       192.0.2.6
www        IN      A       10.11.12.15
```

Example 6-2. Zone with AAAA record

```
; Zone file for example.com
@          IN      SOA     ns.example.com. hostmaster.example.com. (
                           2002102000; Serial
                           28800        ; Refresh       8 hours
                           7200         ; Retry              2 hours
                           604800       ; Expire        7 days
                           86400 )      ; TTL                1 day
           IN      NS      ns.example.com.
           IN      NS      ns2.example.com.

ns         IN      A       10.11.12.13
ns2        IN      A       192.0.2.6
www        IN      A       10.11.12.15
           IN      AAAA    2001:db8::3210
```

Setting up the reverse entry for this AAAA record is a little more complicated, as we will need to talk to the provider of our IPv6 address space to get the appropriate reverse zone under ip6.arpa delegated to our nameserver. Delegation is the process of assigning responsibility for a zone to a particular set of servers, if you're not familiar with it you may want to consult *DNS and BIND* by Paul Albitz and Cricket Liu (O'Reilly). The move from ip6.int to ip6.arpa is, at the time of writing, proceeding apace, but you may still want the ip6.int domain delegated. Less than one in five of the reverse queries we see uses the ip6.int domain. Most resolvers check ip6.arpa only now, but some resolvers try ip6.int if lookups in ip6.arpa fail.

With IPv6 the provider of our address space will usually be our ISP, or for large organizations, the RIRs. However, if you are using transitional address space, such an address in the 6to4 2002::/16 block or an address in the local addressing range, then it may be harder to get the zone delegated. The system for delegation of 2.0.0.2.ip6.arpa is not yet operational, but is likely to involve nothing more than visiting a web page (probably *https://6to4.nro.net/*) using 6to4. If you find yourself in the situation where you cannot get the zone corresponding to your address space delegated, you can run a nameserver for the zone without delegation. In this case, the records will only be visible to hosts directly querying your nameserver, but that may be sufficient for internal needs, such as preventing programs requesting reverse DNS mappings from timing out or giving errors.

Once we have the appropriate ip6.arpa zone delegated to our nameserver, the zones for reverse domains are typically simpler than those for forward lookups, as shown in Examples 6-3 and 6-4. The format of the zone files for ip6.int and ip6.arpa is identical, so if you are maintaining both zones, you only need to maintain one file. Remember to contact the administrators of any DNS servers that you have listed as nameservers for these zones so that they can configure their servers to act as DNS secondaries for these zones.

Example 6-3. Reverse zone files for IPv4 subnet 10.11.0.0/16

```
; Zone file for 11.10.in-addr.arpa
@       IN      SOA         ns.example.com. hostmaster.example.com. (
                            2002101900; Serial
                            28800           ; Refresh        8 hours
                            7200            ; Retry          2 hours
                            604800          ; Expire         7 days
                            86400 )         ; TTL            1 day
        IN      NS          ns.example.com.
        IN      NS          ns2.example.com.
13.12       IN      PTR         ns.example.com.
15.12       IN      PTR         www.example.com.
```

Example 6-4. Reverse zone files for subnet 2001:db8::/64

```
; Zone file for 0.0.0.0.0.0.0.0.8.b.d.0.1.0.0.2.ip6.int or
;               0.0.0.0.0.0.0.0.8.b.d.0.1.0.0.2.ip6.arpa
@       IN      SOA         ns.example.com. hostmaster.example.com. (
                            2002101900; Serial
                            28800           ; Refresh        8 hours
                            7200            ; Retry          2 hours
                            604800          ; Expire         7 days
                            86400 )         ; TTL            1 day
        IN      NS          ns.example.com.
        IN      NS          ns2.example.com.
0.1.2.3.0.0.0.0.0.0.0.0.0.0.0.0             IN      PTR         www.example.com.
```

Calculating the reverse nibble format for reverse zone entries can be a bit of a chore, so you may want to use a tool like Peter Bieringer's ip6calc, available from *http://www.deepspace6.net/projects/ipv6calc.html*. For example, `ipv6calc -in ipv6addr -out revnibbles.arpa ::1` will output `1.0.0.0.0.0.0.0.0.0.0.0.0.0.0.0.0.0.0.0.0.0.0.0.0.0.0.0.0.0.` `0.0.0.0.0.0.0.0.ip6.arpa.`. Once you have added the forward and reverse DNS entries, you can check they match up and are visible to the rest of the world using *http://www.maths.tcd.ie/cgi-bin/check_dns.pl*.

So, now that we know what the zone files and DNS records look like, how do we actually add them to our DNS configuration? This depends on what DNS server software is being used. We'll look at the ISC's BIND package, Dan Bernstein's djbdns, the Microsoft DNS server and NSD.

BIND

BIND is the best known DNS server available. BIND 8 has the beginnings of support for IPv6, enough for AAAA records and the new reverse domains.[*] The BIND 8.4 family of releases includes IPv6 transport. BIND 9 has actually offered full IPv6 support for longer than BIND 8 has, but isn't as fast as BIND 8, so the 8.4 release is to accommodate people with very heavily loaded nameservers who want to offer a service over IPv6.

Most of the Unix-like operating systems we consider ship with BIND, but new versions of BIND can be obtained at *http://www.isc.org/products/BIND/* or as extra software packaged by the vendor.

Within BIND, zones are stored as text files, like those shown in Example 6-2 and Example 6-4. Each zone is listed in the file *named.conf*. To add a record you can just edit the appropriate zone file, but remember to update the serial number in the SOA record. After changing the zone file you have to reload the zone by either restarting the server or by using the `ndc reload` (BIND 8) or `rndc reload` (BIND 9) commands.

Example 6-5 shows the part of the *named.conf* file for `ns.example.com`. It shows four zone files for which `ns.example.com` is the master. The configuration allows `192.0.2.6` (i.e., `ns2.example.com`) to perform zone transfers. The zone files would correspond to those shown in Examples 6-2, 6-3, and 6-4. Note that we use the *same* zone file for the `ip6.arpa` and `ip6.int` domains.

Example 6-5. Example named.conf file

```
zone "example.com" {
        type master;
        file "example.com.fwd";
        allow-transfer { 192.0.2.6; };
};
```

---

[*] Technically, no extra support is necessary for the "reverse nibble" format now used in `ip6.int` and `ip6.arpa`, because they only use PTR records.

Example 6-5. Example named.conf file (continued)

```
zone "11.10.in-addr.int" {
        type master;
        file "example.com.4rev";
        allow-transfer { 192.0.2.6; };
};

zone "0.0.0.0.0.0.0.0.8.b.d.0.1.0.0.2.ip6.arpa" {
        type master;
        file "example.com.6rev";
        allow-transfer { 192.0.2.6; };
};

zone "0.0.0.0.0.0.0.0.8.b.d.0.1.0.0.2.ip6.arpa" {
        type master;
        file "example.com.6rev";
        allow-transfer { 192.0.2.6; };
};
```

djbdns

DJBDNS is Dan Bernstein's attempt to strip what it means to be a nameserver and a caching resolver down to the bare essentials, and implement only that, with the aim of improving security. In this case, there are two pieces of software you need to think about.

The first is dnscache, which is the caching resolver program. This can successfully retrieve AAAA records. It does not, unless patched, use IPv6 transport.

The second is tinydns, the authoritative nameservice program. Here there are two options. Tinydns includes support for arbitrary record types, which can be input using an octal notation. Example 6-6 shows a little Perl script that can output the records.* This script is passed a host name and an IPv6 address. For example tinyaaaa `www.example.com` `2001:db8::3210`, will output a line such as:

```
:www.example.com:28:\040\001\015\270\000\000\000\000\000\000\000\000\000\000\062\020
```

which can be added to the end of the */service/tinydns/root/data* file. You then update tinydns's database by using the supplied makefile from the tinydns data directory: `cd /tinydns/root ; make`. PTR records can be handled via tinydns's "^" record type indicator as usual. Thus, the line for `www.example.com` in */service/ tinydns/root/data* would be:

```
^0.1.2.3.0.0.0.0.0.0.0.0.0.0.0.0.0.0.0.0.0.0.0.0.8.b.d.0.1.0.0.2.ip6.arpa:www.
example.com.:86400
```

Felix von Leitner provides a patch for djbdns. It provides easy-to-use tools for the creation of AAAA and reverse records, and also includes support for IPv6 transport. The patch can be found at *http://www.fefe.de/dns/*. Like all unofficial patches, you may have trouble receiving timely support.

---

* Recent versions of ip6calc can also do this.

Example 6-6. Perl code to output AAAA records for tinydns

```
#!/usr/bin/perl
# Script specifically for creating quad A record lines for unpatched tinydns.
# Input taken is the dns name and the address in the usual format;
# ifconfig format is fine.
# Uses the expandv6 function given earlier.
require 'expand.pl';
$name = $ARGV[0] || die ("No name");
$addr = $ARGV[1] || die ("No address");
$addr = &expandv6($addr);
$addr =~ s/://ig;

for ($offs=0;$offs<length($addr);$offs=$offs+2) {
        $fqv6[$ind]=substr($addr,$offs,2);
        $tmp = $fqv6[$ind];
        $ind++;
}

printf(":$name:28:");

foreach $component(@fqv6) {
        printf("\\%03o", hex("$component"));
}

printf("\n");
```

Microsoft DNS

The DNS server service in Windows 2003 Server family supports IPv6 records and even supports IPv6 transport. Management can be performed using the DNS program under Administrative Tools.

You can add static AAAA records to a zone by selecting a zone, going to the Action menu, choosing Other New Records and selecting IPv6 Host (AAAA). You'll then be prompted for the name of the host and the IPv6 address in the usual format.

Before you can add PTR records you will first need to create the appropriate reverse zone. You can do this by selecting Reverse Lookup Zones and then choosing New Zone from the Action menu. Choose Primary Zone or Secondary Zone, as appropriate. Next enter the "Reverse lookup zone name" directly rather than using the Network ID. Note that when creating an IPv6 reverse zone you need to enter a zone name ending in ip6.int or ip6.arpa before you can continue.

Once the zone exists, a PTR record can then be added by selecting the zone, choosing New Pointer (PTR) from the Action menu. You must enter the PTR (without the part represented by the zone) into the "Host IP number" field and the hostname into the "Host name" field.

Alternatively, if you feel comfortable directly changing zone files more directly you can use the dnscmd/RecordDelete and dnscmd /RecordAdd, or edit the zone files in *C:\WINDOWS\system32\dns*.

Many people are familiar with the automatic "register-themselves-in-DNS" behavior of Windows hosts. This behavior extends to IPv6 addresses.* Enabling dynamic updates is a property of a zone and can be enabled at the time a zone is created, or can tweaked later by choosing Properties from the Action menu and then adjusting Dynamic Updates under the General tab.

NSD

NSD is an authoritative-only Nameserver developed by NLNetLabs in association with RIPE. It's designed to be high performance and to be used by very busy nameservers. For example, it is in use serving the root zone and .nl.

NSD's zone files are listed in the *nsd.zones* file. The zones themselves are in the same text format as BIND zone files, so you can edit these in the way described for BIND above. After editing, remember to run nsdc rebuild to build the database from the new files.

From version 2.0.0 of NSD, IPv6 has been enabled by default but can be manually disabled using --disable-ipv6. (Earlier versions of NSD required you to enable IPv6 support yourself using either --enable-ipv6 or by adding -DINET6 to FEATURES—and originally IPv6 support was restricted to KAME-based platforms.) Table 6-1 shows the location of BIND configuration files.

Table 6-1. Location of BIND configuration files

OS	Location
FreeBSD	/etc/namedb/named.conf
Solaris	/etc/named.conf
Red Hat	/etc/named.conf
Tru64	/etc/namedb/named.conf
AIX	/etc/named.conf
Mac OS	/etc/named.conf

IPv6 Transport

We have covered how to add IPv6 addresses into the DNS, which is (initially at least) likely to be running over IPv4. In this section we discuss how to get DNS running over IPv6. The first step here is to make sure that your DNS server can answer queries over IPv6. This may require a configuration option or, in some cases, a patch to the software. Let us quickly run through the details of the necessary changes for each server.

BIND

Needs version 8.4 or 9 and listen-on-v6 must be given in the options stanza of *named.conf*. Example 6-7 shows a typical options stanza for a network—we listen

---

* We haven't seen it ourselves, but we've heard reports.

for queries on all IPv4 and IPv6 addresses, but restrict the answering of queries to our own IPv4 and IPv6 subnets (in this example the IPv4 network is NATed).

Example 6-7. Options in named.conf for IPv6 transport

```
options {
        directory "/etc/namedb";
        pid-file "run/named.pid";

        listen-on { any; };
        listen-on-v6 { any; };
        query-source address * port *;
        query-source-v6 address * port *;

        allow-query    { 127.0.0.1; 10.0.0.0/8; 2001:db8:1cc1::/48; ::1; };
        allow-transfer { 127.0.0.1; 10.0.0.0/8; 2001:db8:1cc1::/48; ::1; };
        allow-recursion { 127.0.0.1; 10.0.0.0/8; 2001:db8:1cc1::/48; ::1; };
};
```

One peculiarity of the BIND 9 `listen-on-v6` directive is that it currently only accepts any or none as possible addresses. This limitation has been addressed in BIND 9.3.0.

djbns

Requires a patch from *http://www.fefe.de/dns/*.

Microsoft

IPv6 transport can be enabled with `dnscmd /config /EnableIPv6 1` command and then restart your nameserver with `dnscmd /restart`. You may need to install `dnscmd` if you are not already using Windows Support Tools.

NSD

Version 1.1 supported IPv6 transport on KAME platforms, version 1.2 and later have wider support. To verify that the server is responding to queries over IPv6, a tool such as `nslookup`, `host` or `dig` can be used.[*] For example, if ns.example.com has address `2001:0DB8::3211`, then we can use the command `dig www.example.com @2001:0DB8::3211` to send a test query. If the query is successful, a selection of records relating to `www.example.com` will be shown, otherwise we'd expect a timeout message. (For this to work as expected, you need a version of `dig` from an IPv6 capable version of BIND.)

Once you are sure that the server is answering queries over IPv6, it should be safe to begin advertising your IPv6 capable DNS server. To do this, just add AAAA records for the hostnames listed as NS records for your zone. Example 6-8 shows our `example.com` zone with an AAAA record for `ns.example.com`.

---

[*] If these commands are not available as a base part of your operating system, they are included as part of the BIND package, which can be downloaded from *http://www.isc.org/*.

Example 6-8. AAAA record for a NS entry

```
; Zone file for example.com
@       IN      SOA         ns.example.com. hostmaster.example.com. (
                            2002102000; Serial
                            28800   ; Refresh      8 hours
                            7200    ; Retry        2 hours
                            604800  ; Expire       7 days
                            86400 ) ; TTL          1 day
        IN      NS      ns.example.com.
        IN      NS      ns2.example.com.

ns      IN      A       10.11.12.13
        IN      AAAA    2001:db8::3211
ns2     IN      A       192.0.2.6
www     IN      A       10.11.12.15
        IN      AAAA    2001:db8::3210
```

There are a few points to remember when you do this. First, remember to add an entry to the corresponding reverse zones. Second, the zone above you may have a glue A record for your nameserver. If so, you should contact them and ask for a glue AAAA record too. So, the example.com administrator would contact their .com registrar to ask for an AAAA glue record for ns.example.com. You may also want to think twice before creating an NS record pointing to a host using an autoconfigured address. See the "Gotchas" section later in this chapter for more details.

Recursive DNS Servers

In the "Configuring Name Resolution" section in Chapter 5 we spoke about configuring DNS clients, and we've just described how to set up the zones for authoritative DNS servers. The third part of the DNS infrastructure consists of recursive servers. These take simple requests from clients ("What is the AAAA record for www.example.com?") and figure out the sequence of authoritative servers that must be contacted to answer the query.

For the foreseeable future, recursive resolvers will need to be dual stacked. Why? There are many domains that don't have any authoritative servers that speak IPv6. Your recursive resolver will need to contact these to answer queries, so it will need to speak IPv4.

If dual-stacking all your recursive servers is not an option, then it is possible to set up *forwarders*. These are DNS servers that receive requests from clients and forward them on to a recursive resolver. Forwarders can also cache the responses from the recursive servers, thus spreading the load. For example, Example 6-9 shows how BIND can be configured to forward requests by adding directives to the options section of *named.conf*. Multiple forwarders can be listed.

Example 6-9. Configuring BIND as a forwarder

```
options {
        forward only;
        forwarders {
                2001:db8:4c6:111::53;
                2001:db8:4c6:222::53;
        };
        // Rest of named.conf follows.
};
```

As with authoritative nameservers, you may want to consider the implications of configuring a recursive nameserver with an autoconfigured address, particularly if you will be hard-coding that address into any configuration files.

AAAA bug workarounds

Several authoritative DNS servers have exhibited bugs when queried for AAAA records. There are two variants of the bug. In one variant, the bad authoritative server returns an error to say the domain does not exist. This answer can be cached by a recursive server, which then assumes that no A records exist for the domain. The end result of this is that the domains served by that nameserver become unavailable.

The second variant of this problem is that the bad authoritative server just doesn't bother replying to queries for AAAA records at all. When the requests time out a request for A records successfully made and things proceed as usual. The end effect of this is a long delay when connecting to the domains served by the bad nameserver.

The correct solution to these problems is to contact the administrator of these problem servers and ask them to have the server fixed. The most commonly impacted servers seem to be DNS-based load balancing systems, of the type used by some busy web sites. Usually the administrators of these servers are eager to resolve such problems, but for some there seems to have been some complications in resolving the problem.

There doesn't seem to be a good workaround for the first variant of the problem but on the whole it doesn't cause any side effects other than making the site in question difficult to contact. The second variant is more irritating, because several web based ad servers have this problem. It means that other web sites displaying the ads may also have to suffer the long delay while the AAAA requests timeout.

There are workarounds for this second variant of the problem. One solution is to get your recursive nameserver to respond quickly for the domain. The easiest way to do this is to configure it to be authoritative for the domain and to give it an empty zone file. Example 6-10 shows example lines from a recursive resolver's *named.conf* that direct two currently problematic domains to the empty zone file shown in Example 6-11.

Example 6-10. named.conf including empty zone

```
zone "uk.adserver.example.net" {
        type master;
        file "blankzone";
};

zone "de.adserver.example.net" {
        type master;
        file "blankzone";
};
```

Example 6-11. Empty zone file

```
; Empty zone file for quick responses.
@       IN      SOA      ns.example.com. hostmaster.example.com.  (
                         2003062700 ; Serial
                         3600     ; Refresh
                         300      ; Retry
                         3600000 ; Expire
                         3600 )   ; Minimum
        IN      NS       ns.example.com.
```

Another solution to this problem that will work with BIND 8 or BIND 9 is to mark these servers as *bogus* in your *named.conf* as you discover them. This will prevent any queries being made to these machines. Suppose you find that 192.0.2.99 does not respond to queries for AAAA records (perhaps by running dig AAAA www.example.com @192.0.2.99) and you also don't want to make queries to 10.76.65.54 because it is a private address being advertised as a nameserver by some organization, then you could use the directives shown in Example 6-12 to make BIND ignore these nameservers from then on.

Example 6-12. named.conf lines to mark a server as bogus

```
server 192.0.2.99 { bogus yes; };
server 10.76.65.54 { bogus yes; };
```

This second technique[*] has both advantages and disadvantages relative to the first one. The first technique only requires you to identify the domain name that is causing problems. The second technique requires that you track down the problematic nameserver once you know the problem domain. However, the second technique fixes the problem for all domains that nameserver is responsible for.

Gotchas

Some problems may arise once other hosts begin to contact you over IPv6. For example, if there is some service that you only provide over IPv4, an initial attempt to

---

[*] Suggested to us by Roland Bless and Mark Doll.

connect to it over IPv6 might fail, producing a warning message before the client falls back to IPv4. Similarly, IPv6 enabled hosts without a connection to the IPv6 Internet may complain about unavailability of routes before falling back to IPv4. These issues don't usually cause operational problems, but may confuse or raise the curiosity of users.

A more serious sort of problem is with IPv6 aware programs that do not correctly fall back to IPv4 in the event of the IPv6 connection failing. This problem is more serious, as skilled intervention by a human is required to resume normal operation. The correct solution to this problem is, of course, to contact your vendor and ask for IPv4 fallback to be correctly implemented. If that's not practical, interim measures might involve either backing out the problem AAAA record or creating a special DNS entry that only has an A record for problem applications.

Examples of these problems are shown in Example 6-13. The first two show warning messages produced on FreeBSD and the final entry shows a buggy telnet client on AIX 4.3.

Example 6-13. Example problems after adding IPv6 DNS entries

```
v6host% rsh www.example.com echo hello
connect to address 2001:db8::3210: Connection refused
Trying 10.11.12.15...
hello

v6noroute% ssh www.example.com
ssh: connect to address 2001:db8::3210 port 22: No route to host
user@www.example.com's password:
Last login: Wed Oct 23 16:04:03 2002 from v6host
www.example.com%

aix% telnet www.example.com
Trying...
telnet: connect: No route to host
aix% telnet 10.11.12.15
Trying...
Connected to 10.11.12.15.
Escape character is '^]'.

FreeBSD/i386 (www.example.com)

login:
```

Note that IPv4 only users should never see any of these problems, as they will ignore IPv6 entries in the DNS.

It is also worth checking that your DNS Secondary servers support any new record types you are using. AAAA records are supported by most nameservers, so this shouldn't be a problem. Some of the more exotic types, such as A6, might not be supported—this could result in a secondary nameserver becoming "lame."

One other interesting question is the topic of updating addresses that you put in the DNS. In the case of static manual addressing or static DHCPv6 the addresses can be managed in the same way as IPv4 addresses always have been, because they are presumed constant enough to advertise.* However, if you are using IPv6 autoconfiguration then address changes may be more frequent—a change of Ethernet card or motherboard may result in a change of address. It may be particularly important to consider this when the address will be written in a configuration file. For example, to fully update an NS record you may have to contact a local registrar to update glue. Likewise for recursive DNS servers, where the address may be manually entered into many *resolv.conf* files. In fact, it might be useful to dedicate a whole /64 to a single authoritative or recursive DNS server. This makes it easy to move such servers within your routing infrastructure, since a /64 can be advertised much more cleanly than multiple /128's, and also facilitates anycast DNS service.

Finally, we would recommend resisting any temptation you might feel to put link-local, site-local or any sort of local addresses in the public DNS; it can only lead to confusion and unpleasant surprises. There are ongoing discussions about how this might be made useful and meaningful, but it is far from clear what the eventual conclusion will be.

IPsec

IPsec is a security system operating at a low level common to both IPv4 and IPv6. It has only recently risen out of relative obscurity with the advent of commonly-available virtual private networks (VPNs), but is deserving of more attention than it gets since it attempts to solve the key security problem of today: application independent encryption and authentication of data. In essence it munges headers and encrypts data packets to provide the following services:

Authentication
> The Authentication Header (AH) provides a way to check that a packet came from a given source and that it has not been modified in transit.

Confidentiality
> The contents of packets may be encrypted, preventing people from determining their contents. This is provided by a protocol called Encapsulating Security Payload (ESP).

Both of these services use shared secret keys. These keys can be manually configured, but automatic configuration is generally more flexible, so IPsec defines a protocol for the management of these keys. This allows the use of certificates for the

---

* Dynamic DNS, used particularly to reflect changes in addressing of a large set of clients, is not covered here.

generation and authentication of these shared secrets. IPsec also defines a compression protocol to get around the problem that encrypted traffic is rarely compressible.

To reiterate a point from "Security" in Chapter 3, the important aspect of IPsec is that it operates far below the application layer. Combined with the system-wide configurability of IPsec, this means it can be used to provide security services to legacy applications. Its use is also required for aspects of Router Renumbering and Mobility, because of the unpleasant security implications of using them in an unauthenticated setting.

The main body of IPsec is defined in RFC 2401. Other RFCs give specific details of the component protocols.

There is a certain degree of alphabet soup to be understood before one wades into the details:

SA

> A Security Association is a key and an algorithm pair used for encryption or authentication between two hosts. It's a one-way association—you need two of these for a given bidirectional conversation.

SAD

> The Security Association Database is the list of currently known SAs.

SPI

> The Security Parameter Index is a part of the SA. It is a number that allows multiple SAs to exist concurrently between two hosts. This potentially allows different encryption algorithms or keys/algorithms to be used for independent conversations (say SMTP and HTTP to the same host). It also allows you to periodically change keys without interrupting the flow of data.

SPD

> The Security Policy Database contains rules that say which SAs must be applied to which packets.

Configuration

To try to understand all this, let's consider an example. Suppose you want to allow people to use telnet, but want to make sure it is encrypted. First, you create an entry in the policy database (SPD) that says that telnet packets that are sent or received must be encrypted.

Now, before telnet packets can be sent you must make sure that the hosts at both ends know the algorithms and keys that will be used for encryption. This can be done by manual configuration or by using a protocol called IKE (Internet Key Exchange). An SPI will also be assigned to identify this key/algorithm pair that has been chosen. The local IP address, SPI, key and algorithm will be stored in the SAD on both hosts.

So, when the `telnet` command is run, the IP stack sees the policy in the SPD saying the packet must be encrypted and consults the SAD to find the correct SA for this packet. It then encrypts the data with the key and sends it off with the SPI in the header.

At the other end, the host receives an encrypted packet, searches its SAD for an entry with matching destination address and SPI. When it finds one, it unencrypts the packet using the specified algorithm/key and passes the data on. The security policy on the receiving host sees that the packet has been decrypted and lets it through. If someone sent an unencrypted packet, then the security policy would cause it to be discarded at this stage.

So, to run through that quickly: the SPD decides if packets need to have IPsec applied, and the SAD contains the list of algorithm/key pairs in use indexed by an identifier, the SPI.

As a concrete of example of this we'll show how to configure FreeBSD and Solaris to encrypt `telnet`.

FreeBSD uses the setkey for manual IPsec configuration. Example 6-14 shows input to the setkey program. The `add` directives create entries in the SA database, we have chosen to create two with SPI 0x534 and 0x776 respectively. We have specified the DES algorithm (in CBC mode) and have given the keys as hexadecimal numbers. The addspd directives create security policies that say packets to or from TCP port 23 on input or output require encryption.

Example 6-14. FreeBSD manual IPsec configuration

```
add 2001:db8:b8::1
        2001:db8:bcc1::1
        esp 0x534 -E des-cbc 0xd4fd9563eede3b07;
add 2001:db8:bcc1::1
        2001:db8:b8::1
        esp 0x776 -E des-cbc 0xa70864e7df39ae89;
spdadd ::/0[23] ::/0 tcp -P out ipsec esp/transport//require;
spdadd ::/0[23] ::/0 tcp -P in ipsec esp/transport//require;
spdadd ::/0 ::/0[23] tcp -P out ipsec esp/transport//require;
spdadd ::/0 ::/0[23] tcp -P in ipsec esp/transport//require;
```

On Solaris, two separate commands are used to configure the SAD and SPD. The `ipseckey` command allows the configuration of keys and algorithms and the `ipsecconf` command allows the definition of policies. Example 6-15 and Example 6-16 shows the corresponding commands for Solaris.

Note that on both ends of the connection we specify the same key and algorithm for a given source, destination and SPI triple.

Example 6-15. Solaris manual IPsec configuration (ipseckey)

```
add esp \
        spi 0x534 \
        src6 2001:db8:b8::1 \
        dst6 2001:db8:bcc1::1 \
        encralg des encrkey d4fd9563eede3b07

add esp \
        spi 0x776 \
        src6 2001:db8:bcc1::1 \
        dst6 2001:db8:b8::1 \
        encralg des encrkey a70864e7df39ae89
```

Example 6-16. Solaris manual IPsec configuration (ipsecconf)

```
{ dport 23 } ipsec { encr_algs des }
{ sport 23 } ipsec { encr_algs des }
```

Most of the platforms we have mentioned have basic IPsec support for IPv6, allowing this sort of manual configuration. (Table 6-2 shows IPSec configuration commands.) However on some platforms support is not complete, particularly in the area of IKE. IKE is supposed to save you the trouble of configuring keys manually by automatically authenticating, generating and exchanging keys between hosts that wish to communication via IPsec. It also makes use of digital certificates to authenticate remote hosts. Unfortunately, if you wish to use it in a coherent and controlled manner it is (at the moment) tricky, because although interoperability details are getting better, implementation quality varies, and ease of administration leaves something to be desired, never mind that running a certification authority is something few people are willing to do! No doubt the details will be sorted out, refined and documented eventually, but for now we will move on.

Table 6-2. IPsec configuration commands

OS	IPsec configuration tools
Solaris	`ipseckey` and `ipsecconf`.
Linux	IPsec available as an add-on from the FreeS/WAN project at *http://www.freeswan.org/*, and USAGI includes a patch for IPsec over IPv6. `pluto` is the configuration daemon.
AIX	Within `smit` choose Communications Applications and Services → TCP/IP → Configure IP Security (IPv6).
WinXP	`ipsec6`
Win2003	`ipsec6`
FreeBSD	`setkey`
Mac OS X	`setkey`
Tru64	`sysman` and `ipsecd`.

Routing

In this section we'll look at some of the aspects of configuring IPv6 routers. We'll begin with the configuration of routing advertisements sent to end hosts, as this is an important area of IPv6 operation that doesn't have an analogue in IPv4. After that we'll move on to the configuration of the inter-router protocols.

Router Advertisements and Renumbering

Router Advertisements, as discussed in the "Neighborhood Watch" section in Chapter 3, are a way of providing configuration information to hosts on your network. Usually you will not need to do much more than turn on router advertisements and your router will automatically advertise the IPv6 prefixes on the interfaces they have configured.

In some unusual situations you may want to adjust parameters. For example, if you run a wireless network or a dial-up network, then you may want to adjust the lifetimes of the prefixes to be short so that the nodes in the network deprecate them quickly after the router stops advertising them or the node moves out of wireless range. If you adjust the lifetime of a prefix, you may also want to adjust how often the prefix is advertised—the maximum time between advertisements should be less than the lifetime of the prefix to make sure it does not accidently become deprecated.

IOS

On Cisco's IOS you have to do very little to enable router advertisements—when you enable `ipv6 unicast-routing` and configure an IPv6 address on an interface, the router will begin to send advertisements and reply to solicitations. More control of router advertisements is available with the `ipv6 nd` commands, which control neighbor discovery in general. These commands are applied on a per-interface basis. If you don't want your router sending router advertisements, then you can use `ipv6 nd suppress-ra`.

JUNOS

On JUNOS, router advertisements are disabled by default but can be enabled using `set protocols router-discovery interface` *ifname*;. The `set protocols router-discovery` hierarchy level also includes statements for configuring which prefixes are advertised and associated lifetimes and timeouts, for example `set protocols router-discovery interface` *ifname* `lifetime 900` sets the advertised life time to 15 minutes.

KAME's rtadvd

rtadvd, as the abbreviation might suggest, is the program responsible for performing the Router Advertisement function on (for example) KAME-equipped FreeBSD routers.[*]

---

[*] Strictly speaking, you are forbidden from sending router advertisements if you are just a host. There are certain cases where it might be useful to do otherwise, but we will not cover them here.

By default, rtadvd does its best to behave sensibly; you must specify a list of interfaces to send advertisements on and, if no specific configuration is found, it will read prefixes for the interfaces from the existing routing table and use those as the basis for its advertisements. This examination of the routing/interface configuration is periodic, and actually extends to deprecating prefixes if they are removed by administrator action (or, indeed, automatically) from the routing table. Of course, its default behavior can be overridden by the administrator by means of *rtadvd.conf*, which, rather bizarrely, is a configuration file in the style of *termcap*.

The configuration file does have the rather pleasant property of only over-riding the attributes you specify, so in the example shown in Example 6-17 we are altering the prefix advertised for the xl0 interface. Since this is a static route that we wish to advertise, we will have to invoke rtadvd with the -s parameter. Full details of rtadvd can be found in the man pages for rtadvd and rtadvd.conf.

Example 6-17. Example rtadvd.conf configuration file

```
xl0:\
        :addrs#1:addr="2001:0db8:ffff:b1be":prefixlen#64:
```

Other route advertisement daemons

Most of the operating systems we've mentioned come with a daemon that can perform route advertisement. Unfortunately, other than the basic ideas, there isn't much in common between the daemons. Only the KAME rtadvd and the Linux radvd daemon operate on more than one platform. The radvd daemon operates on both Linux and BSD systems and is bundled with most Linux distributions or available directly from *http://v6web.litech.org/radvd/*. It is maintained by Nathan Lutchansky and Pekka Savola.

Table 6-3 shows the daemon/command for each of our platforms. You should be able to consult vendor documentation for the details of each.

Table 6-3. Route advertisement daemons

OS	Daemon name
FreeBSD	rtadvd
Solaris	in.ndpd
Linux	radvd
Tru64	ip6rtrd
AIX	ndpd-router
Mac OS	rtadvd
Windows	netsh interface ipv6 set interface interface=*ifname* advertise=enabled netsh interface ipv6 add route prefix=*prefix* publish=yes

Softly softly

Occasionally it may be useful to prohibit RAs or other "noise" across a network. This is often found at exchange points, where it would be inappropriate for members to pollute the commons with advertisements that other routers or hosts might accidentally start using. Example 6-18 shows a configuration file for doing just this on a Cisco router.

Example 6-18. Example IOS configuration for a quiet interface

```
interface Ethernet0/0
 description A quiet interface, suitable for peering LAN
 ip address 192.0.2.1 255.255.255.0
 ipv6 address 2001:db8:ace:fad::1
 ip access-group 101 in
 no ip redirects
 no ip proxy-arp
 ipv6 enable
 no ipv6 redirects
 ipv6 nd suppress-ra
!
```

Multiple Routers

Interesting things start to happen if you have more than one router making announcements on the same segment. If they are configured with addresses on the same subnet, then the EUI-64 algorithm will ensure that your host is assigned the same address by each router—but it will have multiple default routes. The behavior that results depends a little on the host's operating system; however, neighbor unreachability discovery should allow a host to fail over to a second default route if it detects that the first router has gone away. Unfortunately there is no way to control which router will be preferred if there are multiple routers available. In drafts of the router discovery RFC, a field was included to allow routers to advertise themselves as high, medium or low priority. This mechanism is supported by some routers and operating systems, but the preference field was not included in RFC 2461 so you cannot depend on it being present. Work is underway to complete the standardization of advertising more detailed routing information to end hosts, including routes to specific prefixes and if those hosts should have a high, medium or low preference for those routes.

If you have multiple routers in *different* subnets on the same segment, your host will receive a different address from each router (although the last 64 bits will probably be the same—that's EUI-64 again). This is fine, technically, but there are other factors you must keep in mind. When making outward connections your host's IPv6 stack will go through an address selection process, outlined in the "Address Selection" section in Chapter 3. So be aware that the address you *think* you're using might not be the address you're *actually* using if multiple prefixes are being advertised on a link.

Routing Protocols

The operation of BGP, OSPF and other routing protocols in an IPv6 environment is startlingly (and mercifully) similar to their IPv4 equivalents. The advantages are obvious—the learning curve is smaller, your existing routing policies will probably migrate, and you can give the illusion of working very hard by staying in late one night and photocopying the IPv4 routing configuration.

Of course, there are gotchas. Some routing protocol implementations don't cope well if your IPv4 topology is different to your IPv6 layout—that is, if some of your routers aren't dual stacked. A workaround might be to use a different routing protocol for IPv6 (for example, if your existing network uses OSPF already, you might use IS-IS for IPv6) but that is not to be taken lightly. Aside from the extra administration overhead for your NOC staff, troubleshooting may become needlessly complex when the two different routing protocols make different decisions on the best route to a customer's site. Though this can also be viewed as a feature: failures of one routing protocol are likely to be independent of the other, providing redundancy when you need it most.

In addition to IOS and JUNOS, we'll also discuss Quagga, and its ancestor Zebra in this section. Zebra is an implementation of various routing protocols for the Linux and BSD operating systems. Although it is useful it seems to have become somewhat unmaintained; Quagga is a project to further extend Zebra, and appears to be kept more up-to-date. Both include support for IPv6 BGP in its bgpd and for OSPF IPv6 in ospf6d. Zebra does not support IS-IS, but Quagga does.

RIP

RIP is one of the simpler routing protocols to implement, and so IPv6 support for RIP appeared in IOS before it was ready for either IS-IS or OSPF. It's also very easy to configure.

Example 6-19 shows how to configure RIP on Cisco IOS. To add ::/0, the default route, to your announcements on a particular interface use the default-information originate option. If you *only* want to send the default route using RIP, you may substitute default-information only.

Example 6-19. Example RIP configuration on Cisco

```
!
! Configure RIPv6 with process name "backbone"
!
ipv6 router rip backbone
!
! Now configure it on every interface we want to run RIPv6 on
!
interface FastEthernet0/0
 ipv6 router rip backbone
!
! Send the default route ::/0 to the router on Serial0
!
```

Example 6-19. Example RIP configuration on Cisco (continued)

```
interface Serial0
 ipv6 router rip backbone
 ipv6 rip backbone default-information originate
```

On JUNOS, RIP can be configured using the protocols ripng group, which acts just like the IPv4 equivalent protocols rip group.

OSPF

Traditionally, OSPF has been one of the most popular internal routing protocols on the Internet, favoured by service providers and enterprises that have outgrown RIP. That said, the protocol changes to support IPv6 were more fundamental than were required by IS-IS and RIP, so it has come a little late to the IPv6 scene. However, it's been ratified and implemented by the major vendors, and is ready for deployment. The good news—on the surface, it's not changed much.

How has OSPF configuration changed on IOS? To run an OSPF command you might be familiar with in IPv4, you probably just want to substitute "ipv6" everywhere you would have typed "ip"—for example, show ipv6 ospf neighbor will list the IPv6 adjacencies that have been formed by the router.

This substitution persists into the configuration. Whereas IS-IS and BGP have been modified to handle IPv4 and IPv6 data together (using address-family subsections of the IS-IS and BGP configurations to separate IPv4 and IPv6) the IPv6 version of OSPF runs as a completely separate process. Where we would configure an IPv4 OSPF process using router ospf 1, we may then configure an IPv6 OSPF process, entirely independently, using ipv6 router ospf 100.

Like most routing protocols, OSPF selects a 32-bit router ID. Usually this will be the IPv4 address of one of the loopback interfaces, but it's a good idea to configure this explicitly with the router-id command. If you don't have an IPv4 address on your router, OSPF won't work until you set this. Any 32-bit number will do as long as it's unique within your network (which is why an IPv4 address is a reasonable choice, if the router has one).

Perhaps the biggest change between IPv4 and IPv6 OSPF configuration on IOS is entirely cosmetic, but removes a dreadful inconsistency. In BGP, the network statement specifies which subnets you wish to advertise. In OSPF for IPv4, the network statement also specifies a list of subnets, but they are *not* directly advertised; OSPF is simply enabled on any interfaces that have addresses within those subnets. Then, the prefixes associated with those interfaces (not the original subnets you specified) are inserted into the routing table. It's enough to make a CCNA weep and a Juniper salesperson jump for joy.

So for IPv6 the network statement has been mercifully removed, and one configures OSPF on a per-interface basis a little like RIP. While configuring an interface, issue `ipv6 ospf 100 area 0` to enable OSPF (use the same process number you specified with `ipv6 router ospf`) and put the interface in area 0.

One artifact of this is that you should explicitly enable OSPF on your loopback interface, if you have one, in order to make sure that its address enters the routing table.

Example 6-20 shows a basic example of how to configure OSPF on a Cisco, and Example 6-21 shows an equivalent configuration under JUNOS.

Example 6-20. Example OSPF configuration on Cisco

```
!
! Configure OSPFv6 with process number 100
!
ipv6 router ospf 100
!
! Give this process an explicit router-id - must be unique in our OSPF network
!
 router-id 192.168.0.101
!
! Log whenever our neighbours appear or disappear
!
 log-adjacency-changes
!
! Turn on OSPF on our loopback and ethernet interfaces
!
interface Loopback0
 ipv6 address 2001:DB8:101::/64
 ipv6 enable
 ipv6 ospf 100 area 0
!
interface FastEthernet0/0
 ipv6 address 2001:DB8:1::1/64
 ipv6 enable
 ipv6 ospf 100 area 0
!
```

Example 6-21. Example OSPF configuration on JUNOS

```
interfaces{
    lo0 {
        unit 0 {
            family inet6 {
                address 2001:db8:101::/64;
            }
        }
    }
    fe-0/1/0 {
        unit 0 {
            family inet6 {
                address 2001:db8:1::1/64;
            }
        }
    }
```

Example 6-21. Example OSPF configuration on JUNOS (continued)

```
protocols {
    ospf3 {
        area 0.0.0.0 {
            interface lo0.0 {
                passive;
            }
            interface fe-0/1/0.0;
        }
    }
}
```

Integrated IS-IS

IS-IS is of the OSI breed, and has the notable distinction of not running over IP. This is why you must to assign a unique NET id for each router; where other routing protocols might borrow IDs from your IPv4 address pool,* IS-IS is truly protocol independent.

Like OSPF, each IS-IS router must be configured with an area name. Also, an IS-IS router needs a NET, or Network Entity Title. This is a large number, in a particular format, but most of the number can pulled from thin air as long as each NET address is unique within your network. Most sites use the IPv4 loopback address of the router and pad it out with zeroes so as to appear in correct format—for example, 192.168.2.1 becomes net 49.0001.1921.6800.2001.00—but you might choose any convenient system you like that ensures that the number remains unique. An example configuration is shown in Example 6-22; this enables IS-IS on the router and turns it on the Fast Ethernet interface, which will have the effect of adding the interface's address range to the IS-IS routing table. It will also start speaking IS-IS to any other routers on that network that are similarly configured.

Example 6-22. IS-IS configuration on Cisco

```
!
! Configure IS-IS in area "backbone"
!
router isis backbone
 !
 address-family ipv6
 redistribute static  ! Optionally, redistribute routes into IS-IS
 exit-address-family
 !
 ! NET here based on second and third segments of our IPv6 address
 ! but any other convention may be used. Leading 49.0001 and
 ! trailing 0000.00 should remain intact.
 !
```

---

* A hairy practice that can go wrong very quickly if one uses IPv4 anycast on your network. If one of the addresses on your loopback interfaces isn't unique, Murphy's Law (no relation, honest) suggests that the likelihood of it being chosen as a router ID is immeasurably increased.

Example 6-22. IS-IS configuration on Cisco (continued)

```
 net 49.0001.0db8.0008.0000.00
 !
 ! Now configure it on every interface we want to run IS-IS on
 !
 interface FastEthernet0/0
  ipv6 router isis backbone
```

An equivalent, though slightly more elaborate, configuration for Juniper routers is shown in Example 6-23. Here the ISO address, needed for IS-IS, is specified on the loopback interface, alongside the IPv4 and IPv6 loopbacks. family iso is also specified on the interfaces we want to run IS-IS on, and some tweaking of the IS-IS options takes place under the protocols section of the configuration.

Example 6-23. IS-IS configuration on a Juniper M-series

```
interfaces {
    fe-1/0/0 {
        description "IPv6 ethernet with IS-IS";
        unit 0 {
            family iso;
            family inet6 {
                address 2001:0770:0800:0003::1/64;
            }
        }
    }

    lo0 {
        description "Loopback interface with ISO address";
        unit 0 {
            family inet {
                filter {
                    input inbound;
                }
                address 127.0.0.1/32;
                address 193.1.195.17/32;
            }
            family iso {
                address 49.0001.0770.0800.0000.00;
            }
            family inet6 {
                address 2001:0770:0800:0000::/128;
            }
        }
    }
}

protocols{
    isis {
        no-ipv4-routing;
        interface all {
            level 1 disable;
        }
```

Example 6-23. IS-IS configuration on a Juniper M-series (continued)

```
    interface fxp0.0 {
        disable;
    }
    }
}
```

One thing to note is that if you want to use IS-IS to route both your IPv4 and IPv6 traffic, then your IPv4 and IPv6 topology must be the same. However, Juniper and Cisco are offering IS-IS *multi-topology* extensions to allow separate IS-IS topologies to operate simultaneously.

BGP

Perhaps the routing protocol that has survived the trip from IPv4 to IPv6 most unscathed is BGP. This is somewhat ironic (or perhaps iconic,) since one of the great unsolved problems in IPv6 is how to reign in the inevitable increase in size of the global routing table.

For a basic BGP-4+ configuration, you need the following information:

- Your Autonomous System (AS) number,
- The prefixes (i.e., addresses) you wish to advertise,
- The AS numbers and addresses of your peers' routers.

If you've done BGP in IPv4 land, none of this will be terribly shocking. If you've not configured BGP before, there is one truism: the routing protocol itself is reasonably simple, but the odd behaviors that arise from connecting many thousand networks together can be complex. In particular, if you attempt to advertise any route other than a /35 or /32, you may encounter difficulty; many sites filter announcements of networks smaller than these, (and a few misguided souls even filter networks that are bigger) and so some parts of the Internet may not be able to reach you.

If you already have an AS number from your IPv4 network, you may re-use this on the IPv6 Internet. Typically BGP is spoken by medium and large ISPs who will have an AS number anyway. Most end sites speaking IPv6 won't usually need to speak BGP and will not require an AS number.* If these sites need to swap IPv6 routing information then they can use one of the other protocols that we have discussed.

One thing that may surprise you, if you are familiar with implementing BGP on Cisco, is what IPv6 does to your existing configuration. The BGP section of the running-config is split into sections by protocol: IPv4 unicast, IPv6 unicast, IPv4 multicast and so on. If you've used multi-protocol BGP before, say for MPLS VPNs, then IPv6 will be easy for you since it's just a new address family. The config for each BGP

---

* Private AS numbers are another option here, if you wish to run BGP for a different reason.

session is split in two—up top go configuration elements that are protocol-independent, such as the remote router's AS number. Further down are protocol-specific configurations such as the routes you wish to filter. This is elegant in many ways, as it allows you to maintain separate route-maps and filter lists for your IPv4 and IPv6 data in each peer. At first glance you may find it disconcerting to do a sh run only to find your lovingly crafted IPv4 route maps missing; don't worry, they're still there, just keep scrolling.

The address-family split is quite intuitive once you're used to it, but one consequence is that you have to explicitly activate your peers under the address-family ipv6 section. If you see the error "% Activate the neighbor for the address family first" on a Cisco, you're either trying a line that needs to go under address-family ipv6, or you need to activate that peer.

As with IPv4, there are differences between internal and external BGP. For example, while you only need to maintain one BGP session with your external peers (typically from the router that connects directly to them), you must still maintain a BGP session with every other router in your own AS, even those routers that aren't directly connected. This is known as the BGP full mesh. Just as with IPv4, Route Reflectors and BGP Confederations may be used to work around this for larger networks.

The configuration example we're about to consider assumes that you want to send only IPv6 information over an IPv6 BGP session, and IPv4 information over an IPv4 session. While the syntax allows you to do otherwise, it's common practice to separate the peerings, even if they run on the same physical link. This keeps next-hops consistent and ensures that transmission problems affecting one protocol* don't affect the other.

Example 6-24 shows a typical BGP-4+ configuration on a Cisco router.

Example 6-24. Example BGP configuration on Cisco

```
router bgp 65001
!
! If your router is IPv6 only, you need to specify a router-id
!
 bgp router-id 192.168.1.2
 bgp log-neighbor-changes
!
! Configure an external peer
!
 neighbor 2001:DB8:FF:AC1::1 remote-as 65002
 neighbor 2001:DB8:FF:AC1::1 description Our upstream ISP
!
! Configure a peer within our own AS, originating from our loopback addr
!
```

---

* "Oops, did I just type no ip address?"

Example 6-24. Example BGP configuration on Cisco (continued)

```
neighbor 2001:770:8:: remote-as 65001
neighbor 2001:770:8:: description Our other PoP
neighbor 2001:770:8:: update-source Loopback0
!
! IPv4-specific configuration - we must make sure not to send
! any IPv4 routing information over our IPv6 BGP sessions
!
address-family ipv4
no neighbor 2001:DB8:FF:AC1::1 activate
no neighbor 2001:770:8:: activate
exit-address-family
!
! IPv6-specific configuration
!
address-family ipv6
!
! start sending (only) our IPv6 routes to this peer, using filter list 41
!
neighbor 2001:DB8:FF:AC1::1 activate
neighbor 2001:DB8:FF:AC1::1 filter-list 41 out
!
! send IPv6 routes to our internal peer, no filtering
! but set the next-hop to our own address instead of the remote router
!
neighbor 2001:770:8:: activate
neighbor 2001:770:8:: next-hop-self
!
! The prefixes that are local to our network
!
network 2001:770::/32
!
exit-address-family
!
! AS-path access-list 41 permits our AS (^$) and our customer, AS 65003
!
ip as-path access-list 41 permit ^$
ip as-path access-list 41 permit _65003$
```

In line with the list above, the details are:

- Our Autonomous System (AS) number: 65001.
- The prefixes we wish to advertise: 2001:770::/32.
- The AS numbers and addresses of our IPv6 peers' routers: AS65002 is directly connected on 2001:DB8:FF:AC1::1, and the other router in AS1 is at 2001:770:8::.

In addition to our own prefix, we have also chosen to advertise routes we have learned from AS65003, so our AS-path access list is configured to permit that announcement.

There is one other thing that might surprise those of us familiar with IPv4 BGP, and it's not a pleasant surprise either. On a Cisco, if your router is IPv6-only, you will need to explicitly configure a router id for BGP. This is normally selected from the IPv4 addresses configured on the router, but where none are available BGP simply won't work until a valid router ID is configured. We have reliable reports that this is almost as maddening as forgetting to configure `ipv6 unicast-routing`.

Finally, don't forget that most of the BGP commands on IOS have changed from variations on `show ip bgp` to `show bgp ipv6`.

On Juniper, the configuration syntax is unbearably similar to that for BGP with IPv4. An example config is shown in Example 6-25.

Example 6-25. Example BGP configuration on Juniper

```
protocols {
    bgp {
        export heanet-networks;
        group ibgp-v6 {
            type internal;
            local-address 2001:770:0800::;
            family inet6 {
                any;
            }
            neighbor 2001:770:8:: {
                description Salinger;
            }
            neighbor 2001:770:8:B::1 {
                description Miranda;
            }
            neighbor 2001:770:88:8:: {
                description Charon;
            }
        }
        group extpeer-v6 {
            type external;
            family inet6 {
                unicast;
            }
            peer-as 65002;
            neighbor 2001:DB8:FF:AC1::1;
        }
    }
}

policy-options {
    prefix-list heanet-v6 {
        2001:770::/32;
    }
    policy-statement heanet-networks {
        term Heanet-v6 {
            from {
                family inet6;
                prefix-list heanet-v6;
            }
```

Example 6-25. Example BGP configuration on Juniper (continued)

```
            then accept;
        }
        term ELSE {
            then reject;
        }
    }
}
```

Example 6-26 shows a simple *bgpd.conf* for Zebra 0.93b. Beware, the syntax for advertising IPv6 prefixes depends somewhat on the version of Zebra/Quagga, so you will want to check the documentation with your version. Fortunately, the bgpd documentation includes a configuration for IPv6 at the end of its info page, which can serve as a handy template.

Example 6-26. Example BGP configuration for Zebra 0.93b

```
router bgp 65295
 bgp router-id 10.0.0.10
 neighbor 2001:db8:a000::c5 remote-as 65481
 address-family ipv6
  network 2001:db8:8000:1::/32
  neighbor 2001:db8a0000:c5 activate
 exit-address-family
```

Of course, just because you're advertising addresses using BGP doesn't mean your peers—or indeed, their peers—will accept them. The rules for this aren't quite as locked down as they are in the more mature IPv4 Internet, so you may get away with some configurations that are frowned upon in certain parts of the network. In particular, if you attempt to advertise a /48, /64 or any prefix longer than a /35, you are likely to find your announcements filtered by at least parts of the IPv6 Internet.

Incidentally, as one grows more familiar with BGP, one might begin to see what all the fuss is about regarding tunnels and their impact on performance. One of the metrics that BGP uses to determine the distance between networks is the AS path length (that is, how many autonomous systems there are between you and the destination.) Without some sort of local configuration, an IPv6-in-IPv4 tunnel appears to be no better or worse than a super-fast dedicated fibre optic link. In reality, that tunnel might transit many different IPv4 networks with varying performance. Stories abound of traffic from Dublin to Vienna being routed via California and Japan thanks to unwise tunnelling.[*]

Recommended filter lists are to be found, however, and as a matter of best practice should be followed, especially if you provide transit to network other than your own.

---

[*] In case you think this is an urban legend, it has been documented: *http://www.ripe.net/ripe/meetings/ripe-45/ presentations/ripe45-tt-ipv6/page12.htm*.

Gert Döring maintains such a Best Current Practice list at *http://www.space.net/~gert/RIPE/ipv6-filters.html* and groups such as Cymru provide "bogon" lists at *http://www.cymru.com/Documents/bogonv6-list.html*.

Multicast Routing

Beyond link-local multicast, the deployment of IPv6 multicast is still at a relatively early stage. IPv6 multicast routing involves additional daemons, but most implementations lack full support at the time of writing. KAME provide PIM implementations `pim6dd` and `pim6sd` so deploying multicast routers based on the KAME platform has become popular.

For now, if you are interested in multicast routing in IPv6, we suggest you join M6Bone, the experimental IPv6 multicast network at *http://www.m6bone.net/*.

Firewalls

In this section we'll look at IPv6 and firewalling, or in particular, packet filtering. Packet filtering, in general, is the process of examining packets as they enter and exit a network and making a decision about allowing them through or dropping them. Usually packet filters allow you to make decisions on factors such as:

- Protocol (e.g., TCP, UDP, or ICMP)
- Source and destination port number/ICMP type (e.g., 80 is HTTP; 25 is SMTP)
- Source and destination IP address
- Incoming and outgoing interface
- TCP flags, sequence numbers and window values
- IP fragmentation offset and size

The rules used to filter packets can either be statically configured or rules may be updated dynamically by the traffic itself. For example, TCP data traffic may only be passed if the normal 3-way handshake has been completed. These sorts of dynamic rules are referred to as *stateful packet filtering*.

Many existing packet filters offer additional features, such as packet normalization (where unusual looking IP streams are normalized before being allowed through the firewall), sequence number rewriting (where TCP initial sequence numbers are made more random), transparent proxying (where HTTP connections are redirected to a proxy server without the client's knowledge) or NAT (where several machines are made to appear as a single IP address).

Most of what is known about IPv4 packet filtering applies directly to the IPv6 situation, as layer 3 (TCP and UDP) and above are largely the same in both IPv4 and IPv6. There are a few differences at the lower layers, though.

Note that the examples in this section are given in a Cisco IOS ACL-*like* format. These are intended as the sort of rules that you may want to include in a packet filter rule set. They will need to be translated so that they have the correct syntax for your platform.

Filtering on IPv6 Addresses

The obvious difference is that we must now filter on IPv6 addresses. Less obvious is the fact that most devices will now have multiple IPv6 addresses, and so you may need to have several rules where one was sufficient in the IPv4 case.

Furthermore, different types of IPv6 address are also common, so you may have to consider the filtering of link-local and anycast addresses.

However, filtering of link-local addresses is not usually necessary, as link-local traffic should not be forwarded between networks. Still, if you happen to have filtering (layer 2) switches that filter within a single logical network, you may have to consider what needs to be done with link-local traffic.

Regardless of their future, site-local addresses will almost certainly require filtering, to prevent the leak of site-local traffic to and from your site. Naturally, this requires deciding where the boundary of your site is and then configuring the packet-filters on the boundary routers to keep site-local traffic completely internal. One of the factors that was held against the original site-local addressing scheme was confusion when a router was a member of more than one site. If you are not using site-local addresses, then it should be safe to block their use at all firewalls within your network.

The use of link-local multicast addresses is central to the correct operation of IPv6, and so you should think very carefully about applying filtering to these addresses. Most of the important link-local multicast traffic is ICMP traffic used for neighbor discovery (see the "ICMPv6" section in Chapter 3).

There are also other special addresses to be considered within IPv6. The loopback address ::1 needs to treated in the same way as 127.0.0.1. The IPv4 address space is also embedded in the IPv6 address space as mapped addresses ::ffff:0.0.0.0/96, compatible addresses ::0.0.0.0/96 and 6to4 addresses 2002::/16.

Filtering ICMPv6

With IPv4, protocols such as ARP are used to provide low-level IP to MAC translations (see the "MAC Layer Address Resolution" section in Chapter 1). ARP is a non-IP protocol, and so has never been an important factor when designing rules for IP packet filters.

In IPv6 these functions are provided by Neighbor Discovery, which is at the ICMP level, so we must now consider this when designing rules. Similarly, as autoconfiguration can now be driven by routers as well as DHCP servers, we must also account for this. So, any packet filtering put in place must allow Router Discovery to happen. We also have to remember that both Neighbor Discovery and Router Discovery use multicast.

One approach to this is to allow ICMP traffic to and from link-local addresses. We also need to allow traffic from the unspecified address :: and to the link-scope multicast addresses to accommodate Duplicate Address Detection. Here's an example of the sort of rules necessary:

```
! DAD (unspec -> link-local multicast)
permit ipv6-icmp from :: to ff02::/16

! RS, RA, NS, NA (link-local unicast -> link-local unicast or multicast)
permit ipv6-icmp from fe80::/10 to fe80::/10
permit ipv6-icmp from fe80::/10 to ff02::/16
```

As a safety net against foot-shooting, recent versions of Cisco's IOS supplement the usual implicit 'deny all' with additional implicit rules permit icmp any any nd-na and permit icmp any any nd-ns. This shows the alternative approach of explicitly allowing the ICMP messages you want, rather than allowing traffic with addresses in the right range.

It is also important to remember that IPv6 is more sensitive to the filtering of ICMP error messages relating to path MTU discovery, so it is not possible to filter out all ICMP messages, as some networks have chosen to do for IPv4.

Ingress and Egress Filtering

Ingress and *egress* filtering usually refer to checking that packets have appropriate source and destination addresses before they enter or leave your site. This sort of filtering is considered important in preventing IP spoofing, and in particular anonymous attacks on hosts.

As packets enter our site we need to check that the source address of the packet does not claim to be within our site. We could check that a packet's destination is one of the following:

1. The filtering router's link-local or global address
2. An appropriate multicast address
3. An appropriate site-local address (if site-local addresses are in use)
4. A global address within the site

The decision to allow or deny traffic with site-local addresses will depend on where the filter is in a site and if that site exchanges site-local traffic with other sites. If site-local addresses are not in use, then it should be safe to block all site-local traffic on border routers.

Naturally you may want to filter incoming traffic to certain addresses and ports, as you would with IPv4. Less important is the screening of packets on ingress for destination addresses not in your site. Such packets are unusual, as odd-ball destination addresses should not be routed toward your site in the first place.

To prevent nodes within our site impersonating nodes in the networks of others we need to check that the source address is within our site or is the router itself. The router itself might include a link-local address and the unspecified address if you are not applying the rules discussed in the previous section, "Filtering ICMPv6," although allowing link-local traffic of a non-ICMP type can also be useful. You may also want to check that the destination address is not without your site, to prevent misrouted traffic from looping.

Example 6-27 shows a simple implementation of these rules. In the example, variables are set to represent the network on the inside of the packet filter host and the address of the packet filter itself.

Example 6-27. Sample ingress and egress filtering rules

```
! Ingress filtering applied to incoming packets on external interface.
deny ipv6 from $inside_network to any

! Egress filtering applied to outgoing packets on external interface.
deny ipv6 from any to $inside_network
permit ipv6 from fe80::/10 to any
permit ipv6 from $filter_ip_address to any out
permit ipv6 from $inside_network to any
```

Suspicious Addresses

In IPv4 there are certain addresses that, if seen on the wire, are considered suspicious. Packets with these addresses are often filtered to prevent any confusion they might cause. The sort of addresses considered suspicious are the loopback address, private addresses, and subnet broadcast addresses.

Example 6-28 shows the sort of rules that you might consider. It includes filtering out all mapped addresses, compatible addresses (or a subset of them that are based on special use IPv4 addresses) and 6to4 addresses that are based on special IPv4 addresses. We also filter well-known site-local multicast traffic, which would normally have no reason to cross a border router.

Example 6-28. Addresses that might warrant filtering

```
! Disallow mapped addresses, as they shouldn't be on the wire.
deny ipv6 from ::ffff:0.0.0.0/96 to any
deny ipv6 from any to ::ffff:0.0.0.0/96

! Denying automatically tunnelled traffic using compatible addresses
deny ipv6 from ::0.0.0.0/96 to any
deny ipv6 from any to ::0.0.0.0/96
```

Example 6-28. Addresses that might warrant filtering (continued)

```
! If some compatible addresses are allowed,
! then these should probably be filtered.
deny ipv6 from ::224.0.0.0/100 to any
deny ipv6 from any to ::224.0.0.0/100
deny ipv6 from ::127.0.0.0/104 to any
deny ipv6 from any to ::127.0.0.0/104
deny ipv6 from ::0.0.0.0/104 to any
deny ipv6 from any to ::0.0.0.0/104
deny ipv6 from ::255.0.0.0/104 to any
deny ipv6 from any to ::255.0.0.0/104

! Disallow packets to malicious 6to4 prefix.
deny ipv6 from 2002:e000::/20 to any
deny ipv6 from any to 2002:e000::/20
deny ipv6 from 2002:7f00::/24 to any
deny ipv6 from any to 2002:7f00::/24
deny ipv6 from 2002:0000::/24 to any
deny ipv6 from any to 2002:0000::/24
deny ipv6 from 2002:ff00::/24 to any
deny ipv6 from any to 2002:ff00::/24

deny ipv6 from 2002:0a00::/24 to any
deny ipv6 from any to 2002:0a00::/24
deny ipv6 from 2002:ac10::/28 to any
deny ipv6 from any to 2002:ac10::/28
deny ipv6 from 2002:c0a8::/32 to any
deny ipv6 from any to 2002:c0a8::/32

! Filter site-local multicast.
deny ipv6 from ff05::/16 to any
deny ipv6 from any to ff05::/16
```

Packages Available for IPv6 Firewalling

There is a great deal of variability in the packet filtering software available on various platforms, so we will not go into details of each package. All software should be able to support the basic rules described in the preceeding sections, so it is only a matter of consulting vendor documentation to determine the correct syntax. However, we will take a moment to mention some of the packages available.

Linux supports IPv6 packet filtering using the ip6tables command, the basic setup of which are covered in Peter Bieringer IPv6 HOWTO at *http://www.bieringer.de/ linux/IPv6/IPv6-HOWTO/IPv6-HOWTO.html*.

FreeBSD and Mac OS Panther also support IPv6 packet filtering using the ip6fw. Documentation is available in the man page and the basic rule sets are listed in */etc/ rc.firewall6*. On Panther rules can also be adjusted using the network control panel. The ip6fw command does not have as comprehensive set of features as provided for IPv4 by the ipfw command.

Recent versions of FreeBSD also ship with an IPv6 capable version of Darren Reed's IPFilter. IPFilter also supports other platforms such as Solaris and BSD/OS. Further documentation is available at *http://coombs.anu.edu.au/~avalon/*. Recent 5.X releases of FreeBSD also ship with the pf packet filter from OpenBSD, which has full IPv6 support.

Cisco support for IPv6 access lists is quite complete and the Cisco document *Implementing Security for IPv6* provides details and examples of how these can be configured. Cisco's firewall products are just beginning to include IPv6 support and should be should be mainstream in the near future.

At the time of writing, Checkpoint have been offering IPv6 for some time and Netscreen have announced comprehensive IPv6 support in their ScreenOS integrated firewall and VPN product.

Windows XP Service Pack 2 (or the *Advanced Networking Pack* for earlier versions of Windows XP) includes a personal firewall called the IPv6 Internet Connection Firewall. It provides basic stateful firewalling for IPv6 for a single host. It is actually a regular Windows Service, so once installed it can be enabled and disabled using the Services Administrative Tool. Fine control over the firewall is available using netsh firewall, including per-port and per-interface controls.

Impact of IPv6 Deployment on IPv4 Filtering

If your IPv6 connectivity is via an IPv6-in-IPv4 tunnel of some sort (e.g., either a configured tunnel or 6to4), then you may have to allow this traffic through your IPv4 packet-filter. As we've mentioned several times, this traffic operates on IPv4 protocol 41.

IPv4 filtering can also be indirectly affected by IPv6 deployment because packets may be sent to dual-stacked hosts via IPv6. This means a service blocked by the IPv4 firewall may be accessible over IPv6, unless the IPv6 firewall is appropriately configured.

While not directly an IPv6 issue, the increased availability of IPsec in the IPv6 world brings up some thorny issues for the network administrator. When ESP is used to encrypt the payload of an IPv6 packet, it is not possible to examine any of the encrypted fields in the packet, which may make it impossible to tell if the packet is a UDP or TCP packet, what the port numbers are and what any TCP sequence numbers might be. Some limited control could be exerted over encrypted traffic by limiting access to IKE, the system used to dynamically establishes keys for IPsec. It runs on UDP port 500, and could be filtered normally. However, if static keys are used, or dynamic keys are established using some other protocol then all bets are off.

Port Scanning

Particular forms of port scanning are rendered ineffective by IPv6's large address space. In particular, if someone chooses an IPv4 address at random then the chances are reasonably good that they will hit a live machine. In the IPv6 world, the chance of them hitting a live machine is hugely reduced. This makes randomly targeting machines for port scanning, virus infection or other malicious traffic a much less practical strategy. Hopefully this means that we will never see anything like the SQL Slammer in the IPv6 Internet.

While not actually a packet filtering issue, it is an issue that is linked with firewalling in many people's minds. In particular, some people have used NAT to try and reduce their statistical exposure to random port scanning, by reducing the number of public addresses they use. It is interesting to see that IPv6 handles this problem by going to the other extreme!

Gotchas

Dealing with autoconfiguration and privacy addressing is something that can make IPv6 packet filtering a little tricky. Remember that if you use autoconfiguration (rather than DHCPv6 or manual configuration of addresses) then a change of network card can result in a change of IPv6 address. So, if your firewall rules mention any autoconfigured IPv6 addresses then the rules need to be kept up to date. One way to get around this is to explicitly assign addresses to hosts that are mentioned in your firewall rules, rather than assigning them automatically.

A variation of this idea is to assign addresses to specific services you offer, rather than to hosts. In this scheme, you might have a host that offers an SMTP and a HTTP service, but you give the host multiple addresses and advertise one address for SMTP and one address for HTTP. The firewall rules can reflect this by only allowing SMTP to the SMTP address and only allowing HTTP to the HTTP address, thus reducing the chance of unexpected interactions between services and firewall rules.

Another way to tackle the problem of autoconfigured hosts changing address is to put the hosts with different firewall requirements in different networks and use router advertisements to assign different prefixes. This allows your firewall to match on prefix rather than worrying about Interface IDs. Remember that you have a lot of subnets to play with in a /48.

Privacy addressing is the technique where a host generates a new, effectively random, address for itself periodically (see the "Neighborhood Watch" section in Chapter 3 for more details). Again, if a host is using these addresses it may complicate packet filtering. However, the prefix of these addresses will all be the same, so if the firewall requirements of all addresses with one prefix are the same, then you don't need to worry about this. The equivalent of statically configuring addresses here is to disable privacy addressing. This can be achieved on Windows (where it is on by default) using the command netsh interface ipv6 set privacy state=disabled. On most other platforms privacy addressing is off by default, but can be turned on if desired: for example, sysctl -w net.inet6.ip6.use_tempaddr=1 on KAME.

When designing firewall rules, remember that you need to let enough ICMPv6 messages through to allow local neighbor discovery and Path MTU discovery to work. In particular, blocking ICMPv6 errors will cause problems because Packet Too Big messages will be lost. The obvious symptom of this broken path MTU discovery is that TCP connections hang when they have to transfer large amounts of data.

In an effort to allow Packet Too Big messages, one of the authors had carefully configured a FreeBSD firewall to pass ICMP messages with the command `allow icmp from any to any`, not realizing that the correct command was `allow ipv6-icmp from any to any`. The incorrect command was actually legal allowing (meaningless) ICMPv4 datagrams in IPv6 packets. The moral? Read your packet filter's documentation carefully to find differences between the IPv4 and IPv6 syntax.

Management

Any moderate-size network will have mechanisms for the automatic configuration and monitoring of the network. We've already talked about IPv6 autoconfiguration, but we'll mention DHCPv6 in this section again. We'll also take a look at the state of SNMP for IPv6.

Running DHCPv6

At the time of writing, the 800-pound gorilla of DHCP implementations, ISC DHCPd, does not support IPv6. More importantly, most of the operating systems we have mentioned do not yet support configuration via DHCPv6.

If you cannot wait, there are a variety of implementations out there. For example, HP provide a `dhcpv6d` for HP-UX, and also include a client. KAME has a minimal DHCPv6 implementation, which isn't really designed for managing addresses, but can provide simple additional configuration information. In particular, it can be used to distribute the address of the local DNS server. The setup of their small server and client programs is described at *http://www.kame.net/newsletter/20030411/*. The only additional advice we can add is to explicitly specify the location of the client and server configuration files using the `-c` option to `dhcp6c` and `dhcp6s`.

There is a port of the KAME DHCPd to Linux available from *http://sourceforge.net/projects/dhcpv6*. It actually includes more complete address assignment features.

With respect to integrating the DHCP and DHCPv6 services, at the moment, the closest you can get is running the two in parallel from the same information and have both servers hand out static addresses to given MAC addresses. DHCPv6 is not currently capable of carrying IPv4 specific information and vice versa.

SNMP

SNMP has two parts that need to support IPv6. The protocol itself, which as the name suggests is extremely simple, doesn't require much modification to run over IPv6. The information that SNMP manages, or MIBs as they are known, requires significantly more work because new MIBS are needed that can contain IPv6 addresses or concepts specific to IPv6. The basic changes for SNMP and IPv6 are in RFC 3291 and there are a new set of IPv6 related MIBs to follow.

Promiscuous IPsec in IPv6 has the potential to fix a lot of the arguments that took place over the security of SNMP—arguments that resulted in the vast majority of management systems exchanging important information over plain-text, essentially unauthenticated UDP packets.

The split between IPv6 support for the protocol and IPv6 for the information is very like the split in DNS between IPv6 transport and IPv6 records. It is possible to have equipment that can transport IPv6 MIBs over IPv4 and vice versa. This means that dual-stacked SNMP devices can be managed from IPv4-only management stations.

If you aim to operate an IPv6-only network, you will want to check with vendors of your switches, routers, management stations and other devices to ensure that they support IPv6 transport. At least JUNOS and recent releases of NET-SNMP* are known to. We'll comment on the support in NET-SNMP as it is used on a wide range of platforms and its syntax is a little unusual.

IPv6 support for NET-SNMP is integrated into the 5.0.X family of releases. You can enable support for IPv6 MIBs and IPv6 transport independently at compile time by giving the `configure` program the option `--with-mib-modules="mibII/ipv6"` or `--with-transports="UDPIPv6"` respectively.

NET-SNMP's SNMP agent is called `snmpd` and when given no options listens on all IPv4 addresses. You can give a list of alternative transports to use on the command line, for example `snmpd udpv6::: udp:0.0.0.0` tells it to listen on the IPv6 unspecified address and the IPv4 unspecified address, resulting in an agent listening on all IPv4 and IPv6 addresses.

You also need to set up access controls for IPv4 and IPv6 addresses in *snmpd.conf*. Three directives are provided for doing this: `rocommunity6`, `rwcommunity6` and `com2sec6`. These are like their IPv4 counterparts but accept IPv6 hostnames, addresses and CIDR blocks. For example `rwcommunity6 private ::1` allows read-write access from the IPv6 localhost address, and `rocommunity6 public 2001:db8:68::/48` allows read-only access from that /48. The *snmpd.conf* manual page explains these directives in more detail.

---

* On Linux, Solaris, and FreeBSD, at least.

NET-SNMP is also used as a SNMP client, and can be told to make IPv6 transport SNMP requests using a similar syntax to that used for `snmpd`. The command `snmpwalk -v 1 -c public udp6:router.example.com` would attempt to use IPv6 to contact `router.example.com` to display a subtree of the available SNMP information (using SNMP Version 1).

Possibly the best news for IPv6 SNMP users is that MRTG, the popular tool for plotting statistics based on SNMP, supports IPv6 from the 2.10 family of releases.

Scripting Network Monitoring

In addition to the sort of network monitoring performed using SNMP, many people have built monitoring systems of their own by scripting common commands to check that networks are reachable, routes are sensible and web servers are responding.

These systems are usually built around `ping`, `traceroute` and other simple commands. Naturally, any such scripts will need to be either duplicated or modified so that they can monitor both IPv4 and IPv6 network services. Probably the only thing of significant note here is to remember that many commands automatically fall back to IPv4 if an IPv6 connection fails. If this is the case for any commands you are using, you'll want to specify that IPv6 must be used on the command line (either by using an IPv6 only command like `ping6` or by using flags like `-6` or `-f inet6`).

Remember that you have some additional facilities, such as multicast and node information queries, when you are designing an IPv6 monitoring system.

Intrusion Detection

Intrusion Detection Systems (IDS) have become popular in some networking circles in the last few years. Unfortunately, vendors of intrusion detection products seem to have been relatively slow to provide IPv6 support. There is even a reported case of break-ins where IPv6 has been configured on systems after they are compromised, because the crackers know that IPv6 is less likely to be analyzed fully by IDSs.

Help is at hand though. Snort 2 has experimental support for IPv6 (available from *http://www.snort.org/*) and Lance Spitzner has been talking about IPv6 and honeypots, which is likely to increase the level of interest and support in this area.

Providing Transition Mechanisms

In this section we'll look at how you might provide infrastructure for two of the transition mechanisms that we discussed in "Transition Mechanisms" in Chapter 4. First we look at 6to4 Relay Routers. These might useful be deployed either by an ISP or at the border of a large organization that has a number of 6to4 users internally.

Second we'll look at the configuration of the KAME *faith* system. This is an implementation of TRT, and so we also cover a DNS server, *totd*, that can convert DNS A records into AAAA records.

We'll also look at how VLANs and other similar mechanisms can be used to provide IPv6 without disturbing existing IPv4 infrastructure.

We'd like to be able to describe good software to allow an ISP manage tunnels to their customers. Unfortunately, at the time of writing, we are not aware of any generally available software for doing this. It is possible that operation of such software is too ISP specific, probably requiring integration with billing systems and customer databases. One quick solution to this problem would be to become a POP for some tunnel broker service such as *http://www.sixxs.net/*.

We'll talk about the more service-oriented transition mechanisms, application proxies and port forwarding in particular, in Chapter 7.

6to4 Relay Routers

Setting up a 6to4 relay router is actually quite a good way for an ISP to begin offering IPv6 services. Currently if an ISP's customers use 6to4 as a way to experiment with IPv6, their traffic may travel around the world before reaching the IPv6 Internet. Provision of a relay router allows an ISP to route this traffic, destined for the IPv6 Internet, via a transit carrier that supports native or tunnelled IPv6 traffic. This should offer more direct routes for customer traffic.

Why offer a relay router and not some other form of IPv6 connectivity? A relay router requires only one router to be configured for IPv6. It offers the ISP a chance to get some IPv6 experience without a huge outlay of time or money. The router itself should be low maintenance once set up (similar to normal router maintenance). The service offered to customers requires no per-customer setup or support services at the ISP's end. Even if the router does fail, the use of anycast means that the traffic should automatically fail-over to the next closest relay router.

To deploy a 6to4 relay router you'll need:

1. A machine capable of IPv6 forwarding that supports 6to4 pseudo-interfaces
2. A connection to the IPv4 network where you can advertise a route to 192.88.99.0/24 at least locally
3. A connection to the IPv6 Internet (either natively or via a tunnel) where you may want to advertise 2002::/16

The requirements for a 6to4 relay router are covered in RFC 3068. This RFC is only eight pages long and should be read by anyone deploying a relay router. It covers the configuration of a relay router, advertising it into local and global routing tables, monitoring and fault tracking.

One issue with 6to4 relay routers is that they can be used as a packet laundering service by unscrupulous network users. For this reason you may wish to restrict who has access to your relay routers at appropriate ingress points.

Example 6-29 shows the configuration of a 6to4 relay router under IOS. The router's loopback address is 192.0.2.4 and we also configure a corresponding 6to4 address 2002:c000:0204::1. The IPv4 anycast address for 6to4, 192.88.99.1, is also configured on the lookback interface. We then configure a 6to4 tunnelling interface. We finally configure OSPF to advertise the anycast address into out IGP. This will result in 6to4 traffic being drawn toward this router. Note that we do not show the configuration of the interface providing IPv4 or IPv6 connectivity.

There is one unusual aspect of this configuration, and that is the "anycast" argument used in the configuration of the 2002:C058:6301:: address on this tunnel interface. This marks the address as an IPv6 anycast address, which for a time was only supported in beta versions of IOS, but became mainstream in 12.2(25)S and 12.3(4)T. Some operators report that Windows XP 6to4 clients work better when the anycast flag is not set on the relay.

Example 6-29. Cisco 6to4 relay router configuration

```
interface Loopback0
 description 6to4 Relay anycast address & Equivalent IPv4 unicast address
 ip address 192.88.99.1 255.255.255.0 secondary
 ip address 192.0.2.4 255.255.255.255
 ipv6 address 2002:c000:0204::1/128
 ipv6 mtu 1480
 no ipv6 mfib fast
!
interface Tunnel2002
 description anycast 6to4 Relay
 no ip address
 no ip redirects
 ipv6 address 2002:C058:6301::/128 anycast
 ipv6 unnumbered Loopback0
 no ipv6 mfib fast
 tunnel source Loopback0
 tunnel mode ipv6ip 6to4
 tunnel path-mtu-discovery
!
router ospf 1
 log-adjacency-changes
 auto-cost reference-bandwidth 10000
 network 192.88.99.0 0.0.0.255 area 0
!
```

One thing to note is that you may want to manually configure your router's BGP/OSPF ID manually if you are using any IPv4 anycast addresses. Otherwise you may risk your router choosing the IPv4 anycast address as its router ID, and this may lead to confusion because router IDs are supposed to be unique.

Faith

Faith is a special case proxy; it does IPv6 to IPv4 translation, but using TCP only. As you might imagine, it's used on dual-stack machines to connect an IPv6-only network to some portion of an IPv4 network. The interesting thing about faithd is that it determines the endpoint of the IPv4 connection by looking at the last 32 bits of the IPv6 destination. It can be useful for general port proxying to NAT friendly services, but also has special support for FTP and rlogin, that are not so NAT friendly. Perhaps the most useful feature of faithd is that it allows you to do TRT for all of the IPv4 address space without configuring 2^{32} addresses on a machine.

Faith is available on KAME-based platforms, and example configurations are included in the man page. We'll show an example of how to allow IPv6 hosts to make telnet connections to IPv4 only hosts. We'll consider four hosts: an IPv6 only client, the dual-stacked host running faithd, the DNS translator and the regular recursive DNS server. We also need a block of addresses to use with faith and a block of addresses for the IPv6 only hosts, we'll use 2001:db8:68:fa17::/64 and 2001:db8:68:1ff::/64 respectively.

On the IPv6 only client, we set the nameserver to be the address of the DNS translator either by editing *resolv.conf* or by using DHCPv6.

On the DNS translator we install Feico Dillema's totd, a translating DNS server, available from *http://www.vermicelli.pasta.cs.uit.no/ipv6/software.html*. This daemon works like a forwarding DNS server, but we configure it so that if it sees a request for a host having no IPv6 DNS record then it takes its IPv4 address a.b.c.d and makes up a IPv6 DNS record 2001:db8:68:fa17::a.b.c.d, making the host appear to be in our block of addresses used for faith.

Example 6-30 shows the configuration file for totd used to achieve this translation. Totd is only a forwarding nameserver, so we first point it at the usual resolving nameserver for the network. Second, we configure the prefix that the IPv4 addresses are to be mapped in to.

Example 6-30. A simple totd configuration

```
; Set the address of the real nameserver.
forwarder 2001:db8:68:1ff:202:b3ff:fe65:604b port 53
; Prefix to map IPv4 addresses into.
prefix 2001:db8:68:fa17::
```

Next, we need to configure your network so that packets for 2001:db8:68:fa17::/64 are routed to the host running faithd. If the router for your IPv6-only subnet happens to be the host running faithd, there will be no configuration needed. Otherwise you will need to adjust the static or dynamic routing to forward these packets to the faithd host.

Finally, we need to configure faithd itself. Example 6-31 shows a sequence of commands to configure faithd. First we enable the use of faith and enable the special faith interface. We then route packets to the faith prefix via that interface.[*] Then we create the *faithd.conf* file, allowing access from clients in our IPv6 only subnet to any IPv4 address. The final step is to start faithd, asking it to proxy the telnet service. If we also wanted it to proxy other services, we could run additional instances of faithd.

Example 6-31. Using faithd to proxy telnet

```
sysctl net.inet6.ip6.keepfaith=1
ifconfig faith0 up

route add -inet6 2001:db8:68:fa17:: -prefixlen 64 ::1
route change -inet6 2001:db8:68:fa17:: -prefixlen 64 -ifp faith0

echo "2001:db8:68:1ff::/64 permit 0.0.0.0/0" > /etc/faithd.conf
faithd telnet
```

The setup is now complete. If a user on the IPv6 only network tries to telnet to v4only.example.com that happens to have IPv4 address 192.0.2.15, then the DNS translator will fabricate the address 2001:db8:68:fa17::c000:020f. The IPv6 only host will make a connection to this address, that will be routed to the faithd host. Faithd will make an IPv4 connection to 192.0.2.15 and relay the data back and forth.

Faithd will work well with NAT friendly protocols that don't embed addresses. It also knows how to do the necessary protocol magic to make FTP work, and can be extended to support other protocols.

Hacking Native Connectivity Around Incompatible Equipment

We all want native IPv6, but some of us have hardware that doesn't support it yet. An across-the-board upgrade is likely to be an expensive proposition, but all is not lost; there are ways one can work around incompatible hardware instead of replacing it or relying indefinitely on the IETF-defined transition mechanisms already discussed.

When your gateway router doesn't support IPv6

For example, the IPv4 router on a LAN doesn't necessarily need to be the same device as your IPv6 router. If you have a dedicated IPv4 router on your LAN, this might already be obvious. You can add a second router to act as your IPv6 gateway, as shown in Figure 6-1.

---

[*] Here the syntax is slightly strange, but follows the recommendations of the faithd documentation!

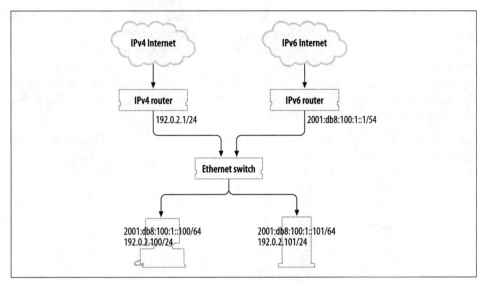

Figure 6-1. Using two routers connected by a switch/VLAN

However, a common option these days is to use an intelligent layer 3 switch, rather than a router, to provide switching and IP routing in the same device. If this switch does not support IPv6 yet, what options do you have? Well, the decoupling still applies.

The way Cisco (at least) configure routing on a layer 3 switch[*] is to create a virtual interface on the VLAN of your choice. This virtual interface can then be assigned an IPv4 address, and that IPv4 address will typically be used as the gateway address when configuring your hosts. Such a configuration is shown in Example 6-32.

Example 6-32. IPv4 configuration of a layer 3 switch

```
interface Vlan1
 description IPv4 gateway for office LAN
 ip address 192.0.1.1 255.255.255.0
!
interface Vlan2
 description IPv4 gateway for server LAN
 ip address 192.0.2.1 255.255.255.0
!
interface Vlan3
 description IPv4 gateway for DMZ
 ip adderss 192.0.3.1 255.255.255.0
!
interface FastEthernet0/0
 description Trunked uplink to IPv6 gateway
 switchmode trunk encapsulation dot1q
 switchport mode trunk
!
```

---

[*] Such as the Catalyst 4000 or 6500 with the appropriate supervisor card.

If your switch software does not support IPv6 yet, then you cannot assign an IPv6 address to this virtual interface. However, you can place an IPv6 capable router on a port on your switch, configure that port in the desired VLAN and give *that* device an IPv6 address. The new router will then announce its presence on the VLAN and your hosts will autoconfigure themselves. Your IPv4 traffic will continue to be routed by the layer 3 switch as before. Meanwhile, your IPv6 hosts will direct IPv6 traffic to the new router instead. The switch is none the wiser.

You can repeat this trick for every VLAN in your network—the layout looks like Figure 6-2. Three separate IPv6 routers are shown serving three different VLANs each with a different IPv6 prefix.

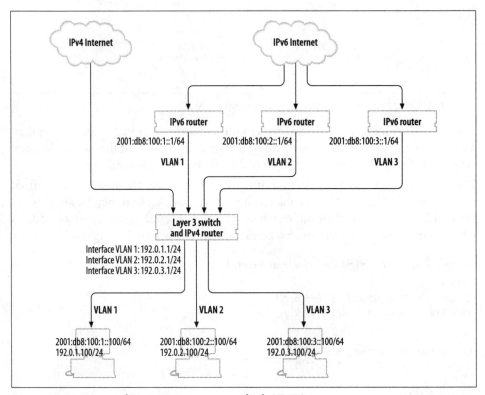

Figure 6-2. Using several IPv6 routers to serve multiple VLANs

Best of all, if your IPv6 router supports VLAN trunking,[*] you may (logically) place this IPv6 device in *every* VLAN, thus providing an IPv6 router on all attached networks. The result looks like Figure 6-3.

---

[*] Note that Linux and FreeBSD both support VLAN trunking if equipped with a modern FastEthernet card, and Cisco routers support it in certain versions of IOS such as the "Enterprise" trains. Our experience is that it doesn't work on Ciscos with plain 10 megabit Ethernet interfaces—check with your support people.

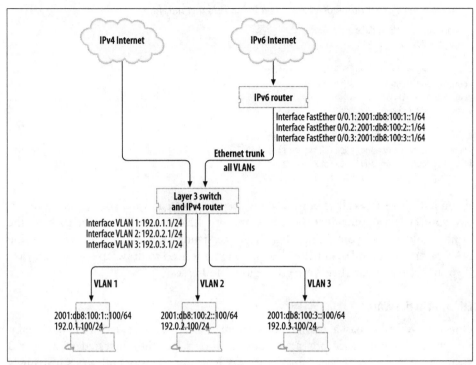

Figure 6-3. Using a single VLAN-aware IPv6 router

To configure your IPv6 router to do this you create a virtual interface in each VLAN and then configure IPv6 on that virtual interface. The config one might use to configure 802.1q VLANs on a Cisco router can be seen in Example 6-33. To do the same on Linux you might use commands like those in Example 6-34.

Example 6-33. Cisco configuration of an IPv6 router on a trunked Ethernet port

```
interface FastEthernet0/0
 description Trunked ethernet interface, gateway for many VLANs
 no ip address
!
interface FastEthernet0/0.1
 description IPv6 uplink for office LAN
 encapsulation dot1q 1
 ipv6 address 2001:db8:100:1::1/64
!
interface FastEthernet0/0.2
 description IPv6 uplink for server LAN
 encapsulation dot1q 2
 ipv6 address 2001:db8:100:2::1/64
!
interface FastEthernet0/0.3
 description IPv6 uplink for DMZ
 encapsulation dot1q 3
 ipv6 address 2001:db8:100:3::1/64
!
```

Example 6-34. Configuration of VLANs on a Linux Ethernet interface

```
# Load the 8021q module
modprobe 8021q

# Add three VLANs to this ethernet interface
vconfig add eth0 1
vconfig add eth0 2
vconfig add eth0 3

# Add IP addresses to the new VLAN interfaces
ifconfig eth0.1 up add 2001:db8:100:1::1/64
ifconfig eth0.2 up add 2001:db8:100:2::1/64
ifconfig eth0.3 up add 2001:db8:100:3::1/64
```

If you have IPv4 access lists or firewalling on your IPv4 gateway, you will want to satisfy yourself with equivalent measures on your IPv6 gateway in order to have the same confidence in your firewalling. If your existing security policy involves using NAT or proxies to hide your IPv4 hosts, you might need to draw up a new policy for IPv6, wherein all your clients are given global addresses.*

Ethernet in the WAN

One ISP we know has a number of customers that connect over Fast or Gigabit Ethernet. The staff there are strict routing purists but they invested in a layer 3 switch to deliver this service, since it gave a high port density and was surprisingly good at acting like a "real" router.

This ISP was rather disappointed when its own IPv6 deployment plans overtook those of the vendor who sold them the switch. They did however see this coming, and had a trick up their sleeve.

Normally, the ISP would reserve a Gigabit Ethernet interface on their switch for the customer's connection, and assign a link IP address directly to that interface, as per a router port. This is shown in Example 6-35. Unfortunately, this does not allow the ISP to provide native IPv6.

Example 6-35. Cisco configuration of IPv4 on a routed port

```
interface GigabitEthernet1/1
 description Customer Metro Ethernet connection
 ip address 192.0.2.1 255.255.255.252
 speed nonegotiate
```

For the workaround, they configured the interface on the IPv4-only device as a switchport, and put it in a VLAN on its own. Then they configured a virtual interface on the same device in the same VLAN and assigned the link IPv4 address to

---

* Of course, that doesn't mean they'll be allowed to *use* them.

that. This is shown in Example 6-36. On a Cisco 7600 (which is essentially a Catalyst 6500 with a special supervisor card) one can safely do this without impacting performance.

Example 6-36. Cisco configuration of a switch port and logical VLAN interface

```
interface GigabitEthernet1/1
 description Customer Metro Ethernet connection
 no ip address
 speed nonegotiate
 switchport
 switchport access vlan 101
 switchport mode access

interface VLAN101
 description Customer IPv4 interface for metro ethernet on Gig1/1
 ip address 192.0.2.1 255.255.255.252
```

This is no doubt offending the routing sensibilities of many WAN networkers out there, but it's important to note that this is just an internal configuration change. The device at the remote end of the link doesn't need to be VLAN aware. Furthermore, no other device needs an IP address on that VLAN.

Well. No other device needs an *IPv4* address. The advantage of configuring the interface as a switchport is that you can then create a separate IPv6 router and connect it to the same Ethernet VLAN, just as described above. You can do this either by connecting the IPv6 router to a switchport in the appropriate VLAN on the IPv4-only device or by connecting the devices using VLAN trunking (as per Example 6-33.)

Figure 6-4 shows all this in action. If an IPv4 packet is sent by the customer, the Ethernet frame will have as its destination the MAC address of the layer 3 switch, and the layer 3 switch will handle it. If an IPv6 packet is sent, the destination MAC address will be the IPV6 router; it will be switched directly to that device and handled appropriately.

Troublesome ATM devices

There's a similar hack that one can use with ATM links. ATM is commonly used to link networks at speeds higher than 2Mbps (where leased lines run out of steam) but lower than about STM-1 level (where SONET and SDH start to make more sense). ATM offers a lot of flexibility in configuring circuits, and we may use some of this to our advantage.

An ATM circuit typically has two numbers associated with it—a Virtual Path Identifier (VPI) and a Virtual Circuit Identifier (VCI). These are expressed as a pair, and a unique VPI/VCI pair describes a single ATM circuit. When one orders an ATM link from a telco, they typically provision a virtual path, specifying a particular VPI. The customer may then define as many private virtual circuits (PVCs) over that path as they wish, by choosing a unique VCI for each one.

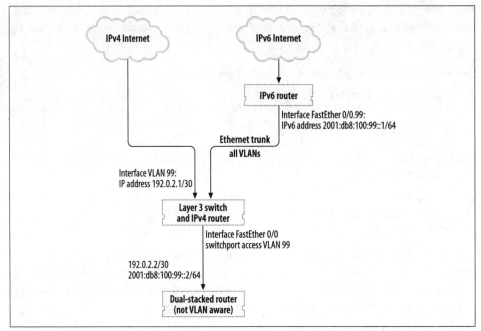

Figure 6-4. Connecting a dual-stacked customer via an IPv4-only layer 3 switch

Normally when used for IP we would configure a single PVC and set its bandwidth to be the same as the bandwidth provided by the telco for the entire virtual path. If the termination points for this PVC are both dual-stacked routers, then we can simply run both IPv4 and IPv6 over the same PVC.

Suppose, however, that one of the routers is IPv4-only. If your circuits land on an ATM switch, rather than directly onto the IPv4-only router, then we can configure a second PVC. The ATM switch can deliver this second PVC to an IPv6-capable router and can be used to provide an IPv6 service without disturbing the original IPv4 connectivity. This is shown in Figure 6-5.

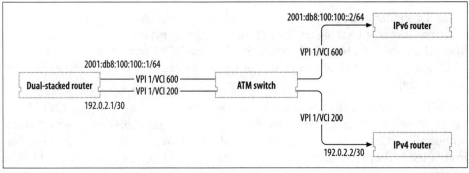

Figure 6-5. Using a second PVC to provide IPv6

Unlike the VLAN workarounds described above, you must set aside some bandwidth to be dedicated to your IPv6 PVC. If you do not, then you risk oversubscribing your link, and your telco will start dropping cells. (Dropping cells is much worse than dropping packets: you tend to lose bits of packets instead of whole ones, and the impact of congestion is made much, much worse.)

MPLS and 6PE

MPLS, or by its full name Multi Protocol Label Switching, is a mechanism to deploy circuit-switched paths around an IP network. Translated for us mortals, the notion is this: there are lots of destination addresses, but often only a small number of paths through a network that are all that frequently used. On a straight IP-only network, every single router does a lookup in its routing table every time it forwards a packet.

With MPLS, all the (relevant) paths in the IP network are set up in advance (usually automatically.) Then the very first MPLS router that encounters a packet will perform the destination lookup, choose the path that will get it to that destination, and will label it. Each subsequent router checks the label (which is a much less onerous task than looking up the destination address,) changes the label if necessary, and then forwards the labelled packet to the next MPLS router. This repeats until the labelled packet reaches its destination in the MPLS network, at which point the label is removed and ordinary routing resumes.

Now, contemporary MPLS networks are usually based on an IPv4 infrastructure. However, a close look reveals that while IPv4 is used in these networks for the setup of labels and paths, it is not used at any point in the transmission of packets. So the packet that gets labelled and passed around doesn't have to be an IPv4 packet at all.

Cisco's implementations of AToM (Any Transport over MPLS) and EoMPLS (Ethernet over MPLS) take advantage of this to allow the operator to set up layer 2 circuits over their MPLS network. One can of course run IPv6 over Ethernet or ATM (the transmission protocol used for AToM). If your equipment has this capability, then this may be an easy way to get high performance IPv6 transmission in your core.

One can also remove the middle-man of an extra Layer 2 protocol and label-and-forward IPv6 packets directly. In this instance, the routers at the edge of the MPLS network (typically called "PE" or Provider Edge routers) must be dual-stacked. This is because they obviously need to be able to transmit IPv6 packets, but they must also run IPv4 BGP and take part in the IPv4 setup underlying the MPLS network.

Cisco's implementation of this is called 6PE. To make this happen, it takes advantage of the flexibility found in multiprotocol BGP. Each PE router sets up BGP sessions, over IPv4, with the other PE routers in the network. (We're assuming, of course, that the core that connects them doesn't have IPv6 capability, hence the need to run these sessions over IPv4). The PE routers are then configured to advertise their IPv6 prefixes over their IPv4 BGP sessions—along with the labels needed to reach them. Without the labels, this would be madness; your precious IPv6 routes would be sent to other routers with a next-hop in IPv4-land. In this configuration, however, the packets are labelled and sent through the MPLS network to the remote router with the complicity of the IPv4-only core.

Accounting for hacks

While the methods described above are workarounds rather than permanent deployment strategies, some do have one distinct advantage in common—you have a router interface which is guaranteed to contain only IPv6 traffic. This makes measuring IPv6 traffic with MRTG and other SNMP tools a doddle; many vendors still don't have separate IPv6 counters for true dual-stacked interfaces.

If your equipment doesn't support per-protocol byte and packet counters and you would prefer not to use the sub-interface methods we have described, then it may still be possible to count traffic using firewall or ACL rules. When considering such an option, remember that enabling ACLs on some platforms carries a performance penalty.

Summary

In this chapter we've covered quite a lot of technical detail on the operating of infrastructure services that keep a network running. The core of this is really the operation of DNS, which everyone running a network will interact with at some time. We've also looked at routing, firewalling and network management, all of which are likely to be issues in moderate sized networks. The other thing that we looked at was 6to4 Relay Routers and Faith as examples of the sort of infrastructure that may be useful for IPv4 and IPv6 interoperation. We've also looked how you can provide IPv6 at layer 2 without upsetting your IPv4 infrastructure.

## CHAPTER 7

Services

A satisfied customer; we should have him stuffed.
—*Fawlty Towers*

In this chapter, we talk about commonly deployed network services, and how they can be configured and offered over IPv6. We have assume a basic familiarity with the services and software discussed, and focus on issues relating to IPv6 deployment.

General Notes

Most of the higher level protocols that you are familiar with can theoretically be transported over IPv6 with almost no modification. All that's generally required is that the clients and servers be modified to make and accept IPv6 connections rather than IPv4.* A good example of this is NNTP: many people are now taking Usenet news feeds over IPv6 as a way to move some bulk traffic from IPv4 to IPv6 while having a minimal impact on customers.

Unfortunately, there are some exceptions to the general case. Some of these exceptions are minor "layering violations" and do not greatly affecting the rewriting of a given application to support IPv6. For example, the Received: header in SMTP can mention the IPv4 address of the host mail was received from, such as [127.0.0.1]. Clearly, this needs only minor changes to operate over IPv6: mail received from the IPv6 localhost would be denoted [IPv6:::1]† instead. More serious problems arise when IPv4 addresses are a semantic part of the protocol itself. Here addresses may be embedded within the protocol to be later interpreted by the other communicants as, perhaps, a message indicating where a connection should be made. Protocols like this have generally needed extension for IPv6 compatibility, but are usually easy to spot because they are the same ones that require special treatment by NAT devices.

---

* We look at how clients and servers can be updated in Chapter 8, although this will usually be done for you by your vendor.

† Yes, there really should be three colons here!

Once the protocol supports IPv6 we have to think about how to deploy the software. On a dual-stacked host you may have the option of configuring a single daemon to provide both the IPv6 and IPv4 service, or you may be able to run independent daemons: the best option depends on the situation. For a resource intensive application with mature IPv6 support, the correct choice is likely to be a single daemon. In a situation where some experimentation and tweaking of the service will be needed, it may be best to opt for independent daemons.

 Remember you may have the option of running an IPv4 and IPv6 service on different hosts by using DNS to advertise a single name for the IPv4 address of one host and the IPv6 address of the other.

Sometimes the function of the daemon in question makes the decision even easier. For example, there is little point in running two NTP daemons to synchronize your clock, because any one machine only has a single clock! If you were running two daemons to provide clock synchronization sources over IPv4 and IPv6, it would make sense to tell only one to control the local clock.

Inetd/TCP Wrappers

Inetd, a daemon that manages many smaller network services, is available on most Unix systems. Traditionally, these services have included diagnostic capabilities like generating and discarding data, management of Unix services such as telnet, FTP, and finger, and sometimes slightly more heavyweight applications such as IMAP and its encrypted relatives.

Most of these services have obvious extensions into the IPv6 world, and so inetd also needs to be changed. AIX, FreeBSD, Tru64 and Solaris all provide an IPv6-capable version of inetd. Some Linux distributions provide a version of inetd, while others use a variant of inetd called xinetd, which also supports IPv6. OS X provides inetd and xinetd, though only xinetd supports IPv6. If your system's inetd does not support IPv6, then you can get xinetd from *http://www.xinetd.org/*.

The services inetd provides are configured in */etc/inetd.conf*. In the traditional format of this file, the third field is either *tcp* or *udp*, to indicate the sort of service inetd should run. This has been extended to also allow *tcp6* or *udp6*, indicating that IPv6 services are provided. For example, the following would configure inetd to listen for telnet connections over IPv6 and IPv4.

```
telnet stream tcp  nowait  root  /usr/libexec/telnetd  telnetd
telnet stream tcp6 nowait  root  /usr/libexec/telnetd  telnetd
```

There are several points to note about this setup. First, it is usually not necessary to configure a separate daemon for IPv4 and IPv6, as an IPv6 daemon can provide services to IPv4 clients if IPv4 mapped addresses[*] are enabled. However, having one

---

[*] Mapped addresses are explained in the "Mapped IPv4 Addresses" section in Chapter 8.

daemon configured for IPv4 and one for IPv6 shouldn't cause a problem. Second, you do not have to configure the same daemon for IPv4 as IPv6—this may provide an opportunity to migrate to a new piece of software. Third, and more insidious, while inetd itself is IPv6 enabled, this does not mean that the daemons it launches are. Very simple TCP daemons may be protocol agnostic, but most of them will need alterations to support IPv6. The good news is that the mainstream server daemons have already been altered.

 On some inetd implementations "tcp6" means only IPv6 connections. KAME-based versions allow you to say "tcp46" to allow both IPv4 and IPv6 connections via a single configuration line. It may be simpler to configure one line for IPv4 and another for IPv6.

One of the most common tools used with inetd is Wietse Venema's *TCP wrappers*. They implement a flexible access control and logging mechanism that can be "wrapped" around services run from inetd.* If you are wrapping IPv6-based services, or wrapping IPv4-based services provided through a tcp6 *inetd.conf* entry, the version of TCP wrappers you're using must have IPv6 support. The most common symptom of getting this wrong is TCP wrappers reporting all connecting IP addresses as 0.0.0.0! You can find the IPv6-enabled version of TCP wrappers at *ftp://ftp.porcupine.org/pub/ipv6/*.

Configuring an IPv6 service in xinetd is easy; just add IPv6 to the flags line of the configuration file for the service in question. In all other respects the configuration is the same as that for IPv4.

HTTP

HTTP can be delivered over IPv6 by a large array of web servers. We'll deal with the two most popular here: Apache (version 2) and IIS. We'll also cover some general issues that may arise when using an IPv6-enabled server.

It may be worth noting that IPv6 has slightly extended the format of URLs to allow IPv6 addresses: see the "When IPv6 Addresses Don't Fit" section in Chapter 8 for details.

Apache

Apache can be downloaded from *http://httpd.apache.org/* and a precompiled version of Apache for Microsoft Windows can be found at *http://win6.jp/Apache2/*. Documentation for Apache can also be found on the Apache web site, including a

---

* Some versions of inetd have special features for cooperating with TCP wrappers: for example, the ENABLE_ TCPWRAPPERS option in Solaris or FreeBSD's -w and -W options. TCP wrappers support can also be a built-in part of an application.

section on installation in the reference manual. Apache 2 is the current release family, though Apache 1.3 is still in widespread use.

Although Apache 1.3 can support IPv6, we do not recommend you use it. Perhaps the most important reason is that Apache 2 is an inherently better platform on which to deploy web services anyway: the code quality, performance and scalability have improved dramatically since Apache 1.x. In more practical terms, the IPv6 patch for 1.x has a tendency to play nastily with other patches, which can be problematic for existing deployments.

While Apache 2 is the preferable option, some people may prefer to stick with Apache 1.3, because of policy or the availability of third-party/in-house modules. In cases like this there are two options. First, Apache 2 can be installed separately to support IPv6, and then hung off an IPv6-only address with minimal impact on system resources. Second, Apache 2 could be used in *reverse proxy* mode, where it proxies the content from a different server, but can serve it over IPv6. This second technique can be used to proxy the content of any web server, not just an Apache server. Consequently, it is already commonly deployed to improve the security or performance of other web servers. Of course, there is an administrative overhead involved with running an extra piece of software to proxy a web server.

Apache as a server on dual-stacked or IPv6 only hosts

The changes required when using Apache for IPv6 alone or for dual IPv4/IPv6 are minimal. If, in your existing configuration, you have specified that the server should operate on a particular IPv4 address, you'll need to updated the configuration to include an IPv6 addresses. You'll want to check for IPv4 addresses in the Listen directive, the definition of virtual hosts, and IP-based access restrictions. Remember that some of these configuration directives may live in Apache's *.htaccess* files.

The default Listen directive, Listen 80, is now equivalent to Listen [::]:80. Note that the IPv6 address is enclosed in square brackets. This results in the server listening on all IPv4 and IPv6 addresses, unless mapped IPv4 is disabled, in which case it will listen only to IPv6, and you'll want to add the line Listen 0.0.0.0:80 to also listen on all IPv4 addresses.

If you choose to upgrade to Apache 2, there is a short list of other changes to watch out for at *http://httpd.apache.org/docs-2.0/upgrading.html*. Example 7-1 shows the changes[*] to the configuration file of www.maths.tcd.ie when it was upgraded from Apache 1.3 to Apache 2. The ServerType directive was removed and the Port and FancyIndexing directives were replaced with Listen and IndexOptions directives respectively. Access restrictions based on IPv4 addresses were extended to cover the equivalent IPv6 ranges. Similar small changes to *.htaccess* files were also made.

---

[*] The changes are in the diff format, explained in the "Conventions Used in This Book" section in the Preface.

Example 7-1. Configuration changes for Apache 1.3 to 2.0 upgrade

```
--- httpd.conf      2002/10/14 18:42:23      1.24
+++ httpd.conf      2002/10/29 11:12:26      1.25
@@ -2,9 +2,7 @@
 # Apache http deamon configuration file
 #

-# Inetd vs Standalone
-ServerType standalone
-Port 80
+Listen 80

 # Do DNS resolution
 HostnameLookups double
@@ -92,6 +90,7 @@
 order deny,allow
 deny from all
 allow from 134.226.81.
+allow from 2001:770:10:300::/56
 </Location>

 <Location /server-info>
@@ -99,6 +98,7 @@
 order deny,allow
 deny from all
 allow from 134.226.81.
+allow from 2001:770:10:300::/56
 </Location>
@@ -159,7 +159,7 @@
 # Icon information for directory indices
 #
 <IfModule mod_autoindex.c>
-        FancyIndexing on
+        IndexOptions FancyIndexing

        AddIconByEncoding (CMP,/icons/compressed.gif) x-compress x-gzip
```

Apache for reverse proxying (IP address-based)

Example 7-2 shows[*] a simple example of reverse proxying an IPv4 web server, running on the same host www.example.com. We assume that IPv4 connections will be served by the original web server and our Apache 2 server only needs to deal with IPv6 connections.

We ask the server to listen on all IPv6 addresses and then load the necessary modules.[†] In the VirtualHost section we specify the name of the server that Apache will pretend to be. The ProxyPass directive tells Apache to pass on incoming requests to

---

[*] We only show the lines of configuration that differ from the default Apache 2 configuration file.

[†] If your version of Apache does not support dynamically loaded modules, then these modules must be compiled in. This can be done by passing the --enable-modules="proxy proxy_http …" option to Apache's configure program.

the server running on 127.0.0.1. The ProxyPassReverse applies any necessary transformations in the response. Note, that we forward the connection using the IPv4 address, rather than the name www.example.com, which may have an associated IPv6 address and so result in a loop.

Example 7-2. Reverse proxying localhost with Apache

```
Listen [::]:80

LoadModule proxy_module libexec/apache2/mod_proxy.so
LoadModule proxy_http_module libexec/apache2/mod_proxy_http.so

<VirtualHost *>
    ServerName www.example.com
    ProxyPass / http://127.0.0.1/
    ProxyPassReverse / http://127.0.0.1/
</VirtualHost>
```

Example 7-3 shows a more complex example, where we use a single Apache server to make two web servers available over IPv6. Here Apache is operating on a machine with two IPv6 addresses, 2002:c000:0204::1 and 2002:c000:0204::2. Connections to the first address are forwarded to 127.0.0.1, as in the previous example. Connections to the second address are forwarded to support.example.com, which we assume resolves to an address of another server. The address 2002:c000:0204::2 should be advertised in DNS as v6support.example.com. If we advertised it as support.example.com, then we would risk a forwarding loop.

Example 7-3. Reverse proxying two servers using multiple IPv6 addresses

```
Listen [2002:c000:0204::1]:80
Listen [2002:c000:0204::2]:80

LoadModule proxy_module libexec/apache2/mod_proxy.so
LoadModule proxy_http_module libexec/apache2/mod_proxy_http.so

<VirtualHost [2002:c000:0204::1]>
    ServerName www.example.com
    ProxyPass / http://127.0.0.1/
    ProxyPassReverse / http://127.0.0.1/
</VirtualHost>

<VirtualHost [2002:c000:0204::2]>
    ServerName v6support.example.com
    ProxyPass / http://support.example.com/
    ProxyPassReverse / http://support.example.com/
</VirtualHost>
```

Apache for reverse proxying (name-based)

Example 7-4 shows a second example of using a single Apache server to make two servers available. Rather than using IP addresses, this time we use *name-based virtual hosting*, enabled with the `NameVirtualHost` directive. With name-based virtual hosting we use the `Host:` header sent by web browsers to decide which server we are reverse proxying for. If the browser sends `www.example.com`, then Apache will forward the connection to `www4.example.com`. If the browser sends `support.example.com` or `support.ipv6.example.com` the connection is forwarded to `support4.example.com`. Browsers that send any other hostname will match the first virtual host section and the request will be forwarded to `www4.example.com`.

Note that we have forwarded these connections to `www4.example.com` and `support4.example.com`, which we expect to resolve to the IPv4 address of the real servers. As we have used names, rather than addresses, these two names could resolve to the same IPv4 address and the real server could also use name based virtual hosting to decide what content should be served. In our previous examples, the proxy's connections to `www.example.com` would have sent the hostname `127.0.0.1`.

Example 7-4. Reverse proxying two servers using name-based virtual hosts

```
Listen [::]:80

LoadModule proxy_module libexec/apache2/mod_proxy.so
LoadModule proxy_http_module libexec/apache2/mod_proxy_http.so

NameVirtualHost *

<VirtualHost *>
    ServerName www.example.com
    ProxyPass / http://www4.example.com/
    ProxyPassReverse / http://www4.example.com/
</VirtualHost>

<VirtualHost *>
    ServerName support.example.com
    ServerAlias support.ipv6.example.com
    ProxyPass / http://support4.example.com/
    ProxyPassReverse / http://support4.example.com/
</VirtualHost>
```

Gotchas

We'll mention a couple of Apache IPv6-specific gotchas here, but there are also a few general points you'll want to think about when offering HTTP over IPv6. We cover those in the "General Issues" section later in this chapter.

Some older versions of Apache disabled IPv6 on platforms that had particular issues with IPv6 mapped addresses, such as Mac OS X. This was rather surprising for people who had enabled IPv6 support on an IPv6 capable platform, but found it didn't work. The Apache development team has now worked around these issues, and versions of Apache from 2.0.48 on should no longer have this problem.

We have also seen a problem with TCP checksum offloading. TCP checksum offloading is an optimization where the network card itself calculates packet checksums, saving time on the main CPU. Unfortunately, some network cards have trouble calculating the checksum for IPv6 packets. On Linux, this can be worked around by disabling the use of the sendfile system call in Apache, by giving configure the flag --without-sendfile before compilation of Apache, or by using the EnableSendfile off directive. We have not heard of this issue on other platforms, but this is probably because Linux makes use of checksum offloading on a wider variety of hardware.

IIS

Naturally, IIS can only serve content over IPv6 if the underlying operating system and DLLs also support IPv6, but thankfully when you enable IPv6 on your Windows system, this should be done for you. The good news is that once the stack has been enabled, as described in Chapter 5, IIS picks up on this automatically; you only need to restart IIS to have it notice that it can listen for requests over IPv6.

Basic support for IPv6 in IIS as shipped with Windows 2003 is pretty complete. IPv6 addresses will be written to log files and variables such as LOCAL_ADDR and REMOTE_ADDR will be set to the IPv6 address for IPv6 connections, though REMOTE_HOST will always be set to the IPv6 address rather than the hostname.

However, some of IIS's non-core features do not support IPv6 at all. One example is the access restrictions based on IP address, which cannot be configured for IPv6 addresses because the GUI provides no way to enter them! Microsoft provides a fuller list of areas lacking IPv6 support at *http://www.microsoft.com/resources/documentation/IIS/6/all/techref/en-us/iisRG_IP6_5.mspx*

Possibly the most significant limitations are on ServerBindings, routing, and SSL. ServerBindings, the rough equivalent of Apache's virtual hosting, can't yet make decisions based on IPv6 addresses. This means that you have to make decisions based on the HTTP "Host:" header. As this header isn't available early enough in the HTTP decoding process when accessing SSL-based sites, you are restricted to just one SSL site on the usual SSL port.

General Issues

Web servers are often highly integrated with other systems via CGI programs, Active Server Pages, PHP and the like. If you are using one of these systems and it deals with IP addresses, then it may need to be updated to expect IPv6 addresses. For example, CGI programs using the REMOTE_ADDR environment variable should be checked.

If you are using reverse proxying, you may also have to think about what addresses accesses come from. For example, if a dual-stacked host is used to provide an IPv6 front end to an IPv4-only web server, then the REMOTE_ADDR variable on the IPv4-only server will show the dual-stacked host's address for all proxied connections. You may be able to use the HTTP_X_FORWARDED_FOR variable as a substitute when the REMOTE_ADDR is that of your dual-stacked host.

One other place where web servers export IP addresses is in log files. Log analysis software should be checked for its reaction to finding an IPv6 format address in a log file—perhaps even for IPv4 connections, if the server uses mapped addresses such as ::ffff:192.0.2.4 for IPv4 connections. For software that has not been updated for IPv6, the most likely reaction is to skip lines it considers malformed. Again, if you are reverse proxying, remember that you will also need to process the logs produced by the reverse proxy.

HTTP Proxies and Caches

Many organizations have deployed HTTP proxies to control access to the web, or proxy caches to reduce demand where bandwidth is scarce. If your web proxy/cache already supports IPv6,* then all you really need to configure are the ACLs corresponding to your IPv6 address space. Unfortunately, support for IPv6 is missing in Squid and some other well-known proxy/cache implementations. We'll use Squid as an example of an IPv4-only proxy cache here, but the examples could be applied to any other system with similar limitations.

Apache 2's IPv6 support extends to proxying and caching, and can be used as a cache/proxy itself. However, in some cases there may be investment in IPv4-only software (such as HTTP virus scanners or other content filtering systems) or hardware (such as high end cache appliances). For this reason, we also consider using Apache to add IPv6 capabilities to another proxy.

We will look at three examples here. First we'll look at using Apache as a proxy cache, as it has all the necessary support. Second, we'll look at using Apache as a parent cache for Squid as a way to allow Squid to fetch pages from the IPv6 Internet. Finally, we'll look at using Apache to allow IPv6-only clients talk to Squid.

Using Apache as a Proxy/Cache

In Apache 2, proxy support and cache support are independent. The proxy module allows both forward proxying, which we'll discuss in this section, and reverse proxying, as described in the "Apache" section earlier in this chapter. Caching support is provided by a separate set of modules, which provide a generic caching layer backed by main memory, disks and possibly other devices in the future. Caching support is currently marked as experimental in the Apache documentation; we won't examine it here.

Using Apache as a proxy is straight-forward. You load the modules required for proxying (there is a generic module and specific modules for HTTP, FTP and CONNECT), you enable proxying, and then set your required access restrictions. Note that proxying can be enabled on a per-virtual-host basis.

---

* We don't know of many proxy/caches that support IPv6 yet. Network Appliance's NetCache supports IPv6, though we have no personal experience of it.

Always remember to restrict access to any sort of proxy, so that only legitimate users can use it. Otherwise, you risk being used as a relay for junk mail or attacks on other organizations.

Example 7-5 shows an example of this basic configuration where Apache listens on IPv4 and IPv6 port 3128, the required modules are loaded and access to the proxy is permitted from 2001:db8:d0:d00::/56 and 192.0.2.0/24. Figure 7-1 shows how the requests make their way from IPv4/IPv6 clients to the IPv4/IPv6 Internet.

Example 7-5. Using Apache as an IPv4/IPv6 Proxy

```
Listen [::]:3128
Listen 0.0.0.0:3128

LoadModule proxy_module libexec/apache2/mod_proxy.so
LoadModule proxy_connect_module libexec/apache2/mod_proxy_connect.so
LoadModule proxy_ftp_module libexec/apache2/mod_proxy_ftp.so
LoadModule proxy_http_module libexec/apache2/mod_proxy_http.so

ProxyRequests On

<Proxy *>
    Order deny,allow
    Deny from all
    Allow from 2001:db8:d0:d00::/56
    Allow from 192.0.2.0/24
</Proxy>
```

Once this Apache proxy is up and running, IPv4 and IPv6 clients can be configured to use port 3128 on this host as a proxy.

Using Apache to Fetch Content for an IPv4-Only Proxy/Cache

The example we consider in this section shows how to continue to use Squid as a cache, but to arrange for Apache to fetch the web pages for Squid, allowing users to fetch web pages from the IPv6 Internet. Figure 7-2 shows this arrangement of Squid and Apache. At the same time, we avoid having to translate client access controls from Squid to Apache. To achieve this, we configure Apache in proxy mode and allow connections from 127.0.0.1. Next we configure Squid to use Apache as a parent proxy. Example 7-6 and Example 7-7 shows the Apache and Squid configurations for this setup. The Apache configuration is easy enough, listening on port 8001 and allowing connections from 127.0.0.1. Squid is instructed to use port 8001 as a parent and the no-query option specifies not to use ICP, the inter-cache protocol. Usually Squid will not ask a parent for material that cannot be cached, such as the output of CGI scripts. The nonhierarchical_direct no option tells Squid to ask its parent for this content.

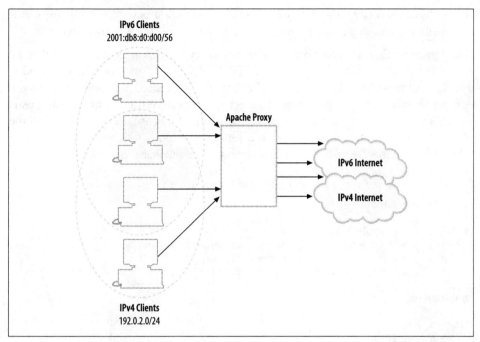

Figure 7-1. Using Apache as a dual-stack Proxy

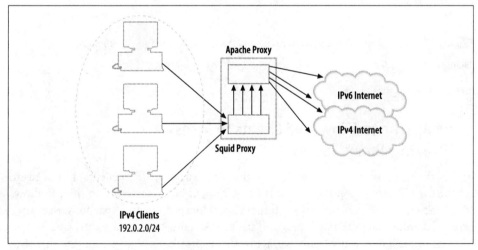

Figure 7-2. A dual-stack parent proxy setup

With this configuration, there are three points of note. First, we used 127.0.0.1 rather than localhost, this is because we don't want Apache binding to ::1 when Squid expects to contact it on the IPv4-loopback address. Second, IPv6-only clients will still not be able to talk to Squid in this setup, as Squid is only capable of listening for IPv4 connections. Finally, while this configuration adds an extra point of failure, Squid is smart enough to detect a non-responding parent and will automatically switch to fetching pages itself if its Apache parent becomes unavailable.

One parameter that we didn't configure in this example was the port numbers that we are permitted to connect to using the HTTP "CONNECT" method. This method is usually used to proxy SSL connections, but can also be abused in various ways, so the port numbers to which a proxy can connect are usually restricted. In Apache this is controlled with the AllowCONNECT directive and in Squid it is usually controlled with the SSL_ports ACL. By default these are both set to allow ports 443 and 564, but if you have adjusted either Squid's or Apache's settings, you will want them to be consistent.

Example 7-6. Proxying using Squid as a cache and Apache to fetch (Apache configuration)

```
Listen 127.0.0.1:8001

LoadModule proxy_module libexec/apache2/mod_proxy.so
LoadModule proxy_connect_module libexec/apache2/mod_proxy_connect.so
LoadModule proxy_ftp_module libexec/apache2/mod_proxy_ftp.so
LoadModule proxy_http_module libexec/apache2/mod_proxy_http.so

ProxyRequests On

<Proxy *>
    Order deny,allow
    Deny from all
    Allow from 127.0.0.1
</Proxy>
```

Example 7-7. Proxying using Squid as a cache and Apache to fetch (Squid configuration)

```
cache_peer 127.0.0.1          parent   8001  7 default no-query

nonhierarchical_direct off
```

Using Apache to Allow IPv6 Clients to Access an IPv4 Only Proxy/Cache

In this situation, we have a Proxy/Cache that only supports IPv4 clients, but needs to support IPv6 clients also. Initially, this situation will be quite common since it allows IPv6 web clients to surf the IPv4 Internet. To achieve this with Apache, we set up a proxy, listening on an IPv6 address and use the Apache ProxyRemote directive to redirect the request to the IPv4-only proxy. In this example we'll also combine this with the ability for the IPv4 cache to fetch IPv6 web pages, using a similar technique to that in the previous section. Figure 7-3 shows the arrangement of Squid and Apache we'll configure.

Suppose that the IPv4-only cache proxy.example.com has IPv4 address 192.0.2.9 and that we want to run Apache on another dual-stacked host with IPv4 address 192.0.2.10 and IPv6 address 2001:db8:d0:d00::a.

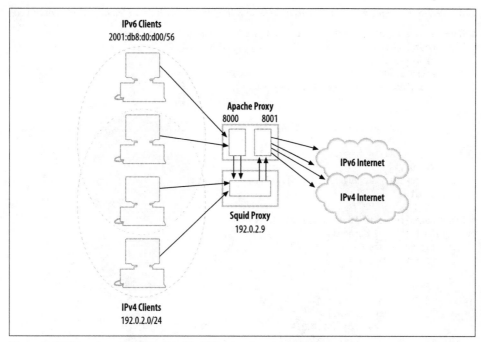

Figure 7-3. Using Apache to provide IPv6 client and parent support

Example 7-8 shows an Apache configuration that defines two virtual hosts. The first virtual host listens on IPv6 port 8000 and forwards those requests to the IPv4-only cache, i.e. 192.0.2.9 port 8000. Note that we restrict access to port 8000 to our IPv6 clients, that in this example we have taken to be 2001:db8:d0:d00::/56. This first virtual host is all that is needed to forward IPv6 client requests to the IPv4-only cache. Once we have tested this setup, we could add an AAAA record for proxy.example.com pointing to 2001:db8:d0:d00::a.

The second virtual host shows again how a single Apache server can perform multiple tasks. It acts in a similar way to the setup described in the previous section, where Apache acts as a parent to an IPv4-only cache, allowing it to fetch pages from IPv6-only servers. The configuration slightly differs from that in the previous section because the IPv4-only cache and Apache are running on separate hosts. Naturally, the IPv4-only cache would be configured to use 192.0.2.10 port 8001 as a parent proxy.

Example 7-8. Proxying using Apache as a cache and IPv6 proxy, with Squid fetching IPv4

```
Listen 192.0.2.10:8001
Listen [::]:8000

LoadModule proxy_module libexec/apache2/mod_proxy.so
LoadModule proxy_connect_module libexec/apache2/mod_proxy_connect.so
LoadModule proxy_ftp_module libexec/apache2/mod_proxy_ftp.so
LoadModule proxy_http_module libexec/apache2/mod_proxy_http.so
```

Example 7-8. Proxying using Apache as a cache and IPv6 proxy, with Squid fetching IPv4 (continued)

```
# IPv6 clients make requests to this host and we forward them to the cache.
<VirtualHost [::]:8000>
        ProxyRequests On
        ProxyVia On
        ProxyRemote * http://192.0.2.9:8000/

        <Proxy *>
                Order deny,allow
                Deny from all
                Allow from 2001:db8:d0:d00::/56
        </Proxy>
        CustomLog /var/log/httpd-v6clients.log combined
</VirtualHost>

# Cache makes requests to this virtual host.
<VirtualHost 192.0.2.10:8001>
        ProxyRequests On
        ProxyVia On

        <Proxy *>
                Order deny,allow
                Deny from all
                Allow from 192.0.2.9
        </Proxy>
        CustomLog /var/log/httpd-parent.log combined
</VirtualHost>
```

This "Apache sandwich" in some respects is a wasteful configuration because requests from IPv6 clients will go to Apache's IPv6 port 8000, be forwarded to the IPv4-only cache's port 8000 and then be forwarded back to port Apache's IPv4 8001 and then on to either the IPv4 or IPv6 Internet. However, it is an example of how IPv6 can be introduced around an IPv4-only proxy allowing IPv4-only and IPv6-only clients access to both IPv4-only and IPv6-only servers.

Small Proxies

In some cases, Apache might be a bit heavy-weight as a proxy. For example, if your favorite browser does not yet support IPv6 then you might want to run a small proxy on your laptop to allow you to browse IPv6 web sites while on the road.

One small proxy that is designed for just this sort of application is www6to4. Example 7-9 shows a basic configuration file for www6to4, which instructs it to listen for connections on port 8000 of the IPv4- and IPv6-loopback addresses. This means that your browser can now be configured to use localhost port 8000 as a proxy. Www6to4 can also be configured to forward requests to another proxy, see the sample configuration files that come with www6to4 for details.

In Example 7-9, we also configure a feature to work around broken DNS servers by shortening the timeout for URLs containing certain patterns.

Www6to4 does have some limitations, as it is designed with a minimalistic feature set in mind. Curiously, it doesn't support URLs with explicit IPv6 addresses. It also does not support access lists for controlling who can make requests through it. For this reason it's best if you only tell it to listen for connections on ::1 or 127.0.0.1.

Www6to4 is available from *http://www.vermicelli.pasta.cs.uit.no/ipv6/software.html*.

Example 7-9. Basic www6to4 config

```
listen-to          127.0.0.1,::1
listen-port          8000

# URLs containing these patterns prompt a short timeout
pattern .gif
pattern .jpg
pattern adserver.example.net
```

SMTP

SMTP is particularly well provided for in terms of Unix mailers. Below we deal with a few of the main contenders. Windows is not so well off, though Exchange should support IPv6 when the Longhorn edition is released.

Spam and IPv6

Unfortunately, and unsurprisingly, we have actually received spam over IPv6 SMTP. Most of the examples we've seen are either spam sent to a mailing list where the list's server speaks IPv6, or spam relayed through a third party, who just happens to have IPv6 connectivity. We have even seen a small amount of spam that originates from IPv6 addresses too.

One tool that has been useful in the fight against spam is DNS-based black hole lists. These are DNS names that you can look up to see if a connecting host has been reported as a spam relay. So, for example, if you get a connection from 192.0.2.4 you look up the name 4.2.0.192.spam-relays.example.com and if it exists, consideration is recommended before accepting the mail.

As you can see, this technique is dependent on IPv4 addresses, but there's no reason the same technique can't be applied to IPv6 addresses, where an address like 2001:... becomes ...1.0.0.2.spam-relays.example.com. (This can have unforeseen side effects if a blacklist includes things like "all addresses in 2.0.0.0/8", which when mistranslate to IPv6 becomes "all addresses in 2000::/4".) IPv4 and IPv6 blacklists are good ideas, but we haven't seen any blacklists with explicit IPv6 support yet.

Sendmail

Sendmail began to support IPv6 around version 8.10 and is now built with IPv6 support on many IPv6-enabled systems automatically. To enable support on a system where IPv6 may not have been detected automatically, you can enable the NETINET6 option in *sendmail/conf.h* before compiling.

 You can display the options that your version of sendmail was compiled with by running this handy command from the sendmail FAQ:

```
echo \$Z | sendmail -bt -d0
```

If you see NETINET6 mentioned, your version of sendmail supports IPv6.

Aside from building sendmail with IPv6 support, you may also need to tell sendmail to listen on both IPv4 and IPv6 addresses. Again, this is usually done automatically if the NETINET6 option has been used, but can be enabled explicitly if needed by adding:

```
DAEMON_OPTIONS(`Name=MTA-v4, Family=inet')
DAEMON_OPTIONS(`Name=MTA-v6, Family=inet6')
```

to your *sendmail.mc* file. Explicit IPv4 and IPv6 addresses can also be specified with address= field of these directives. For example

```
DAEMON_OPTIONS(`Name=IPv6, Family=inet6, address=2001:db8:d0c:ff::1')
```

will get sendmail to listen for IPv6 connections to 2001:db8:d0c:ff::1.

One gotcha particularly pertinent to sendmail is the problem of broken nameserver software misbehaving when sendmail queries for AAAA records. An unfortunately common occurrence was Spamcop, where sendmail queried for an AAAA record, to see if the mail came from a blacklisted host. The DNS software in question replied with SERVFAIL as an answer, indicating temporary name server failure, although there indeed may have been A records (or indeed other kinds of record) for the host in question. The side effect here was that blacklisted hosts could send email. This also happened in some cases where sendmail was looking for an IP address to deliver mail to, resulting in mail being delayed or even bounced as undeliverable!

Luckily, sendmail has a way to work around this behavior. You should use this line in your sendmail.mc configuration file:

```
define(`confBIND_OPTS',`WorkAroundBrokenAAAA')dnl
```

This option tells sendmail to attempt a lookup for an A record if there is a temporary failure while performing an AAAA record lookup.

Postfix

Postfix currently requires patching to support IPv6. One well regarded patch set is Dean Strik's patch from *http://www.ipnet6.org/postfix/ipv6.html*, which also provides

---

TLS support for postfix. This patch is automatically applied by some systems, for example if you choose to install Postfix from FreeBSD's ports collection, then you have the option to automatically apply it. Work to integrate these patches into the main 2.2 Postfix releases is underway.

Once postfix has been built and installed with the patch, IPv6 will be enabled and no further configuration is really necessary. If you want to set the value of a configuration option to an IPv6 address, then generally you can just use the address enclosed in "[]". The *IPv6-ChangeLog* file, included in the patch, details new configuration options and features provided.

Qmail

Qmail also requires patching for IPv6, but exactly what the best way to do this is unfortunately not as clear as for Postfix. While various patches providing IPv6 for Qmail have been available, the patch from *http://pyon.org/fujiwara/* seems to be the best choice.

Applying this patch will produce an IPv6-capable qmail-smtpd that can then be hung off an IPv6 socket, invoked either via your current IPv6-capable tools, or by patching tcpserver in the ucspi package using the patch available at *http://www.fefe.de/ucspi/*.

Exim

Exim ships with good IPv6 support, though you may need to add HAVE_IPV6=YES to *Local/Makefile* if it is not enabled by default on your operating system. The one quirk is how IPv6 addresses are specified in config files, where ":" has traditionally been used as a separator. You must replace each colon with a double colon, leading to configuration lines like:

```
hostlist relay_from_hosts = 127.0.0.1 : ::::1 : 192.0.2.4
```

Alternatively, if the list begins with a less-than symbol, then the next character will be used as a separator instead. For example, to use a ";" character as a separator you'd say:

```
hostlist relay_from_hosts = <; 127.0.0.1 ; ::1 ; 192.0.2.4
```

POP/IMAP

We've seen that there are many options for IPv6 mail transport agents on Unix-like systems, both in terms of out-of-the-box support and patches for the remaining well-known systems. In terms of POP and IMAP we are similarly well-provided for.

WU-IMAP

The University of Washington's IMAP server (available from *http://www.washington. edu/imap/*) doesn't much care if it is run over IPv6, IPv4 or something completely different.* So, if your inetd supports IPv6, and you're already using this IMAP daemon, then running IMAP over IPv6 is as easy as editing your */etc/inetd.conf* and adding a line like:

```
imap    stream  tcp6    nowait  root    /usr/sbin/tcpd imapd
```

If you need logs of where your IPv6 IMAP connections are coming from, then unfortunately WU-IMAP can't do this for you. However, you can use TCP wrappers to do it instead. For example, consider the following line in */etc/hosts.allow*:

```
imapd: ALL : severity mail.info : allow
```

This will allow all connections to the program imapd, syslogging them to the mail facility at level info. Naturally, your vendor's inetd (or xinetd) may provide additional logging options.

Courier-IMAP

Courier-IMAP is a POP 3 and IMAP server available from *http://www.courier-mta.org/imap/*. It works with Qmail style Maildir mailboxes and has lots of nice features, like supporting POP and IMAP with TLS.

When you compile Courier-IMAP, it automatically enables IPv6 if it detects support for IPv6 in the operating system. In our experience this is a no-brainer once installed, and it generally just works.

Qpopper

The Qpopper program, available from *http://www.eudora.com/qpopper/* does not support IPv6 out of the box. Patches are available from *http://www.imasy.or.jp/~ume/ipv6/* for versions 3.1 and 4.0 of the daemon. We haven't used these patches personally, but they are used in the FreeBSD ports system, and so should be well tested and supported.

Cyrus Imapd2

The Cyrus imapd, often used at sites where the IMAP users do not have normal logins to the IMAP server, supports IPv6 from version 2.2.0. Cyrus can be obtained from *http://asg.web.cmu.edu/cyrus/download/*. Patches are available for earlier versions of Cyrus at *http://www.imasy.or.jp/~ume/ipv6/*.

NNTP

As mentioned earlier, NNTP transport has been a popular choice for conversion to IPv6. Strangely though, despite seemingly significant deployment, the standard news

---

* IP over albatross anyone?

servers have been slow to ship with built-in IPv6 support, usually requiring patches. It is possible that this tells us something about the sort of people who run news servers…

The 2.4.X family of INN releases ship with IPv6 support. To enable it you must configure it with the --enable-ipv6 flag. For IPv6 support to work, innd must be started via inndstart, but this is the usual configuration. You may also need to specify a bindaddress6 in *inn.conf*, enclosed in double quotes. For more details, see the usual INN man pages.

Version 5.0 of Diablo supports IPv6. Though the support is experimental it has been used in CVS versions of Diablo for several years and it seems to work well. Advice on installing, the Diablo download page, release notes, hints for upgrading and mailing lists can be found off *http://www.openusenet.org/diablo/*.

Leafnode is commonly run by those who don't want to run a whole news server, just to allow a few users to read a few Usenet groups. Leafnode has supported IPv6 for a few years, though if you are compiling it yourself you'll need to run configure with the --with-ipv6 option.

NTP

NTP, the Network Time Protocol, is an important but often overlooked piece of infrastructure, despite Y2K making time-keeping a lot more relevant to the average network. Probably the foremost implementation of it is the NTP daemon series that David Mills is responsible for.

Mills's Ntpd

The 4.1.X* family of release versions of ntpd do not support NTP over IPv6. Version 4.1.74, which was a development snapshot of the code that became the 4.2.0 release of ntpd, was the first version to support IPv6. All releases after this (including 4.2.0) should support IPv6 if your operating system does.

Details of the most recent production, development snapshot and development versions of ntpd can be found at *http://www.ntp.org/*, including downloads of releases, snapshots and details of how to get development versions, if you need bleeding-edge features.

The network support in ntpd, as currently implemented, will only try to use the first address returned for any hostname. This has some serious implications for IPv6-capable ntpd—it will not fall back to IPv4 if an NTP server cannot be reached over IPv6. Indeed, ntpd will not fall back to other IPv4 addresses if the contacting server's first IPv4 address does not work out. This means that upgrading to a version of ntpd that can speak IPv6 may result in it losing contact with your NTP servers.

---

* For small X.

So, how can you avoid getting out of touch? One simple option is to tell ntpd to use only IPv4 by using the -4 command line option. Naturally, this isn't very useful if you actually want to use IPv6. Another option is to use the -4 option in */etc/ntp.conf*, for example, if you have a peer that you know only speaks NTP over IPv4, then you can change peer ntp.example.com to peer -4 ntp.example.com.

This suggests the following plan for upgrading hosts running ntpd:

- Before adding AAAA DNS records in order to advertise an NTP server as having an IPv6 address, make sure you have installed a version of ntpd that can speak IPv6.

- When upgrading ntpd, check that you can contact all the hosts listed as peers or servers in */etc/ntp.conf*. You can do this using ntpq -pn server.host.name or by starting ntpd and monitoring it with ntpq. If you find that a host that cannot be contacted, then see if trying IPv4 using ntpq -pn4 server.host.name works. If it does, use peer -4 or server -4 in the *ntp.conf* config file.

Other Time-Synchronization Software

Other IPv6-capable NTP software is appearing now that IPv6-capable ntpd servers are becoming more common. OpenBSD provide their own IPv6-capable ntpd and also an IPv6-capable rdate that can use SNTP. Another implementation of the Simple NTP protocol that is protocol-independent is available from *http://www.viagenie.qc.ca/fr/ipv6/ntpv6/utilisation.shtml*, though we have not used it ourselves. Dan Bernstein's popular clockspeed package does not yet support IPv6, though patches have been produced. We've yet to see IPv6 time synchronization software for Windows.

Protocols other than NTP are sometimes used for setting clocks. Many of these, like time and daytime, are simple enough to make the transition to IPv6 easy, but there doesn't seem to have been much interest in this given NTP's mind-share.

Syslog

At the time of writing, at least Solaris and FreeBSD support remote syslogging over IPv6. This means that you can log to a remote host using the @hostname syntax in */etc/syslog.conf* and you can also receive messages sent from another host.

Unfortunately, many operating systems, including IOS, don't yet seem to support logging over IPv6, so this service is not yet as useful as it might be.

Note that FreeBSD's logger command-line utility can send a syslog message to any remote host over IPv4 or IPv6. This can be useful for testing IPv6 support on other platforms.

Printing

There are as many protocols for printing as there are programs for sending mail, and IPv6 support varies from platform to platform and from protocol to protocol.

Windows 2003 supports printing using SMB over IPv6, which works in the usual Windows way. Windows 2003 also supports printing via the standard TCP lpr printing port, allowing it to send jobs to Unix print servers.

For people using traditional Unix printing, Solaris's lp system and FreeBSD's lpd both work over IPv6. Those using LPRng,* a reimplementation of the BSD print spooler, seem to be out of luck. It once claimed to support IPv6, but we had no luck getting version 3.8.21 to work and there do not seem to have been any recent efforts to fix this.

CUPS is also acquiring IPv6 support and should have full IPv6 support in version 1.2.

IPv6, ACLs, and DNS

One of the authors spent an afternoon trying to figure out why printing had stopped working from his workstation. Access to the printer was controlled by the */etc/hosts.lpd* file, and his machine was listed. The problem was that the print server had recently had its IPv6 address added to the DNS, and there was a typo in the workstation's reverse IPv6 DNS (see the "V6 lookups" section in Chapter 6 for details about IPv6 forward and reverse DNS), so the print server wasn't able to verify the workstation's hostname when it connected over IPv6.

In general, if:

1. Your clients have IPv6 connectivity
2. Your servers advertise IPv6 in the DNS
3. Your applications are IPv6 capable

then you need to make sure that any access control mechanisms allow IPv6 access. If those ACLs use hostnames, then you need to make sure your DNS is set up correctly. If your hosts use privacy addressing you'll need to account for that, too.

FTP

Most vendors that support IPv6 ship their systems with an IPv6-capable FTP daemon. Of course, you may need to tell inetd to run it—we covered the configuration of inetd in the "Inetd/TCP Wrappers" section earlier in this chapter. Note that even though IIS has support for IPv6, at the time of writing the Microsoft FTP server does not.

If you are running an anonymous FTP server, you may be running a more exotic FTP daemon. Wu-ftpd has been around for many years, but no new releases of it have been made for quite some time. As a consequence, no officially released version has IPv6 support, but patches are available from KAME,† and when (if?) the 2.8 release is

---

* LPRng can be obtained from *http://www.lprng.org/*.

† You can get wu-ftpd releases from *http://www.wu-ftpd.org/* and KAME patches are available from *ftp://ftp.kame.net/pub/kame/misc/*.

made it should support IPv6. Some systems have shipped wu-ftpd with the patch, including Red Hat 8. Red Hat 9 moved to vsftpd Version 1.1.3 for anonymous FTP, which doesn't support IPv6, but if you upgrade to Version 1.2* you can get IPv6 support by changing the listen directive in *vsftpd.conf* to listen_ipv6.

A better choice for an anonymous IPv6 FTP server might be PureFTPd, which has supported IPv6 for a few years on Unix-like platforms. Unfortunately, the Windows version seems to lag behind its cousin in this regard. PureFTPd is available from *http:// www.pureftpd.org/*.

One final note on FTP daemons is that, like HTTP daemons, if you process the log files from the daemon, you may need to update your log processing software to deal with IPv6 addresses. Since there isn't an FTP equivalent of CGI,[†] you don't need to worry about CGI scripts and other active content.

Remote Login Services

Remote login services are important, particularly for remote configuration of routers and other devices. We'll look at SSH and telnet, both of which are supported by IOS, JUNOS and most of the Unix-like systems we are looking at.

Telnetd

Like FTP, which has also been shipped with Unix-like systems for years, most vendors who ship IPv6 actually support telnet over IPv6, the main exception being some versions of Linux that shipped with an IPv4-only telnetd while generally supporting IPv6. The main gripe with telnet is that it may not encrypt the passwords sent for login, or even the data that is transferred subsequently. This could be rectified with IPsec, but in general ssh is now preferred.

SSH

OpenSSH has shipped with IPv6 support for a long time, so the Linux, BSD, and other vendors that use OpenSSH have mature support for IPv6. The only problem we've seen with OpenSSH was a bad interaction between the X11UseLocalhost option and IPv6, but this seems to have resolved itself. OpenSSH is available from *http:// www.openssh.com/*.

Very little extra work is needed to offer SSH over IPv6. If you are using the ListenAddress directive, then you may want to also specify an IPv6 address, though

---

* Available from *http://vsftpd.beasts.org/*

† There used to be a way to tell an FTP server to execute a command locally, from an FTP client. This capability was invoked via "site exec," and thankfully died long ago.

---

by default OpenSSH will listen on both IPv4 and IPv6 addresses. Another place where addresses may be explicitly used is in the known_hosts file. If you manually maintain a known_hosts file, then you'll want to add corresponding IPv6 addresses where IPv4 addresses appear.

Solaris's version of SSH is derived from OpenSSH and seems similarly well behaved. As we noted in the "Tru64" section in Chapter 5, the Tru64 ssh client is a little quirky, and early versions of the corresponding server need a Tru64 update before they will serve IPv6 clients.

If All Else Fails...

In some cases you may use software that simply does not support IPv6. In some cases this software can be made to effectively operate over IPv6 using *port forwarding*. We use the nc6 program, available from *http://www.deepspace6.net/projects/netcat6.html*, and inetd to do port forwarding. The nc6 program allows you to make a connection to a network service and copies its input/output to that network service. For example, you could say nc6 mail.example.com smtp to get a connection to the SMTP server on mail.example.com.

 There are other more sophisticated solutions using programs, such as ssh. Examples of clever port forwarding tricks can be found in *SSH, The Secure Shell* by Barrett and Silverman (O'Reilly). These tricks work over IPv4, IPv6, and a mix of both.

So let's consider the example of cvsup. This is a program used by the FreeBSD project for replicating source code trees. cvsup is written in Modula 3 and the version of Modula 3 used does not yet support IPv6. This means that the client and server parts of cvsup can neither make nor receive IPv6 connections.

However the protocol used by cvsup does not care about what it is transported over, thus on a cvsup server we can add a line to *etc/inetd.conf* saying:

```
cvsup stream tcp6 nowait nobody /usr/local/bin/nc6 nc6 127.0.0.1 cvsup
```

This causes inetd to listen for TCP connections on the cvsup port, and if it gets a connection then nc6 is started and it forwards the connection to 127.0.0.1, where it can be served by the IPv4-only cvsup daemon.

Likewise, a cvsup client can pretend to run a cvsup server on 127.0.0.1 and use nc6 to forward that connection to our (now IPv6 capable) cvsup server. For example, we could add:

```
cvsup stream tcp nowait nobody /usr/local/bin/nc6 nc6 -6 cvsup.example.com cvsup
```

to *letc/inetd.conf* on the client and then configure the cvsup program to use *127.0.0.1* as a server. When the cvsup program runs, its connection will be forwarded to cvsup.example.com over IPv6.*

Note that you'll probably want to restrict access to the client's port forwarding. This could be achieved with TCP wrappers, or some similar mechanism.

While this example uses Unix tools, Windows also supports port forwarding—the server side forwarding of this example can be achieved with a command like:

```
netsh interface portproxy add v6tov4 listenport=5999 connectaddress=127.0.0.1
connectport=5999
```

in which 5999 is the port number for the cvsup service.

So, this allows us to use cvsup on IPv6 clients and servers, as long as they have an IPv4 loopback interface configured. Admittedly, this technique isn't pretty—it requires extra programs at both ends of the IPv6 connection and extra copies of the data transferred as it makes its way through nc6. However, it may be useful as a last resort.

Summary

In this chapter, we spent a lot of time on HTTP before moving on to other services. HTTP is important because it still accounts for a significant percentage of Internet traffic† and is an ideal candidate for offering over IPv6, especially if you use Apache as a server.

Naturally we can't cover everything. IRC, LDAP and SQL come to mind as notable exceptions from our discussions, but rather than give an exhaustive list, we hope we've given you an idea of the level of IPv6 support available out there and the problems you can encounter deploying these services. To keep up to date with the availability of IPv6-enabled software, keep an eye on the list of Applications on Peter Bieringer's pages, *http://www.bieringer.de/linux/IPv6/status/* and *http://www.deepspace6.net/docs/ipv6_status_page_apps.html*, or on sites like the KAME site.

We've also encountered a few general principles for deploying IPv6 services in this chapter: you may need to explicitly enable IPv6 at compile time or at run time, you may need to update log file processors, you may need to update ACLs. One thing we didn't cover explicitly is testing your service—remember to check it works over IPv6, IPv4 and any other way in that it can be accessed.

Overall we've seen that a lot of software is now offering IPv6 support comparable with the IPv4 support. However, this code has yet to accumulate the man-centuries of testing associated with IPv4 and hence we have to expect the odd glitch.

---

* Assuming that the client has IPv6 connectivity and that cvsup.example.com has AAAA records in the DNS.

† HTTP's main competitor for the top spot is now peer-to-peer file sharing applications. These are also obvious candidates for moving to IPv6.

## CHAPTER 8

Programming

> *If 10 years from now, when you are doing something*
> *quick and dirty, you suddenly visualize that I am*
> *looking over your shoulders and say to yourself,*
> *"Dijkstra would not have liked this," well that would*
> *be enough immortality for me.*
> —*Edgar Dijkstra*

The sockets programming interface is probably the most commonly used interface for writing TCP/IP based applications. The sockets API is largely protocol agnostic, so adding support for IPv6 has proved to be relatively easy. To prevent inconsistencies* between the implementations, some standards have been produced to encourage a unified API (RFC 3493 and RFC 3542).

Familiar sockets function calls such as socket, connect, bind, listen and accept all remain unchanged, apart from the introduction of a new address family AF_INET6 that is used instead of AF_INET. IPv6 socket addresses are stored using a struct sockaddr_in6 rather than a struct sockaddr_in; so much is self-explanatory. More interestingly, a struct sockaddr_storage is provided which is large enough to store any protocol address. This is intended to make it easier to write protocol-independent code. Previously, struct sockaddr was sometimes used for this purpose, but the size chosen for this structure was too small on many systems.

Apart from the structures, the main change to the API for IPv6 is the provision of functions for looking up and printing IPv6 hostnames and addresses. The most important of these are getaddrinfo and getnameinfo. These are replacements for gethostbyname and gethostbyaddr, but designed with protocol independence in mind. As a part of this, they act on complete sockaddr structures, rather than just the host address.

---

* Having seen the mess of different commands for pinging, configuring interfaces, and displaying information in Chapter 5, we should be grateful that someone took time to standardize the programming interface.

We'll consider some basic sockets programming in this section, focusing on how the API has been expanded. This is not intended to comprehensively cover sockets programming under IPv6, but rather to provide enough information for those who need to IPv6-enable existing code that they maintain. For a more thorough coverage of sockets programming, including IPv6, see Volume 1 of *UNIX Network Programming* by the late W. Richard Stevens et al. (Addison-Wesley).

Note that this chapter focuses on C, as it is the parent language of the sockets API. We do mention some other programming languages in the "Languages Other than C" section later in this chapter.

Relevant Functions

First let's briefly review the well-known functions and how they behave when used for IPv6. We will also look at some of the new functions added to the API with IPv6.

Socket Functions

socket
>   The socket function creates a new socket. It takes three arguments: the protocol family you wish to work in, the type of socket within that family and a sub-protocol specifier for when multiple options might be available. For example, s = socket(PF_INET, SOCK_STREAM, 0); returns an IPv4 TCP socket and s = socket(PF_INET, SOCK_DGRAM, 0); creates a UDP IPv4 socket. To produce an IPv6 socket, we just use the protocol family PF_INET6 rather than PF_INET.

bind
>   A socket, being a network connection, has two ends: local and remote. The bind function assigns an address to the local end of a socket's link. This step can usually be skipped in the case of outgoing connections because the local address is unimportant and can be assigned automatically.
>
>   In the case of incoming connections, this step is essential, and specifies the address on which the program will listen for new connections.
>
>   Bind takes three arguments: the socket on which it operates, a pointer to the address structure and the length of the address structure. For example, bind(s, &ss, sizeof(ss)); would give the local address stored in the struct sockaddr_ storage called ss to the socket s.
>
>   The only change to the bind function is that it understands a struct sockaddr_ in6 as a valid address for a socket created with the protocol family PF_INET6.

connect
>   The connect function attempts to assign the remote end of a socket to a specified address by making a connection. It is only used for outgoing connections and its arguments are the same as those for bind. This function may take a

---

noticeable amount of time to return since it actually establishes the connection, where possible.

As with BIND, the only change to connect is to allow IPv6 addresses as the address to connect to for PF_INET6 sockets.

listen

In the case of SOCK_STREAM sockets, the listen function indicates that we wish to use this socket for accepting incoming connections. It takes two parameters: the socket to act on and the number of outstanding connections allowed at one time.

IPv6 support requires no changes to listen.

accept

For a socket on which we have called the listen function, this function waits for a new connection and then returns a new socket representing the new connection. It takes three arguments: the socket on which we are listening, a pointer to somewhere where the remote address of the new socket can be written and a pointer to where the size of that address can stored.

In the IPv6 world, an IPv6 address will be returned by accept when a connection is accepted on a PF_INET6 socket.

send, sendto, sendmsg

These functions can be used to send data to sockets. The send function allows a block of data to be sent over the socket. The sendto function allows the remote address to be specified when the socket has not been connected. The sendmsg function allows multiple blocks of data and additional control information to be passed to a socket.

For PF_INET6 sockets, sendto and sendmsg may be passed IPv6 addresses. There are additional control messages defined for IPv6. These control messages can be used for things like sending/receiving IPv6 header options or discovering what interface packets were received on.

recv, recvfrom, recvmsg

These functions receive data from a socket. Similar to the send family of functions, recv just receives data, recvfrom receives data and gives the source address on that data and recvmsg can receive data and a host of other control information.

For PF_INET6 sockets, recvfrom and recvmsg will return IPv6 addresses.

getsockname, getpeername

These functions determine the local and remote address of a socket. Naturally, they return IPv6 addresses on PF_INET6 sockets.

Address Resolution Functions

As we can see, the majority of changes to the low-level socket functions are to allow IPv6 addresses, in the form of sockaddr_in6 structures, to be passed to and from these functions.

The next question is, how do we populate these structures? We will examine the traditional address resolution functions, followed by their equivalents within IPv6, and finally look at the protocol-independent address resolution functions introduced to make the programmer's life easier in our multiprotocol world.

We also note which of the functions use static storage, making them unsuitable for use in threaded programs.

inet_aton

> inet_aton takes a string representing an IPv4 address and converts it into a struct in_addr. It takes a pointer to the string and a pointer to the structure. Variants of this function include inet_addr and inet_network. None of these functions understand IPv6 addresses.

inet_ntoa

> This function converts a struct in_addr to a string in standard dotted quad form. As such, it does the opposite to inet_aton. It takes a pointer to the structure and returns a pointer to an internal static buffer. As the address family is not specified, there is no way for this function to operate on IPv6 addresses.

gethostbyname

> This function takes a hostname and returns a structure that contains a list of the addresses corresponding to that hostname. The translation is done using DNS, /etc/hosts or whatever other mechanism is configured.

> While this function could potentially return addresses of different types, it can only return one type of address per invocation, and existing code rarely checks the address type field. For this reason, gethostbyname will not usually return IPv6 addresses. This function uses static data storage for the returned structure.

gethostbyaddr

> This function takes a pointer to a struct in_addr, the length of the address and the address family and converts it to a structure containing the hostname. Again, the conversion is done by DNS, /etc/hosts or whatever configured methods are available.

> As you can specify the address family to this function, it could be used to convert a struct in6_addr into a hostname. This function also uses static data storage for the returned structure.

gethostbyname2

> This function is the address-family agnostic version of gethostbyname, which takes a parameter indicating the address family in that we are interested in, as

well as the hostname. Like the other gethostby* functions, the result is returned in static data storage. gethostbyname2 is a relatively recent addition to the address resolution suite and may not be implemented on all platforms.

getservbyname

This function converts a service name and protocol to a structure containing the port number. For example evaluating getservbyname("www", "tcp")->s_proto will give 80 (in network byte order). The returned structure is in static storage.

getservbyport

This function performs the inverse translation of getservbyname. Again, it uses static storage.

inet_pton, inet_ntop

These functions are the address-family agnostic versions of inet_aton and inet_ntoa. They can be told the address family and the caller must provide a buffer into which the result will be written. This means these functions can be thread friendly.

getipnodebyname, getipnodebyaddr

These functions are replacements for gethostbyname and gethostbyaddr. They are address-family agnostic, use dynamic storage and allow the use of flags to give more control over the name to address translation process. A function, freehostent, is provided to free the dynamic storage allocated by these functions.

So, for the construction of sockaddr_in6 and sockaddr_in we now have getservbyname to construct the port number, followed by inet_pton or getipnodebyname to get the in_addr or in6_addr.

There is a problem with this situation: you want a sockaddr or a sockaddr_storage to pass to the socket functions and do not really want to have to build one yourself by populating a sockaddr_in6 or sockaddr_in. To this end, getnameinfo and getaddrinfo have been introduced.

getaddrinfo takes a node name, a service name and some hints and converts them into a list of protocol families and sockaddrs, ready to be passed to the socket functions. The hints can include:

- The protocol family of interest (or PF_UNSPEC to indicate any protocol family is acceptable)
- The protocol type (SOCK_STREAM, SOCK_DGRAM, and so on)
- The AI_PASSIVE flag, to indicate you plan to bind to the address (in this case the hostname may be NULL)
- The AI_NUMERICHOST flag, to indicate that the node name should be in numeric format and so name resolution via DNS et al. should not be used

- The AI_ADDRCONFIG flag says that getaddrinfo should only return IPv4 addresses if an IPv4 address is configured on the host and that it should only return IPv6 addresses if an IPv6 address is configured on the host

- The AI_CANONNAME flag, to indicate we want to know the node's canonical name

A freeaddrinfo function is provided to free the memory allocated by a call to getaddrinfo. Also, a function gai_strerror is available to translate error codes into error messages.

getnameinfo performs the inverse conversion. It takes a complete sockaddr and converts it into a hostname and a service name (in dynamic storage provided by the caller). A number of flags can be provided to change the behavior:

- if NI_NUMERICHOST is specified, then no address resolution is attempted and the hostname is returned in numeric format.

- if NI_NAMEREQD is specified, then an error will be returned if name resolution fails for the address; without this flag the address is returned in numeric format if resolution fails.

- NI_NUMERICSERV indicates that the numeric form of the service is required.

- NI_NOFQDN indicates that for local hosts, the hostname should omit the domain name and only contain the node name portion of the fully-qualified domain.

- NI_DGRAM indicates that the sockaddr was associated with a SOCK_DGRAM socket, rather than a SOCK_STREAM socket.

Since getaddrinfo and getnameinfo provide fully-populated sockaddr structures, they can fill in some of the more complicated fields, such as the scope ID associated with IPv6 scoped addresses.

Some Simple Examples

We will now look at a few examples of code written from scratch and old code that has been updated to deal with IPv6. The examples are written for Unix-like systems, but the situation on Windows should be very similar apart from the use of *Winsock2.h* and *Ws2tcpip.h* rather than the Unix socket headers. You need to make sure you use a recent version of the Windows Platform SDK to get headers and libraries that include IPv6 support. The SDK is available from *http://msdn.microsoft.com/*.

Parsing and Printing Names and Addresses

In this example, we look at how you might use getaddrinfo and getnameinfo. The program in Example 8-1 reads a list of hostnames, one per line. For each name it calls getaddrinfo with the PF_UNSPEC flag to get a list of the addresses associated with that name. Then for each of the addresses we call getnameinfo with the NI_NUMERICHOST flag to convert that address into the numeric form, rather than resolving the address by DNS or some other method.

Example 8-1. C resolver code

```c
#include <sys/types.h>
#include <sys/socket.h>

#include <ctype.h>
#include <netdb.h>
#include <stdio.h>
#include <stdlib.h>
#include <string.h>

int
main(int argc, char **argv) {
        int error;
        char *p, name[NI_MAXHOST], addr[NI_MAXHOST];
        struct addrinfo hints, *res, *r;

        while (fgets(name, sizeof(name), stdin) != NULL) {
                /* Cut the string at first whitespace */
                for (p = name; *p; p++)
                        if (isspace(*p)) {
                                *p = '\0';
                                break;

                        }
                printf("%s\t", name);

                /* Try to look up the name */
                memset(&hints, 0, sizeof(hints));
                hints.ai_family = PF_UNSPEC;
                hints.ai_socktype = SOCK_STREAM;
                error = getaddrinfo(name, NULL, &hints, &res);
                if (error) {
                        printf("*** %s\n", gai_strerror(error));
                        continue;
                }

                /* For each address, print it in numeric format */
                for (r = res; r != NULL; r = r->ai_next) {
                        if ((error = getnameinfo(r->ai_addr, r->ai_addrlen,
                            addr, sizeof(addr), NULL, 0,
                            NI_NUMERICHOST|NI_NUMERICSERV)))
                                printf("?%d? ", error);
                        else
                                printf("%s ", addr);

                }
                printf("\n");
                freeaddrinfo(res);
        }

        exit(0);
}
```

In Example 8-2 we can see the reaction of this program to various names. Note that getaddrinfo can parse numeric addresses as well as resolving hostnames.

Example 8-2. Resolver code output

```
www.example.com      2001:db8::3210 10.11.12.15
ns2.example.com      192.0.2.6
10.0.0.1      10.0.0.1
ff02::1       ff02::1
```

A UDP Echo Server and Client

UDP echo is a simple service that receives a UDP packet and sends the exact same payload back to the sender. Example 8-3 shows a protocol-independent echo server. The strategy taken in this program is to find all the protocols that we should listen on, create a socket listening on them, and then create a new process providing the echo service on that socket.

The first block of code sets up a hints structure for getaddrinfo, telling it that we are interested in passive addresses, i.e., an addresses that we will bind to. We use a NULL hostname, indicating that we are interested in the wildcard address (this was usually represented by INADDR_ANY in IPv4). The service name is given as "echo," which will be translated to port number 9. The fact that we have given SOCK_DGRAM as the socket type means that we will be offered addresses suitable for UDP or other datagram-based protocols.

The next block of code iterates over the returned addresses creating a socket in the right protocol, binding it to the returned wildcard address and then forking a new child process to handle the socket. Our main parent process then closes its copy of the socket and moves on to the next service.

Example 8-3. Protocol-independent UDP echo server

```c
#include <sys/types.h>
#include <sys/socket.h>

#include <netinet/in.h>
#include <netdb.h>

#include <stdio.h>
#include <stdlib.h>
#include <string.h>
#include <unistd.h>

char buf[4096];

int
main(int argc, char **argv) {
        int error, fd, launched, len;
        socklen_t slen;
```

Example 8-3. Protocol-independent UDP echo server (continued)

```
        struct addrinfo hints, *res, *r;
        struct sockaddr_storage ss;

        memset(&hints, 0, sizeof(hints));
        hints.ai_family = PF_UNSPEC;
        hints.ai_socktype = SOCK_DGRAM;
        hints.ai_flags = AI_PASSIVE;
        if ((error = getaddrinfo(NULL, "echo", &hints, &res)) != 0) {
                fprintf(stderr, "Couldn't find service echo %s\n",
                    gai_strerror(error));
                exit(1);
        }

        for (r = res, launched = 0; r != NULL; r = r->ai_next, launched++) {
                if ((fd = socket(r->ai_family, r->ai_socktype, 0)) < 0) {
                        perror("socket");
                        exit(1);
                }
                if (bind(fd, r->ai_addr, r->ai_addrlen) < 0) {
                        perror("bind");
                        exit(1);
                }
                switch (fork()) {
                case -1: /* Error */
                        perror("fork");
                        exit(1);
                case 0: /* Child becomes echo */
                        while (1) {
                                slen = sizeof(ss);
                                len = recvfrom(fd, buf, sizeof(buf), 0,
                                    (struct sockaddr *)&ss, &slen);
                                if (len >= 0)
                                        sendto(fd, buf, len, 0,
                                            (struct sockaddr *)&ss, slen);
                        }
                        exit(0);
                default: /* Parent releases socket and moves on. */
                        close(fd);
                }
        }

        freeaddrinfo(res);
        printf("%d echo services launched.\n", launched);
        exit(0);
}
```

The client, shown in Example 8-4 has a similar structure. It accepts a hostname and a service name on the command line and finds all matching addresses with getaddrinfo. It sends a packet to each of these addresses and waits for a response. No provision is made for timing out if the response is not forthcoming; undoubtedly in your own programs you would need more assiduous error checking.

Example 8-4. Protocol-independent UDP echo client

```
#include <sys/types.h>
#include <sys/socket.h>

#include <netinet/in.h>
#include <arpa/inet.h>
#include <netdb.h>

#include <err.h>
#include <stdio.h>
#include <stdlib.h>
#include <string.h>
#include <unistd.h>

char buf[4096];

int
main(int argc, char **argv)
{
        int error, fd, len;
        const char *out;
        struct addrinfo hints, *res, *r;

        if (argc != 3 && argc != 4) {
                fprintf(stderr, "Usage: %s host service [message]\n", argv[0]);
                exit(1);
        }
        out = (argv[3] != NULL) ? argv[3] : "Hello World.";

        memset(&hints, 0, sizeof(hints));
        hints.ai_family = PF_UNSPEC;
        hints.ai_socktype = SOCK_DGRAM;
        if ((error = getaddrinfo(argv[1], argv[2], &hints, &res)) != 0) {
                fprintf(stderr, "Couldn't find host %s service %s %s\n",
                    argv[1], argv[2], gai_strerror(error));
                exit(1);
        }

        for (r = res; r != NULL; r = r->ai_next) {
                if ((fd = socket(r->ai_family, r->ai_socktype, 0)) < 0) {
                        perror("socket");
                        continue;
                }
                if (sendto(fd, out, strlen(out), 0, r->ai_addr, r->ai_addrlen) < 0) {
                        perror("sendto");
                        close(fd);
                        continue;
                }
                if ((len = recv (fd, buf, sizeof(buf), 0)) < 0) {
                        perror("recv");
                        close(fd);
                        continue;
                }
```

Example 8-4. Protocol-independent UDP echo client (continued)

```
                fwrite(buf, len, sizeof(char), stdout);
                putc('\n', stdout);
                close(fd);
        }
        freeaddrinfo(res);

        exit(0);
}
```

The use of separate processes in the server and the sequential sending to each address in the client highlights an interesting issue: where an IPv4 daemon may have only managed one socket a protocol-independent server may have to manage several. To do this effectively will require either multiplexing between the sockets (with calls to select, poll, or similar) or by using multiple threads/processes. As many daemons already either multiplex clients or run an instance of themselves per client, this should not require significant code rearrangement in most cases. We'll see the details of this in our TCP server example.

A TCP Client and Server

In this section we look at how a TCP client and server can be changed to support IPv6. Our example will involve updating the networking part of a distributed ray tracer. In this case there are clients that connect to the server to find out what calculations need to be done, and the server then collects the results of these calculations. Note that each client deals with only one server, but the server must deal with many clients.

Each client uses a single TCP connection and the code for creating the connection is contained in a single function, shown in Example 8-5. This code is pretty much a textbook example of IPv4 TCP client code; we look up the hostname using gethostbyname, convert the port number to network byte order using htons, set up the sockaddr_in structure and then call socket and connect.

Example 8-5. Original IPv4 client

```
int connect_to_server(const char *hostname, int port)
{
        int server_fd;
        struct sockaddr_in server_address;
        struct hostent *addr;

        /* We need to find the network address. */
        if ((addr = gethostbyname(hostname)) == NULL) {
                herror("Couldn't resolve server name");
                exit(1);
        }
        if (sizeof(server_address.sin_addr.s_addr) < (size_t)addr->h_length)
                die("s_addr is too small to hold h_addr.\n");
```

Example 8-5. Original IPv4 client (continued)

```
        server_address.sin_family = AF_INET;
        memcpy(&server_address.sin_addr.s_addr, addr->h_addr, addr->h_length);
        server_address.sin_port = htons(port);
        /* Now connect to server. */
        if ((server_fd = socket(PF_INET, SOCK_STREAM, 0)) < 0) {
                perror("Couldn't make socket");
                exit(1);
        }
        if (connect(server_fd, (struct sockaddr *) & server_address,
            sizeof(server_address)) < 0) {
                perror("Couldn't connect to address");
                exit(1);
        }
        return (server_fd);
}
```

We replace it with a textbook example of protocol-independent client code, shown in Example 8-6. Here we call getaddrinfo to convert the hostname and port number to a list of addresses and we then try to connect to each until we are successful. The only (slight) complications are converting the port number into a string and freeing the addrinfo linked list.

Example 8-6. Protocol-independent client

```
int connect_to_server(const char *hostname, int port)
{
        int server_fd, error;
        struct addrinfo hints, *res, *r;
        char serv[6];
        const char *what;

        /* We need to find the network address. */
        memset(&hints, 0, sizeof(hints));
        hints.ai_family = PF_UNSPEC;
        hints.ai_socktype = SOCK_STREAM;
        snprintf(serv, sizeof(serv), "%d", port);
        if (error = getaddrinfo(hostname, serv, &hints, &res)) {
                fprintf(stderr, "Couldn't resolve server name %s: %s\n",
                        hostname, gai_strerror(error));
                exit(1);
        }
        if (res == NULL) {
                fprintf(stderr, "No addresses for server %s\n", hostname);
                exit(1);
        }

        /* Now connect to server. */
        for (r = res; r != NULL; r = r->ai_next) {
                if ((server_fd = socket(r->ai_family, r->ai_socktype, 0)) < 0) {
                        what = "Couldn't make socket";
                        continue;
```

Example 8-6. Protocol-independent client (continued)

```
                }
                if (connect(server_fd, r->ai_addr, r->ai_addrlen) < 0) {
                        what = "Couldn't connect to address";
                        close(server_fd);
                        continue;
                }
                freeaddrinfo(res);
                return server_fd;
        }

        perror(what);
        freeaddrinfo(res);
        exit(1);
}
```

The original server is also a textbook example, using listen, accept, and select. First we deal with the matter of setting up the listening socket. The original setup code, shown in Example 8-7, creates a socket, binds it to the INADDR_ANY address using a specified port number, calls listen, and returns the ready-to-use listening socket.

Example 8-7. IPv4-only TCP server

```
int make_listener(int port)
{
        int listen_fd;
        struct sockaddr_in listen_address;

        /* We need a socket to listen on. */
        if ((listen_fd = socket(PF_INET, SOCK_STREAM, 0)) < 0) {
                perror("Couldn't make socket!");
                exit(1);
        }

        listen_address.sin_family = AF_INET;
        listen_address.sin_addr.s_addr = htonl(INADDR_ANY);
        listen_address.sin_port = htons(port);
        if (bind(listen_fd, (struct sockaddr *)&listen_address,
            sizeof(listen_address)) < 0) {
                perror("Couldn't bind to address");
                exit(1);
        }
        if (listen(listen_fd, BACKLOG) < 0) {
                perror("Couldn't set up listen");
                exit(1);
        }
        return listen_fd;
}
```

The replacement code is a little more complex, as the server must try to listen on as many sockets as there are address families returned by getaddrinfo. This function may now produce multiple sockets, so its prototype is changed to allow it to create an array of sockets and to return the number of sockets in the array.

Then we try to call socket, bind and listen for each address. The addresses may include protocols that are not operational on the system, so if one fails we continue to the next (Example 8-8). We only give up if we create no listening sockets.

Example 8-8. Protocol-independent server

```
int make_listener(int port, int **fd_array)
{
        int fd, error, good, *listen_fd;
        struct addrinfo hints, *res, *r;
        char serv[6];
        const char *what;

        /* We need to find addresses to listen on. */
        memset(&hints, 0, sizeof(hints));
        hints.ai_family = PF_UNSPEC;
        hints.ai_socktype = SOCK_STREAM;
        hints.ai_flags = AI_PASSIVE;
        snprintf(serv, sizeof(serv), "%d", port);
        if (error = getaddrinfo(NULL, serv, &hints, &res)) {
                fprintf(stderr, "Couldn't get bind addresses: %s\n",
                        gai_strerror(error));
                exit(1);
        }
        if (res == NULL) {
                fprintf(stderr, "No addresses to bind to.\n");
                exit(1);
        }
        /* Get enough space to store sockets. */
        for (r = res, good = 0; r != NULL; r = r->ai_next, good++)
                ;
        if ((listen_fd = malloc(sizeof(int) * good)) == NULL) {
                perror("Couldn't malloc socket array");
                exit(1);
        }
        /* Now bind sockets to these addresses. */
        for (r = res, good = 0; r != NULL; r = r->ai_next) {
                if ((fd = socket(r->ai_family, r->ai_socktype, 0)) < 0) {
                        what = "Couldn't make socket";
                        continue;
                }
                if (bind(fd, r->ai_addr, r->ai_addrlen) < 0) {
                        what = "Couldn't bind to address";
                        close(fd);
                        continue;
                }
                if (listen(fd, BACKLOG) < 0) {
                        what = "Couldn't set up listen";
                        close(fd);
                        continue;
                }
```

Example 8-8. Protocol-independent server (continued)

```
                listen_fd[good++] = fd;
        }

        if (good == 0) {
                perror(what);
                exit(1);
        }
        freeaddrinfo(res);
        *fd_array = listen_fd;
        return good;
}
```

Pseudocode for the original version of the server's main loop is shown in Example 8-9. It creates lists of sockets that it is interested in reading from or writing to and then waits for them to become ready using select.

When sockets becomes ready, the code checks to see if it is the listening socket, and accept the new connection if it is. Then we iterate through the remaining sockets, checking to see what needs to be read and written.

Example 8-9. IPv4 only select loop

```
fd_set ready_read, ready_write;

while (work_to_do) {
        FD_ZERO(&ready_read);
        FD_ZERO(&ready_write);
        FD_SET(listen_fd, &ready_read);
        for (fd = 0; fd <= max_fd; fd++)
                ... FD_SET for clients ...

        select(max_fd+1, &ready_read, &ready_write, NULL, NULL);

        if (FD_ISSET(listen_fd, &ready_read))
                ... Accept new connection ...

        for (fd = 0; fd <= max_fd; fd++) {
                if (fd != listen_fd && FD_ISSET(fd, &ready_read))
                        ... Read results from client ...
                if (FD_ISSET(fd, &ready_write))
                        ... Send work to client ...
        }
}
```

To support multiple protocols, we must convert this loop to support multiple listening sockets. When we examine the original loop, we see that all we need to be able to do is check if a socket is a listening socket or not. In some cases it is practical to run through the array of listening sockets, checking each one. Another way to check is to use another file descriptor set to remember which of the descriptors represent listening sockets. Example 8-10 shows pseudocode for a main loop using both these techniques.

Example 8-10. Protocol-independent select loop

```
fd_set ready_read, ready_write, listeners;

for (i = 0; i < listen_count; i++)
        FD_SET(listen_fd[i], &listeners);

while (work_to_do) {
        FD_ZERO(&ready_read);
        FD_ZERO(&ready_write);
        for (i = 0; i < listen_count; i++)
                FD_SET(listen_fd[i], &ready_read);
        for (fd = 0; fd <= max_fd; fd++)
                ... FD_SET for clients ...

        select(max_fd+1, &ready_read, &ready_write, NULL, NULL);

        for (i = 0; i < listen_fd[i]; i++)
                if (FD_ISSET(listen_fd[i], &ready_read))
                        ... Accept new connection ...

        for (fd = 0; fd <= max_fd; fd++) {
                if (!FD_ISSET(fd, &listeners) && FD_ISSET(fd, &ready_read))
                        ... Read results from client ...
                if (FD_ISSET(fd, &ready_write))
                        ... Send work to client ...
        }
}
```

Case Study: MMDF

As a case study, we consider the changes made to a locally-maintained version of
MMDF* by one of the authors to make it IPv6-capable. MMDF is a mail transfer
agent (MTA), similar in purpose to Sendmail or Postfix. It interacts with the network in three ways.

- To accept incoming mail by SMTP.
- To send outgoing mail by SMTP.
- To look up DNS records for the routing of mail.

These components of MMDF are relatively modularized—there is an SMTP channel
daemon that runs from inetd for accepting mail, an SMTP channel program that
sends mail by SMTP and a table system for looking up hosts in the DNS.

---

* Note that the version of MMDF in question was written a long time ago, and while it is relatively well
  designed, the coding practices do not always meet up with modern expectations. If you find yourself updating an old application, we expect that you will see similar code.

Incoming SMTP Channel

A server handling an incoming SMTP connection, must get the address of the remote machine so that it can be included in the Received: headers of the email. This address is obtained by calling getpeername, but the code must now expect a response containing an IPv4 or IPv6 address. We achieved this by using a sockaddr_storage rather than a sockaddr_in. MMDF's old code had a limit of 250 bytes for a hostname; we replaced this with the new constant NI_MAXHOST, which is the length of the longest hostname you will need to deal with.

The original MMDF code then called gethostbyaddr to try to convert the address into a hostname. We replaced this call with a getnameinfo call. For the SMTP header, we need to know if the address can be resolved to a hostname or not, so we can first call getnameinfo with the NI_NAMEREQD flag, to determine the hostname. To prevent spoofing we then must look up the hostname and check if it matches the original address. We can do this by converting all addresses into numeric form via getnameinfo with the NI_NUMERICHOST flag and then using strcmp to see if they match. Example 8-11 shows pseudocode for this process.

If any part of this process fails, we just use the NI_NUMERICHOST flag to get a numeric printable version of the address. In this case the address appears in enclosed in [ ], but the SMTP standard* suggests that an IPv6 address should have IPv6: prepended to it. We can check if it is an IPv6 address by examining the ss_family field of the sockaddr_storage structure.†

Example 8-11. Checking that an address matches a hostname

```
int main(int argc, char **argv) {
        struct sockaddr_storage raddr;
        socklen len_raddr = sizeof raddr;
        char them[NI_MAXHOST];
        int is_numeric;

        ...

        if (getpeername(0, (struct sockaddr *)&raddr, &len_raddr) < 0)
                smtpsend("421 Can't get your address.");
        if (getnameinfo((struct sockaddr *)&raddr, len_raddr,
            them, NI_MAXHOST, NULL, 0, NI_NAMEREQD) == 0 &&
            checkthem(them, (struct sockaddr *)&raddr, len_raddr) == 0){
                is_numeric = FALSE;
        } else if (getnameinfo((struct sockaddr *)&raddr, len_raddr,
            them, NI_MAXHOST, NULL, 0, NI_NUMERICHOST) == 0) {
                is_numeric = TRUE;
```

---

* RFC 2821.

† Though this technique is not foolproof if IPv4 mapped addresses are in use. See the "Mapped IPv4 Addresses" later in this chapter and the IN6_IS_ADDR_V4MAPPED function mentioned in Example 8-12.

Example 8-11. Checking that an address matches a hostname (continued)

```
        } else {
                smtpsend("421 Can't format your address.");
        }
        ...
}

int checkthem(const char *them, const struct sockaddr *raddr, int len_raddr) {
        char addr1[NI_MAXHOST], addr2[NI_MAXHOST];
        struct addrinfo hints, *res0, *res;

        if (getnameinfo(raddr, len_raddr, addr1, NI_MAXHOST,
            NULL, 0, NI_NUMERICHOST) != 0)
                return -1;

        memset(&hints, 0, sizeof(hints));
        hints.ai_family = PF_UNSPEC;
        hints.ai_socktype = SOCK_STREAM;
        if (getaddrinfo(them, "smtp", &hints, &res0) != 0)
                return -1;
        for (res = res0; res != NULL; res = res->ai_next) {
                if (getnameinfo(res->ai_addr, res->ai_addrlen,
                    addr2, NI_MAXHOST, NULL, 0, NI_NUMERICHOST) != 0)
                        continue;
                if (strcmp(addr1, addr2) == 0) {
                        freeaddrinfo(res0);
                        return 0;
                }
        }
        freeaddrinfo(res0);
        return -1;
}
```

Outgoing SMTP Channel

The old MMDF code for the outgoing SMTP channel used variables of type long for the storage of IPv4 addresses, a common practice in older code. These could have been replaced with a union of in_addr and in6_addr; however, instead we decided to move to using full sockaddr structures, otherwise functions would have to be modified to take an additional parameter stating the address family. An alternative solution would have been to store a pointer to the addrinfo linked list returned by getaddrinfo—this has advantages that we outline in the "How Long Is a sockaddr?" section later in this chapter.

Once a decision to change the data structures had been made, the remaining code changes were to replace the parsing and printing of addresses with calls to getaddrinfo and getnameinfo.

DNS Table Code

MMDF's DNS table code stored IP addresses using an array of in_addr structures. Again, we decided to move to using a sockaddr_storage structure to avoid having to store the address family separately. Also, the number of addresses that could be cached was increased to allow for 1 IPv4 and 1 IPv6 address per MX record. If hosts publishing many IPv6 addresses become common, say as part of a multihoming scheme, then this limit may have to be revisited.

Fortunately, no change to the code for looking up MX records was required. However, the code for converting MX records into addresses must be updated to look for AAAA records. This is a straightforward replacement of gethostbyname with getaddrinfo. If MMDF had implemented its own resolver, then converting it would have been significantly more complex, because address selection and sorting would have to be considered. Thankfully, applications that have forsaken the system resolver are rare.

Other Considerations for Developers

Here we will look at a few tips regarding informal standards that have emerged among those producing IPv6-enabled code.

Switching Between IPv4 and IPv6

In many cases, it may be desirable to give the end user the choice of IPv4 or IPv6 operation. The way this has been implemented in most command-line utilities is to use either type of address by default, and to add flags -4 and -6 to restrict the program to using IPv4 and IPv6 addresses respectively. This is easy to implement by setting the appropriate family in the hints passed to getaddrinfo.

The following code shows how you can set a variable family based on command-line arguments and then use that when constructing the hints argument for getaddrinfo.

```
if (argc > 1 && strcmp(argv[1], "-4") == 0) {
        family = PF_INET; argc--; argv++;
} else if (argc > 1 && strcmp(argv[1], "-6") == 0) {
        family = PF_INET6; argc--; argv++;
} else
        family = PF_UNSPEC;

memset(&hints, 0, sizeof(hints));
hints.ai_family = family;
hints.ai_socktype = SOCK_STREAM;
error = getaddrinfo(host, service, &hints, &res);
```

How Long Is a sockaddr?

One inconsistency in the sockets API is the presence or absence of a length field as a common member of all sockaddr structures. While we were busily engaged in writing IPv4-only code, this wasn't really an issue; we knew that functions like getpeername would always return sizeof(struct sockaddr_in) bytes. When writing address-family agnostic code, this suddenly becomes a problem. So, how do we keep track of address lengths within code?

One option is to add a length argument whenever an address is passed around. The sockets API, getnameinfo and getaddrinfo all use this method. However, currently existing code often passes around sockaddr structures in a way that makes directly using a length and a sockaddr tricky.

One nice way to do this is to pass around the addrinfo linked list returned by getaddrinfo, as these structures contain all the information needed. As getaddrinfo dynamically allocates this memory, a downside to this technique is that you must manage that memory and call freeaddrinfo to avoid memory leaks.

If neither of these options are easily applicable, one stopgap technique that has been frequently used is to define a macro as follows:

```
#ifndef SINLEN
#ifdef HAS_SA_LEN
#define SINLEN(s) ((*s).sa_len)
#else
#define SINLEN(s) ((*s).sa_family == AF_INET ? \
                    sizeof(struct sockaddr_in) :\
                    sizeof(struct sockaddr_in6))
#endif
#endif
```

This macro is not terribly clean, as it assumes the program will be dealing with IP of some sort, but it is obvious how it can be extended to other address families and localizes knowledge of address families within a program. A macro similar to this, named SA_LEN, was considered for inclusion in the sockets API drafts, but has not been included in any final standard. Beware though, older versions of glibc do implement SA_LEN!

RFC 3493 does say that if sockaddr_in6 has a length field, then including *netinet/in.h* will result in SIN6_LEN being defined. This macro can then be used to decide what approach to take. For example, if you need to build your own IPv6 sockaddr structure.

```
        struct sockaddr_in6 sa6;

        memset(&sa6, 0, sizeof(sa6));
        sa6.sin6_family = AF_INET6;
#ifdef SIN6_LEN
        sa6.sin6_len = sizeof(sa6);
#endif
        sa6.sin6_port = htons(port);
        inet_pton(AF_INET6, "::1", &sa6.sin6_addr);
```

When IPv6 Addresses Don't Fit

Another issue that has arisen for many people while updating code to support IPv6 is that of colon characters. Many applications have used colons as separators in their own configuration languages, and this can cause conflicts when IPv6 addresses are added to those languages. The common solution to this problem has been to delimit IPv6 addresses with square brackets. For example, in the case of URLs, a colon character is used to separate the hostname from the port, so we write:

http://www.example.com:8000/
> www.example.com, port 8000, IPv4 or IPv6.

http://127.0.0.1:80/
> IPv4 localhost, port 80.

http://[::1]:8080/
> IPv6 localhost, port 8080.

This is currently described in RFC 2732, but should be included in the next update to the definition of URIs.

The use of square brackets is not universal though; for example the MTA Exim uses doubled-colons in IPv6 addresses to represent a single colon, which means that the unspecified address :: becomes ::::! Where possible it is probably best to follow the trend of using square brackets for the sake of consistency.

Services on Dual-Stacked Hosts

An application that contacts multiple services on a single host needs to cycle through *all* the addresses for *each* service it wants to contact. For example, an email client might talk to the POP and SMTP services on a server and while the SMTP service is available over both IPv4 and IPv6, the POP service might only support IPv4. If the client made an SMTP connection first to the server's IPv6 address and from then on only used that IPv6 address to contact the server, POP connections to the server would fail. If the client tries all addresses for every service, then everything should be OK. Make sure your applications try all the addresses before giving up.

Mapped IPv4 Addresses

The prefix ::ffff:0.0.0.0/96 contains what are known as IPv4 mapped addresses. The last 32 bits of an address in this range is an IPv4 address. The intention of these mapped addresses is to allow an IPv6 application to transparently handle IPv4 connections on a dual-stack node.

For example, if mapped addresses are enabled, and an IPv6 SMTP server binds to the unspecified address, ::, then it can receive an IPv4 SMTP connection from a host 192.0.2.5 and it will appear to the SMTP server as if the connection came from ::ffff:192.0.2.5. The traffic generated on the wire will all be IPv4 traffic.

Similarly, you could ssh -6 ::ffff:127.0.0.1, and while SSH thinks it is communicating over IPv6, the connection is actually to the IPv4 version of localhost, and login records will show the connection as being from 127.0.0.1.

In summary, IPv4 mapped addresses are a programming device that makes an IPv6 application use IPv4 on a dual-stacked node. They shouldn't actually appear on the wire,* as they should have been translated into IPv4.

While this is quite a neat idea, it does come with certain risks. These have been documented by Jun-ichiro itojun Hagino, and basically fall into two categories. The first is that if an IPv4 mapped address finds its way onto the wire, it may result in normal packet filtering to be bypassed. For example, hosts usually explicitly reject packets from 127.0.0.1 that do not come from them themselves, but a packet to ::ffff:127.0.0.1 might slip by.

The second risk is that access control lists might be accidently bypassed when mapped addresses are in use. Consider an SMTP server that is configured to reject mail from 192.0.2.0/24, which is replaced with a server using IPv6 mapped addresses. Connections from ::ffff:192.0.2.0/120 now need to be rejected, but it is not clear that the implementor of the software or the administrator of the SMTP server will remember to do this.

As a result of this, mapped addresses have been disabled by default on some systems, and applications that need to accept both IPv4 and IPv6 connections should bind a socket for both protocols. Applications that wish to avoid tripping over mapped addresses can explicitly disable mapped addresses using the IPV6_V6ONLY socket option.

On most KAME stacks you can control the default use of mapped addresses using the sysctl command. Setting sysctl net.inet6.ip6.v6only=0 allows the use of mapped addresses and sysctl net.inet6.ip6.v6only=1 disables them. The stack defaults to disallowing mapped addresses on FreeBSD 5, OpenBSD, and NetBSD and allowing them on FreeBSD 4 and Mac OS X.2. Some platforms do not support mapped addresses at all, for example the Microsoft stack.

The following code fragment explicitly enables or disables the use of IPv6 mapped addresses on the socket fd according to if the variable mapped, logging an error if the code fails to set the value.

```
if (family == AF_INET6) {
        int flg = mapped ? 0 : 1;
        if (setsockopt(fd, IPPROTO_IPV6, IPV6_V6ONLY, &flg, sizeof (flg)) < 0)
                syslog(LOG_ERR, "setsockopt (IPV6_V6ONLY): %m");
}
```

* This isn't strictly true, as the use of IPv4 mapped addresses has been suggested for SIIT in RFC 2765.

If the use of mapped addresses is important to your application, then you will want to use code like the fragment above to explicitly enable or disable them.

Tools for Auditing Sockets Code

There are several tools available for auditing source code that needs to be changed to support IPv6. Sun's "Socket Scrubber" is available is available as source code, so it can be compiled for most platforms. It is available for download from Sun's web site.

Socket Scrubber searches through files or directories looking for source code and picks out lines that you may need to look at. The socket scrubber is actually based on spotting certain strings in code, so it may produce some false alarms. For example, suppose you have a function like this:

```
void printmessage(void) {
        printf("Plug the TV into the socket.\n");
}
```

then socket scrubber will mark that line for attention because it contains the word "socket," even though it is in a string.

The Windows Platform SDK mentioned in the "Some Simple Examples" section earlier in this chapter also provides a source code audit tool called *Checkv4.exe*. This tool checks C files specified on the command line and highlights areas of concern. On Tru64 an IPv6 porting assistant is also available from *http://h30097.www3.hp.com/internet/ipv6portingassistant/*.

Online Guides to Coding for IPv6

There are many online guides to porting and coding for IPv6. We mention a few of them here, but your search engine of choice should be able to locate others.

1. The well known KAME article on implementing address-family independent code is at *http://www.kame.net/newsletter/19980604/* and is a concise guide. Don't be fooled by the date in the URL—the article has been updated as necessary over the last few years.

2. Other groups have also produced recommendations. The LONG project's guide can be found off *http://long.ccaba.upc.es/* and contains worked examples. The IETF is also working on *http://www.ietf.org/internet-drafts/draft-ietf-v6ops-application-transition-03.txt*.

3. Vendors such as Sun and HP provide information about porting, and make them available as whitepapers on their web sites—your vendor may also provide a guide based on their own experiences.

Languages Other than C

When programming, choosing the right tool for the job is half the battle. We've given a lot of coverage to C, but we know that it is a pretty blunt instrument for many tasks. Thankfully, C is not the only language to have support for IPv6. Languages, such as C++ and Perl, that are close to the C API, can grow IPv6 support relatively quickly. There are Perl modules such as Socket6, Net::IP and Net::DNS that provide explicit support for IPv6. The same goes for other scripting languages such as Python, PHP, and Ruby.

A language in a slightly different class is Java. From version 1.4 of J2SDK/JRE, it can deal with IPv6. Sun provide a document detailing the changes at *http://java.sun.com/j2se/1.4.2/docs/guide/net/ipv6_guide/*.

Summary

In this chapter, we covered the basic information required for adding IPv6 support to applications, including how the basic sockets API has been expanded to accommodate IPv6 and new functions for doing name/address translation. Naturally, there is quite a bit more to the basic API in RFC 3493 that we have not covered, including:

- The functions if_nametoindex, if_indextoname, if_nameindex, and if_freenameindex to find a list of interfaces and convert them from names to integers, which can then in turn be used to control multicast.

- Various socket options for controlling multicast transmission (IPV6_MULTICAST_IF, IPV6_MULTICAST_HOPS, IPV6_MULTICAST_LOOP) and reception (IPV6_JOIN_GROUP, IPV6_LEAVE_GROUP).

- The IN6_IS_ADDR_* family of functions that allow the classification of unicast and multicast addresses.

The prototypes for new functions introduced by the basic API are shown in Example 8-12. The advanced API goes even further allowing fine control of IPv6's routing, destination options and hop-by-hop headers. Coverage of these advanced features is beyond the realm of deployment and those interested should consult RFC 3493 and Stevens's *UNIX Network Programming*.

Example 8-12. Prototypes for new sockets API functions

```
#include <net/if.h>

unsigned int if_nametoindex(const char *ifname);
char *if_indextoname(unsigned int ifindex, char *ifname);
struct if_nameindex *if_nameindex(void);
void if_freenameindex(struct if_nameindex *ptr);

#include <arpa/inet.h>
```

Example 8-12. Prototypes for new sockets API functions (continued)

```
const char *inet_ntop(int af, const void *src, char *dst, socklen_t size);
int inet_pton(int af, const char *src, void *dst);

#include <netdb.h>

int getaddrinfo(const char *nodename, const char *servname,
        const struct addrinfo *hints, struct addrinfo **res);
void freeaddrinfo(struct addrinfo *ai);
char *gai_strerror(int ecode);
int getnameinfo(const struct sockaddr *sa, socklen_t salen, char *host,
        size_t hostlen, char *serv, size_t servlen, int flags);

#include <net/in.h>

int IN6_IS_ADDR_UNSPECIFIED(const struct in6_addr *a);
int IN6_IS_ADDR_LOOPBACK(const struct in6_addr *a);
int IN6_IS_ADDR_V4COMPAT(const struct in6_addr *a);
int IN6_IS_ADDR_V4MAPPED(const struct in6_addr *a);
int IN6_IS_ADDR_LINKLOCAL(const struct in6_addr *a);
int IN6_IS_ADDR_SITELOCAL(const struct in6_addr *a);
int IN6_IS_ADDR_MULTICAST(const struct in6_addr *a);
int IN6_IS_ADDR_MC_GLOBAL(const struct in6_addr *a);
int IN6_IS_ADDR_MC_LINKLOCAL(const struct in6_addr *a);
int IN6_IS_ADDR_MC_NODELOCAL(const struct in6_addr *a);
int IN6_IS_ADDR_MC_ORGLOCAL(const struct in6_addr *a);
int IN6_IS_ADDR_MC_SITELOCAL(const struct in6_addr *a);
```

CHAPTER 9
The Future

*Predicting the future is easy. It's trying to figure out
what's going on now that's hard.*
—*Fritz R.S. Dressler*

This chapter is an attempt to do two things. First, to summarise the current thinking
on unresolved issues, so you can make your best guess about how things are likely to
turn out in the future. Our summary will present both sides of a case—where we feel
they actually exist—and as such, is liable to lose us all the friends we have gained
throughout the rest of the book! Second, we deal in some detail with various up-and-
coming subject areas where IPv6 uses its features to good effect—for example, how
large scale mobility and globally unique addressing can support third generation
mobile services (also known as 3G). We do this so that people seeking to understand the traditional telco background or the traditional IETF/Internet components
of the 3G puzzle can both benefit.

Unresolved Issues

In this section we'll look at some of the unresolved issues around site-local
addresses, anycast, DNS, and multihoming.

Site-local addresses have been an area of hot debate within the IETF IPv6 working
groups. Many IPv6 deployments will be able to entirely ignore the site-local address
debate, because global addresses adequately serve their needs. Nonetheless, we'll try
to explain what the fuss is about.

Anycast is another technology like unicast, multicast and broadcast. The details of
anycast in IPv6 have not yet been sorted out. It is not as emotive a subject as site-
locals, but once fully defined anycast should prove a useful feature of IPv6.

For IPv6 DNS, the issue that remains unresolved is how to inform nodes of what the
address of the local DNS server is. DHCPv6 is one solution to this issue, but others
are being considered for situations where DHCP isn't an option. We'll take a quick
look at the other possibilities.

How to do multihoming in IPv6, without routing tables growing to an unmanageable size, is another area of lively debate within the IETF. Again, we'll outline some of the proposals, but resolving this issue may well take longer than any of the others we have mentioned.

Site-Local Addresses

Let's refresh your memory on site-local addresses for a moment.

Site-local addresses share some properties with RFC 1918 private address space, and for IPv4 people, it is best to understand them in that context. As you might recall, private address space is just a section or sections of global address space earmarked for use within organizations. To use it, you just pick a portion of space between some ranges, and start configuring them. No one organization can be said to have exclusivity over the particular space they use, and it is generally used only within an organization.

The non-uniqueness property means that such local-use addresses are "easy to obtain"—in other words, getting them does not require the oversight of an address allocation agency. Network administrators and creators everywhere value this category of IP address space, since this allows network growth to take place with a minimum of ISP or RIR related bureaucracy. One oft-cited reason for private numbering, security, has definitely been a motivating factor in their use by some. However, we feel that real security benefits are not easy to obtain simply and only by using private address space.

Unfortunately private addressing has been *so* popular that experienced network managers soon learned to recognize the fundamental problem of non-globally unique allocations: when two sufficiently large networks that use private address space networks meet, then invariably both of them are using some portion of the same address space. This creates Fear, Uncertainty, and Doubt, since the intercommunication of the networks more-or-less requires that at least one of them renumbers. Various power struggles generally follow, until the least well-defended group is convinced to perform the tedious renumbering task. The problem turns up in other areas too. For example, company VPNs usually require publicly numbered access networks (be they dialup, wireless or whatever), to avoid a numbering collision between the access network and some privately numbered element of the company's network. Further NATing can't always be used to get around this because VPNs are usually tied to IP address endpoints. (We also discuss using NAT as an attempt to get around this problem in the "NAT" section of Chapter 1.)

 If you absolutely must number a network *now* and you are looking for a good one to use, our advice is to avoid 10/8 and choose something from 172.16/12 or perhaps the middle ranges of 192.168/16, as 10/8 seems to be the most popular private address block by quite some way.

Ideally, we would like to accommodate these nice features of private addressing within IPv6 somehow, while trying to ameliorate the bad effects. However, these requirements for site-locals would seem to be flawed: how can you have space large enough to number any given network, which doesn't have to be registered with an upstream registry, yet is also well-managed enough to limit the chance of addressing collisions? Other problems with the concept of site-local addressing have also been identified. For example, the meaning of the word "site," absolutely crucial to the correct definition of the address space, is highly nebulous and means different things to different people at different points in an organization.

There is even a school of thought that says that "site-local" as a concept shouldn't be touched by the addressing system at all; it should be enforced by the routers, for example by means of routing filters. These people point out that the enforcement of communication scope ultimately rests with the routing equipment, and so should not be part of the addressing policy.

However, there are quite legitimate reasons to have unique, if not globally-routed, address space. One example of this is point of sale (PoS) networks, where communications are only ever to back-end billing systems. Another is Internet-unconnected community networks, perhaps formed by WiFi point-to-point communications, where there may be local gaming servers or other services, but no Internet gateway. If there's no upstream, where do you get your address space? And, if your upstream is prone to withdrawing service at inconvenient moments, shouldn't your internal network be resilient against (for example) name-to-address mapping problems? There are some ways to fix these problems, including Node Information Queries, but a stable address space is definitely a useful thing.

With this in mind, it's clear that the site-locals as originally proposed fundamentally don't fix the problems they were designed to fix. So we either need a new proposal, or need to decide the problem wasn't worth fixing in the first place! There is, however, clearly *some* need for an ability to number with minimal bureaucratic pre-requisites, and there's a real hunger for an addressing method that won't result in painful clashes and renumbering when corporate networks merge.

One take on this situation is that it should be a lot easier to get globally unique addresses than it is with IPv4, so the motivation to use private numbering should simply go away. Nevertheless there's a valid need for address space possessing the above properties and this is probably fulfilled either by a low-overhead global registry or by a simple rule that produces a (probably) unique prefix. It is this sort of *unique local IPv6 unicast addressing* that is being proposed by the IETF to replace the original site-local addressing system. Now that the original site-local addressing scheme has been deprecated by RFC 3879, the new scheme should be finalized shortly.

There might be a temptation to try to appropriate some site-local-like space from elsewhere in the routing table, but this is unwise until a standard solution is finalised. In particular, don't be tempted to use 2002:: addresses with RFC 1918 private addresses encoded in them—this is expressly forbidden by the 6to4 definition in RFC 3056 and some IPv6 implementations will recognize these address and decline to process them.

Anycast

An anycast address is a slightly strange animal. Originally defined in RFC 1546 for IPv4, it is another example of a different type of scope of address. You are, by now, familiar with uni- and multicast addresses reaching—by definition—one interface and multiple interfaces respectively. Anycast is like multicast in that multiple interfaces can be the potential target destinations of a packet, but only *one* of the interfaces in question actually receives the packet. Usually it will be the "nearest" interface to the sender, as determined by the routing system.

Anycast is potentially very useful for creating all manner of highly-available systems. However, there's a catch: the address used by the server to reply might not be the anycast destination address used by the client. This creates various technical complications currently under examination. Naturally, we'd like to avoid the need to rewrite applications, while also allowing services to continue to examine the reply addresses as usual.

One interesting example is the subnet-router anycast address, formed by setting all the bits after the subnet boundary to zero*—for example, the subnet-router anycast address for the network containing 2001:db8:1:2:3:4:5:6 and with a subnet mask of /64 is 2001:db8:1:2:0:0:0:0 or simply 2001:db8:1:2::.

Reservations have been made for other well-known anycast addresses in each IPv6 subnet; these are described in RFC 2526. When this RFC was written, only one address had been defined, for use in mobile IPv6.

The usual deployments of anycast in the Internet today actually derive from multiple advertisements of a PI prefix. One example is described in RFC 3258, which explains how to distribute multiple authoritative name servers with one IP address. The technique used is roughly an anycast technique, but is described as "shared-unicast." Our expectation is that anycast of some kind will become important as an infrastructure for delivering highly available services as the standards develop; but one of the most useful roles it could play is in the deployment of automatically discovered DNS services, which we discuss below.

DNS

Given that IPv6 has done so much for the zero-configuration cause, wouldn't it be nice to finally remove the last part of static configuration by inventing a way for DNS

---

* Think "network address" in IPv4.

servers to be discovered and used automatically? As it is, the IPv6 solution to the "thousand computers on a dock" problem* allows only for the broadcast/multicast name resolution that typically goes with older Windows networks. This system works fine for local file and printer sharing. Until you try to resolve an Internet name, all works well. Clearly the problem needs to be addressed, and not everyone wants to or can run a DHCPv6 server.

The pros and cons of the various competing suggestions are discussed in *http:// www.ietf.org/internet-drafts/draft-ietf-dnsop-ipv6-dns-configuration-04.txt* but we'll explain a couple of them here.

Note that DNS discovery almost always refers to discovery of a recursive DNS server, i.e., a server that will resolve if possible arbitrary names, rather than an authoritative-only server.

Anycast recursive DNS

In theory, you could create an anycast group "all-dns-servers," like "all-routers," and simply send a query in the right format to that address. Then any one of a number of servers could reply. Problem solved; the address itself remains the same throughout all networks, so all operating systems could ship with this address hard-coded. There are, however, a number of problems with this scenario. First, anycast requires, according to RFC 1546, an alteration in the TCP stack to enable truly stable TCP communication, although it can and is performed today with un-altered stacks. In fact the problem is not with TCP per-se, but more with applications where the reply address that a response is received from is supposed to be exactly the address to which you sent the original packet. There are a variety of ways of solving this problem; you can fix the client to accept answers from arbitrary sources (opening a variety of interesting and time-consuming security holes) or you can fix the server to rewrite replies so that they appear to come from the address they were sent to. Of course, if two requests are sent to an anycast address, they may be received by two entirely different servers if the routing topology changes. Thus, anycast is particularly vulnerable to transient changes in routing. Having said that, these are largely theoretical problems since DNS travels mostly over UDP, and routing within an organization should be reasonably stable.

One proposal assigns the recursive DNS three well-known *unicast* addresses. These addresses would then be injected into the routing system as host routes by the DNS servers themselves. There are some fears about how to assign these addresses within the IETF: drafts of this proposal use site-local addresses for the well-known addresses. However, there was no special requirement for site-local addresses and the proposal stands regardless of the fate of site-local addressing.

---

* For a discussion see Christian Huitema's IPv6 book, *IPv6, The New Internet Protocol* (Prentice Hall).

DNS discovery

Another approach to the problem is, instead of having well-established addresses, to give the client the mechanism to discover DNS servers if they are available.* A variety of suggestions have been made, including inserting the information in RAs, or using a dynamic service discovery protocol such as SLP. However, work is still very much ongoing to decide on the best method for DNS discovery. At the moment, the most workable solution is to use DHCPv6 for informing clients of DNS server addresses.

Multihoming

Multihoming in IPv6 has generated a large amount of controversy. Why? The multihoming issue has come to the fore as a consequence of the deprecation of PI addressing in favour of routing table aggregation. There is a pent-up demand for a better multihoming paradigm than the one we currently have, but unfortunately there is no anointed successor waiting in the wings. Below we review some of the previous and future contenders for the new multihoming paradigm.

One of the important efforts that has been made with respect to multihoming is to understand what multihoming means to different people. New proposals will have to fulfil the criteria desired by multihomers that have been outlined in RFC 3582, such as redundancy, load-sharing, and so on. Only one approach has really gotten all the way through the standards process, and that is RFC 3178, for multihoming at site exit routers. It relies on creating additional tunnelled connections between your two upstream providers, preferably over different media, but perhaps predictably, it is not a complete solution, and the document is informational rather than describing an actual standard for a new paradigm.

8+8

The idea of 8+8† is to turn the existing rather flat structure of the IPv6 address into something more useful for routing. The latter half of an address still identifies an end system, and is called an ESD (end-system-designator). The first half is rather charmingly called *routing goop*, or RG, and is an indicator of the point of attachment to the Internet. This separation is to be enforced by higher level protocols however, such that addresses with the same ESD are taken to refer to the same machine, no matter what RG is in front of them. This means that TCP checksums, IPsec SAs, and so on, must alter behavior to cope with this new definition of what is an acceptable address, a definition that aids the survivability of higher-layer connections in the event of provider failure.

---

* Sometimes this is called stateless DNS discovery to distinguish it from DHCPv6 configuration.

† Mike O' Dell has a draft at *http://arneill-py.sacramento.ca.us/ipv6mh/draft-odell-8+8-00.txt.*

The other interesting concept in 8+8 is the approach to public versus private routing topology. Today private routing topology, that is to say, details of subnets within an organization, are reflected in the global unicast addresses that are used to communicate between systems, most often in the 32 bits between the middle of an IPv6 address and the start. This detail is actually of no use to anyone apart from the origin system; 8+8 attempts to make use of the fact that exposing private topology is not necessary by encoding public topology in the RG *dynamically* by site egress/ingress routers to reflect changes in connection. Furthermore, the RG encoding plan is itself capable of expressing other kinds of routing than the purely hierarchical model beloved of CIDR and derivatives. The RG encodes a *path* rather than a destination, and has extremely subtle and powerful capabilities. Those wanting to know more should read the draft. Sadly, 8+8 does not seem to have received much attention recently.

MHAP

MHAP is the Multihoming Aliasing Protocol. It also relies on placing additional semantics within the IPv6 global unicast address space. There are locators and identifiers; the system relies on using an "on-demand" routing setup where connections provoke an attempt by the originating router to locate the destination network, by some process involving talking to more knowledgeable routers. When the correct information is returned, the originating router then uses the real addresses and aliases the ones used by the actual originating host to the real addresses.

The MHAP proposal is described in *http://arneill-py.sacramento.ca.us/ipv6mh/draft-py-mhap-intro-00.txt*; however it seems that it has also fallen into neglect.

Geographical addressing

One question raised by the various attempts to get multihoming into a sensible state has been whether or not the default free zone really needs to be composed of routers that have complete copies of the routing table.

Geographical addressing is an attempt to respond to this. In this scheme address blocks are assigned to cities and geographical areas. Customers in those areas can use the addresses regardless of what ISP they connect through and ISPs operating in a city can provide aggregated routes by peering at an exchange point for that city.

Steve Deering and many others, including CAIDA, have considered geographical addressing as a possible move forward. However, the details of geographical addressing changes the type of controls that ISPs have over the routing of customers' traffic, and so it has not proven popular with ISPs. A good essay on geographical addressing can be found at *http://www.caida.org/outreach/papers/1996/aai6/aai6.html*.

SCTP

An alternative to implementing the requirements of multihoming as discussed above in the routing system is actually implementing them in the transport protocols—i.e.,

TCP and its cousins. This has a number of advantages: you don't need so many expensive routers, and certain multihoming failure modes don't kill ongoing connections by changing the addresses of their end points. You can read more at RFC 2960, RFC 3257 and *http://www.ietf.org/internet-drafts/draft-coene-sctp-multihome-04.txt*. SCTP has been implemented for several IP stacks, but is nowhere near wide acceptance.

Layer 3 Shim

In this approach, a multihomed site can use multiple address blocks provided by multiple providers. If a link to one of the providers fails, then a special protocol can arrange for existing connections to be *rehomed*. The IP layer takes care of this rehoming so that upper layer protocols never need to know it has happened. In a sense, this is a little like Mobile IPv6, except that hosts are usually connected to many networks. The advantage is that things continue to be much as they were; the disadvantage is that things continue to be much as they were.

Better the devil you know?

We'll finally mention what may happen if a new multihoming solution cannot be agreed on: people will go back to using provider independent addressing. If the need is severe enough it seems likely that RIRs would decide to allocate addresses to large organizations that needed to multihome. This is not a terribly palatable thought for those hoping that IPv6 would be a clean-up for the global routing table, but it is at least a known quantity with known behaviour.

Up and Coming Subject Areas

The subject we'll look at here is what may happen when the worlds of IP networks and mobile telephony collide.

Cellular Devices

Cellular devices are, loosely, devices that are expected to be hand-held, and operating in a cellular network of some kind. Mobile phones of various generations would be cellular devices, as would *some* kinds of laptop, or computers where power management is very important. They are typically small in size and in capability: they have limited CPU power, RAM, and battery capacity. The battery capacity issue is particularly relevant when the only network connection costs you significant amounts of power to transmit. Signalling traffic, such as RAs and pings, which in wired networks would be essentially "free," can be very keenly felt by a small device.

If you are looking at implementing IPv6 for such a device, then RFC 3316 is the RFC to read. It outlines some of the considerations for IPv6 on a device meeting the above definitions.

P2P Applications

It seems clear that peer-to-peer applications are going to be an important chunk of what networks are used for in the future. While P2P file sharing applications have acquired a tarnished name, due primarily to copyright concerns surrounding the files being shared, these applications also address hard problems related to how you distribute files efficiently. For example, Bittorrent is already the method of choice for downloading the most recent Linux distributions. Furthermore, the BBC are releasing their old program archives to the public. Actually distributing this content via a centrally managed server farm could be expensive for the BBC in terms of bandwidth and maintenance costs. However, they are looking at P2P file sharing as a way to distribute the load of providing access to the archives.

Of course, peer-to-peer applications extend beyond simple file sharing. Microsoft's *Three Degrees*, while it does share files, is more like a remote-collaboration application. And then, of course, there are applications like telephony and messaging.

SIP, IM, and VoIP

SIP is the Session Initiation Protocol, a protocol designed for doing the sort of call setup usually associated with telephone networks. IM is Instant Messaging, an application that lies somewhere between email, pager/GSM text messages, and IRC. VoIP is a way of transporting voice telephone calls over an IP network. All of these applications are contributing to a blur between the telephone networks and computer networks.

These communication applications also all benefit from some core features of IPv6: lots of addresses, IPsec and QoS support. Although these applications will definitely be running on cellular devices, one of the more compelling successes of IPv6 will be the amount of equipment, from desktops to cellular devices, using the same address space. This means that you might be able to make a call from your mobile phone that goes straight to your friend's desktop computer. For the protocols themselves, running over IPv6 means easier communication between the devices without having to resort to NAT.

One perhaps underemphasized benefit of IPv6, when combined with the right infrastructure (primarily Teredo), is that you can easily write scalable and debuggable applications for VoIP, gaming, and things we haven't even imagined yet. All this is available to clients primarily connected to the *IPv4* Internet.

Where the future of these applications leads isn't yet clear, but it seems that IPv6 will probably be involved in that future. While these services may provide you with new ways of communicating at home or in the office, they may also be used in the next generation mobile telephone networks, which brings us nicely to our next topic.

Supporting Notes for Understanding 3G

Like most large telecommunications efforts, the governing standards umbrella body, the 3GPP, is a combination of a large number of interested organizations, including ETSI (the European telecomms industry body), T1 Telecommunications (T1), the China Wireless Telecommunication Standard Group (CWTS), the Korean Telecommunications Technology Association (TTA), the Association of Radio Industries and Businesses (ARIB), and the Telecommunication Technology Committee (TTC) in Japan. It's this group which dictates what is and is not 3G, with input from its members and other interested parties, such as the IETF. The 3GPP has a structure slightly reminiscent of the IETF Areas and Groups: there are specific areas of concern (e.g., terminals, or handsets) investigated by Technical Specification Groups, but TSGs are themselves further divided into Working Groups (WGs), which do the actual technical work.

3G was originally conceived in 1986, although it was not called "3G" at the time. Prior to 1996 the work was mostly in research, but the standardization efforts ramped up after that, and it is expected that serious deployment will begin within a short time frame.

Architecture

The 3G (a.k.a. UMTS)* architecture can be divided into two main domains: the packet switched (PS) domain, and the circuit switched (CS) domain. For the purposes of this book, we will only examine the packet switched domain.

Core network elements comprise the GGSN, the SGSN and the IMS. The GGSN is a customized router between the GPRS network and other networks, such as the general Internet.† The SGSN is an intermediate router between the GGSN and radio network. It is responsible for administrative functions other than routing: AAA, mobility management, and billing, among others. The IMS, essentially the server farm, is where content and IP infrastructure servers live.

In turn, the radio network (UTRAN) has Radio Access Network Controllers (RNCs) and base stations, which connect the handsets (UE or User Equipment) to the core network. The radio network is capable of transmitting data at various increments from 64 kbps to 2 Mbps. The actual data rate depends on propagation, velocity of the handset, bandwidth available, and so on.

We can usefully distinguish between two kinds of mobility that we might want to support in networks: micro and macro. Micro mobility would be (for example) moving between base stations. Macro mobility would be moving your point of layer 3

---

* Universal Mobile Telecommunications System.

† Think of the GGSN as being a NAS, if that terminology is familiar to you.

attachment to the network, e.g., perhaps moving between GGSNs. In the initial releases of 3G, micro mobility is taken care of below IP layer by using tunnels to create an apparently flat IP network.

Whereas IP attempts to preserve a tightly-layered, hourglass-type model, 3G has a layered model that is more intertwined; for example, the voice codecs are exactly geared to the bandwidth increments supplied by the radio interface, and so on.

Probably the clearest motivation for 3G from the telco point of view is that the integration of IP actually helps to reduce the cost of running the network.* Ultimately, the goal is to carry voice traffic over packets, enabling statistical multiplexing to kick in. This should save costs on traditional support infrastructure, such as circuit-switched E1-minimum increment backhaul. Furthermore, the mass market economics of IP, when brought to bear upon the production of telecomms equipment, should result in further savings.

3G from the IETF Point of View

A 3G network is, in certain respects, not unlike a "generic" ISP's network. The functional roles that can be identified within an ISP network, namely a core network, an access network, and a distribution network, can also be identified in a 3G network. Needless to say, it is a lot more complicated than that, but for the purposes of focusing on IPv6, we will keep this functional model in mind while we are reviewing the 3G system architecture.

From IPv6's point of view, the most important 3GPP concept is the PDP Context. A PDP Context is a "connection" between the user equipment (UE), such as a mobile phone, and the GGSN. It is this connection over which the packets are transferred. Think of the PDP as a PPP connection of some kind and you won't be far wrong, though they actually use a protocol called GTP. These PDP contexts are brought up and down as handsets detach and re-attach to the network. IPv6 runs over the PDP contexts, and it is these that are considered to be the IPv6 *link*.

The GPRS system supports static and dynamic address allocation in both stateless and stateful varieties. For autoconfiguration, GPRS nodes have no MAC address, so this means that the procedure is based on PPPv6, described in RFC 2472.

Other services running over IP are also important in a 3G network, such as DNS, which is used internally. The details are too involved to examine here, but the IETF and the 3GPP are working on the many issues of mutual interest.

---

* Capital and license costs are orthogonal to this issue, of course.

IPv6 in a 3G Network

Oddly enough, although IPv6 might have been considered an "easy win" for mandating on handsets, the 3GPP actually nominated the IMS (server farm) as being the section of 3GPP networks that has mandatory IPv6 support.

Work is ongoing in the IETF to characterize situations that will arise in 3G networks and to identify the important transition mechanisms for 3G. To some degree the answers that will be important to a particular 3G operator are likely to depend on the 3G equipment already in place. Until the detail of this is more clear, it's probably more useful to attempt to answer a very simple questions about IPv6 in 3GPP: What does IPv6 bring to a 3G network that IPv4 doesn't provide?

Lots of addresses
This is naturally the most obvious argument for IPv6. Attempting to number the expected quantity of handsets from public IPv4 address space is simply infeasible. Numbering handsets using private IPv4 space is a short-term solution, but has limits, particularly if we want to expand the range of peer-to-peer services available via 3G networks. For many the prospect of being able to run a phone call directly over IP from some kind of mobile phone to a desktop PC is quite attractive.

IPsec
IPsec is a useful protection mechanism for the end-user, but it is also useful also for the network manager. It allows secure communications between the server farm and the handset without involving additional protocols. Of course, the persistent problem of key management is still present.

Privacy addressing
This provides a standard way for devices to vary their addresses that may enhance the privacy of customers.

In addition to features, IPv6 also brings questions. For the 3G network designer, there are two obvious questions that we will address below.

What addresses do we assign to handsets?
This question is actually two questions. First, should an operator assign static addresses? And second, how many and of what type are the addresses we hand out to each handset?

Thankfully, there is no technical necessity to statically assign addresses to handsets. The autoconfiguration mechanism built into IPv6 and the PDP negotiation process should be sufficient for normal operation of 3G networks. Given the whole network will initially be maintained by GTP tunnels, it seems that assigning a /64 to each handset should be sufficient. If devices need to do subnetting of any kind, say a handset connected to a laptop that is acting as a router, there is perhaps a case for allocating a /48 per handset. However, a /64 should be sufficient even for personal area networks, since (for example) a Bluetooth connection to your headset can be operated as a separate link to the PDP context, and can use link-local addresses.

From a network planners perspective, it is sensible to reserve space for handsets from a portion of a /48, and perform standard subnet allocation for the remainder of your address space.

Will I run out of addresses?

This, in principle, depends on many variables, including size of allocation, customer takeup, and so on. But in reality even with a HD ratio adjusted /64 per PDP context, and only addresses from 2xxx:: used, there are still 490 trillion addresses available. This should be plenty of room for the next few years.

Summary

As we've seen over the course of the book, much of IPv6 is finalized. Certainly enough is now concrete that IPv6 could step in as a replacement for IPv4, we would lose no features, and we would also be able to gratefully dispose of NAT.

However, as you might expect of a living and growing protocol, not everything in IPv6 has been finalized yet. This is in fact good: not only does it keep us networking folk in jobs and thinking about interesting things, but it also means that we have not spent our time solving problems that do not exist yet.

In this chapter, we ran through some of the more controversial outstanding issues, illustrated our take on them, and talked a little bit about where you might expect to see IPv6 ending up in the future. Hopefully these will help you in your planning and preparation.

Glossary

This glossary is intended as a quick reference for terms you may be unfamiliar with. More complete descriptions of the most entries can be found by consulting the index.

3G

Shorthand for Third Generation mobile services.

3GPP

3rd Generation Partnership Project, a group set up to work on standards for third generation mobile telecommunications.

6bone

The original test network for IPv6 consisting of sites joined by tunnels. The 6bone is now beginning its retirement, due for completion by 06/06/2006.

ACL

An Access Control List is a way of specifying who can access a particular file, network or service. Different vendors and different software all have their own way to specify ACLs.

anycast

A way of sending a packet so that it is destined to any one of a group of machines. Compare this with multicast.

API

An Application Programming Interface is a standard set of data structures, functions and methods made available to programmer to allow access to some facility,

such as a network protocol or a windowing interface.

APNIC

The Asia Pacific Network Information Centre is the RIR for the part of the world you'd guess it would be.

ARIN

The American Registry for Internet Numbers is the RIR for North America and some other countries in the Caribbean and Africa.

ARP

The Address Resolution Protocol, used by IPv4 to translate IPv4 addresses into lower layer addresses, such as Ethernet MAC addresses.

AS

Autonomous Systems are routing black boxes out of which a BGP network is built. Within an AS, routing will be managed by an IGP, between ASs routing is managed by BGP.

ATM

Asynchronous Transfer Mode, a layer 2 technology that moves small chunks of data called *cells* around a network.

bit

A bit is the basic unit of data storage on most computers. It can remember if something had value 0 or 1. Bits are combined together to remember more complicated things such as address, words and images.

BOF

Birds of a Feather, a group of people, usually at a conference, meeting to discuss a particular common interest.

BGP

A protocol for connecting networks together in a fashion resistant to failure.

broadcast

A broadcast packet is one that is delivered to all machines on a network.

CIDR

Classless Interdomain Routing, a way of splitting IPv4 addresses into a network part and a host part without using the Class A, B and C system.

CIFS

Common Internet Filesharing System. A Microsoft protocol for sharing files; also known as SMB.

CLNP

The ConnectionLess Network Protocol, part of the ISO protocol stack, specified in ISO 8473.

CPE

Customer Premises Equipment. In other words, the kit that ends up on-site, at the customer premises.

DAD

Duplicate Address Detection, a process IPv6 nodes conduct to make sure an address is unused before they use it.

default free zone

The part of the Internet that does not have a 'default route' and so it has to calculate a route to every network on the Internet, using a combination of an EGP and a IGP.

deprecate

To deprecate something is to pension it off and, with a slightly disapproving tone, mark it as no longer suitable for general use. This happens to addresses in IPv6, old facets of protocols in the IETF, and sometimes even entire operating systems. Of course, many people wonder if we will be able to deprecate IPv4 some day.

DHCP

DHCP is the dynamic host configuration protocol. It is used to allow an IPv4 host find its IP address and other information, such as the local name server, without having to store this information locally.

discontiguous

Things are discontiguous if they are not adjacent, or immediate neighbors.

DNS

The Domain Name Service, a distributed database translating between hostnames and addresses. Other information can also be stored in the DNS, such as mail routing information or telephone numbers.

DoS

Denial of Service; usually means a type of malicious network traffic that is sent with the intention of removing access to a network, a machine or individual, often using overwhelming amounts of traffic.

dual stack

A dual-stacked node is one that has a working IPv4 and IPv6 stack. While both IPv4 and IPv6 are in use, dual-stacked routers and proxies will form an important part of keeping the Internet operating smoothly for everyone. Since TCP and UDP are more-or-less the same in IPv4 and IPv6, some vendors actually produce only dual IP level stacks and use a common stack above that.

EGP

An Exterior Gateway Protocol is a protocol, such as BGP, that is spoken between routers in different networks to establish a routing table. At one time there was an EGP called EGP.

flag day

A flag day is a time when everyone has to coordinate to make some change. For example, if everyone had to shut down their computer one day, uninstall IPv4 and install IPv6, that would be a flag day. Naturally, a design aim of the IPv6 deployment process is to avoid flag days.

GPRS

General Packet Radio Service, a way to use 2nd generation mobile phone networks for packet data. GPRS is considered to be 2.5G.

jitter

Varying amounts of latency. If a TCP connection is suffering from serious jitter, performance is very difficult to predict, and it generally causes users to be annoyed and/or confused. On the other hand, if the latency is large but constant, performance is predictable and generally more manageable for users.

IANA

The Internet Assigned Numbers Authority, the traditional body associated with standardizing IP addresses, protocol numbers, port numbers and the like. These responsibilities now largely fall with ICANN.

ICANN

Internet Corporation for Assigned Names and Numbers, in their own words, is a global, consensus-driven, non-profit organization formed to assume responsibility for the IP address space allocation, protocol parameter assignment, domain name system management, and root server system management.

ICMP

The Internet Control Message Protocol, used to communicate errors and other diagnostic messages across within IP. An expanded and revised version of ICMP is included in IPv6.

IETF

The Internet Engineering Taskforce. The people who write RFCs and Internet-Drafts in an effort to make the Internet interoperable, comprehensible and manageable.

IGP

An Interior Gateway Protocol is spoken between routers in a network to learn about routes within that network. IS-IS and OSPF are IGPs. Compare to EGP.

IKE

Internet Key Exchange is a protocol for establishing keys and algorithms to be used by IPsec.

IMAP

The Internet Message Access Protocol is like POP on steroids.

IMS

Internet Multimedia Subsystem. A complicated way of saying "server farm" in 3G networks.

Internet-Draft

These are the working documents of the IETF that may, in time, become RFCs.

IPsec

A technique for providing privacy, authentication and other security related services at the IP level.

IPv4

The version of the Internet Protocol mainly in use within the Internet.

IPv6

A new version of the Internet Protocol, designed to address issues that have arisen with IPv4.

IS-IS

IS-IS is a routing protocol from the OSI protocol suite. It routes from *Intermediate System* to *Intermediate System*. It is sometimes used in the IP world as an IGP.

ISP

Internet Service Providers are people who are in the business of providing others with a connection to the Internet.

KAME

A group, based in Japan, working to provide IPv6 and IPsec for the BSD family of operating systems. They have also provided patches to make well-known software IPv6 capable.

LACNIC

The Latin American and Caribbean Internet Addresses Registry is the RIR for, well, Latin American and the Caribbean. It is a young RIR and was fully recognized in 2002.

LIR

A Local Internet Registry. Like an RIR, but operating on a organizational level within a country, rather than a continent wide level.

machine

Another name for a computer, as in 'reboot that machine' or 'have you finished installing those Solaris machines'.

MLD

Multicast listener discovery is a part of ICMPv6 that allows a router to find out what multicast addresses are being listened for on a link.

MPLS

Multipath labelled switching is a technique for routing packets quickly through a network based on labels that are assigned when the packet enters the network. Has a chewy ATM flavour.

MTU

Maximum Transmission Unit, the size of the largest packet that can be transmitted on a link.

multicast

A way of sending a packet to a certain group of machines. Multicast can be much more efficient than broadcast.

multihoming

A network with multiple connections to the Internet, usually for reasons of improved reliability, is described as multihomed. An analogy is an ISP is your home network within the Internet, and if you have multiple ISPs then you have multiple homes.

NAT

Network Address Translation, a technique for rewriting the addresses on packets as they enter and leave a network. Usually used to allow many hosts to use a single public IPv4 address.

ND

Neighbor Discovery, the broad equivalent of ARP in IPv6.

NNTP

The Net News Transfer Protocol, used for transporting Usenet News around the Internet.

NTP

The Network Time Protocol is a fiendishly clever system for keeping clocks in sync using the Internet.

OSI

A family of protocols once considered to be in competition with IP. It is now best known for the layered paradigm used in its design.

OSPF

Open Shortest Path First is an IP routing protocol used within a organization, making it an example of an IGP. OSPF has been updated to support IPv6.

PA

Provider Aggregate is a term used to describe addresses assigned to someone that are a subset of the addresses assigned to their network provider. cf. PI

P2P

Person to Person or Peer to Peer. A method of filesharing or communicating that is not centralized.

PI

Provider Independent addresses are addresses assigned directly to an organization, rather than borrowing addresses from their network provider. cf. PA

PIM

Protocol Independent Multicast is a protocol for routing multicast traffic. It comes in two flavours, sparse and dense.

POP

The Post Office Protocol is used to allow users to collect their mail from a mail server.

PPP

The point-to-point protocol is for transporting packets from a variety of protocols over a point-to-point link. It was most commonly used for traditional dialup Internet services, but has variants such as PPPoE (PPP over Ethernet) and PPPoA (PPP over ATM) have become more common as DSL has become available to more people.

prefix

A prefix is a block of IPv4 or IPv6 addresses determined by fixing the first n bits of the address. For example, `192.168.8.0/24` is the collection of IPv4 addresses that look like `192.168.8.`*anything*. Similarly, `2000::/3` is the collection of IPv6 address that start with the digit 2 or 3.

QoS

Quality of Service—the ability to ensure that network traffic ends up where it is supposed to, when it is supposed to be, and within the right amount of the time.

RFC

The standards documents for the Internet, produced by the IETF. RFC stands for Request For Comments.

RIP

The Routing Information Protocol is one of the simplest IP routing protocols. RIPng is a version of RIP running over IPv6.

RIPE

Réseaux IP Européens, the European Regional Internet Registry, for some definition of Europe.

RIR

Regional Internet Registries work to allocate resources needed for the operation of the Internet, such as addresses. They also usually provide support to those administering Internet infrastructure and help with the development of standards and policies.

SIP

The Session Initiation Protocol is a standard for initiating multi-media conversations between various kinds of endpoints (such as 3G phones, desktop PCs, laptops, etc.).

SMB

Server Message Block, a Microsoft protocol for sharing files also known as CIFS.

SMTP

The Simple Mail Transfer Protocol is used to get email from A to B in the Internet.

ToS

Type of Service—several bits in an IPv4 packet used to identify service requirements of the that packet. The Traffic Class field serves a similar function in IPv6.

transit

A network on the Internet provides transit if it carries traffic that neither originates nor terminates locally. This is usually thought of in terms of BGP Autonomous Systems, so an AS provides transit if traffic flows through that AS that is neither to nor from that AS. For example, a small ISP that carries traffic only for their own customers is not a transit network, but a large ISP that carries traffic for multiple smaller networks and between other large ISPs is a transit network.

TSIG

Transaction SIGnature. A particular way of signing a DNS transaction so that you can have more confidence it's correct.

tunnel

Tunnelling is a way of getting packets from one point in a network to another without the intermediate networking understanding those packets. This usually involves wrapping extra headers around the packets that the intermediate network does understand. The most common example in the IPv6 arena is wrapping IPv6 packets in IPv4 so that they can traverse the IPv4 Internet.

tunnel broker

A tunnel broker is someone who can provide you a IPv4 address that you can tunnel IPv6 packets to. They will usually provide you with IPv6 addresses for your end of the tunnel too.

UMTS

Universal Mobile Telephony Service. A third generation mobile standard.

Unicast

The usual way packets are sent, where they only have a single destination. Other options include anycast, broadcast and multicast.

userland

The part of an operating system outside its kernel or core. This includes all the tools typically run by the user.

USAGI

USAGI is a project to provide IPv6 and IPsec support for Linux.

VLAN

Virtual LAN, a method of defining one or more logical networks within a single physical Ethernet. They are usually used to keep particular machines on separate networks while sharing the same switching infrastructure.

Index

Numbers

3G
    3GPP, 255
    architecture, 255
    definition, 259
    IETF and, 256
    introduction, 255
    IPv6 and, 257
    RNCs and, 255
3GPP (3rd Generation Partnership
       Project), 259
6bone addresses, 80, 259
6over4, 71
6to4, 67
    addresses and, 79
    configuring, 137–139
    DJB's AutoIPv6, 69
    relay routers, 185
    Teredo, 70
8+8, 251

A

A6 records, DNS lookups, 146
AAAA bug workarounds, DNS and, 155
Abilene, xxiii
accept function, 223
ACL (Access Control List), 259
address
    preferred, 41
address resolution functions
    gethostbyaddr, 224
    gethostbyname, 224
    gethostbyname2, 224
    getipnodebyaddr, 225

getipnodebyname, 225
getservbyname, 225
getservbyport, 225
inet_aton, 224
inet_ntoa, 224
inet_ntop, 225
inet_pton, 225
addresses
    6bone, 80
    6to4 and, 79
    aggregation, 5
    anycast, 34, 249
    CIDR, 4
    classes, 3
    DAD, 37
    deprecated, 41
    dotted quad form, 3
    filtering
        ICMPv6, 176
        IPv6, 176
    global Unicast addressing, 29
    grouped, 23
    interface IDs, 22
    IPv4, mapped, 241
    length, 241
    link-local addresses, 22
    link-local addressing, 29
    MAC layers
        resolution, 9
        stateless autoconfiguration and, 40
    multicast, 31
        hardware support, 33
        scope value, 32
        solicited node multicast, 33
        unicast prefixes, 32

We'd like to hear your suggestions for improving our indexes. Send email to *index@oreilly.com*.

H

Hagino, Jun-ichiro itojun, xxi
Hain, Tony, xxi
hardware, multicast addresses, 33
headers
    compression, 50
    Destination Options header, 47
    extension headers, 47
    Fragment header, 47
    Hop-by-Hop Options, 47
    packet structure, 20
        fixed-length, 20
    Routing header, 47
hexadecimal notation, 23
Hexago, xxiii
hexdigitnotation, 23
Hinden, Bob, xxi
home, address selection and, 46
home addresses, nodes, 51
Home Agent, Mobile IPv6, 51
home networks, Mobile IPv6 nodes, 51
Hop-by-Hop Options header, 47
HTTP, 199
    caches, 205
    proxies, 205
Huitema, Christian, xxi
Huston, Geoff, 19

I

IAB (Internet Architecture Board), xvii
IANA (Internet Assigned Numbers
        Authority), 261
ICANN (Internet Corporation for Assigned
        Names and Numbers), 261
ICMP (Internet Control Message
        Protocol), 261
    name resolution, 41
ICMPv6, 34
    address filtering, 176
    Echo Requests, 34
    errors, 34
    message types, 43
IDS (Intrustion Detection Systems), 184
IESG (Internet Engineering Steering
        Group), xvii
IETF (Internet Engineering Task Force), xvi,
        261
ifconfig, 120–122
IGMP, multicast addresses and, 31
IGP (Interior Gateway Protocol), 54, 261
IIS (Internet Information Service), 204

IKE (Internet Key Exchange), 261
IM (Instant Messaging), 254
IMAP (Internet Message Access
        Protocol), 213, 261
    Courier-IMAP, 214
    Cyrus Imapd2, 214
    WU-IMAP, 213
IMS (Internet Multimedia Subsystem), 261
in6_addr, 225, 238
INADDR_ANY, 228, 233
inet_addr, 224
inet_aton function, 224
inetd, TCP wrappers, 198
inet_network, 224
inet_ntoa function, 224
inet_ntop function, 225
inet_pton function, 225
infrastructure, deployment and, 94
ingress filtering, 177
in.ndpd, 114
installation
    applications, 139
        SSH, 141
        web browsers, 139
    email clients, 141
    routers, 116
        Cisco, 117
        Juniper, 118
    workstations
        AIX, 114
        FreeBS, 115
        Linux, 111
        Macintosh, 110
        Solaris, 114
        Tru64, 115
        Windows, 108
interface configuration, 122
interface IDs, 22
intermittent connection, 80
internal routing
    protocols, 11
    RIP, 11
Internet Draft, xvi, 261
IOS, 117
    routing and, 162
ip6fw, 179
ip6tables, 179
IPsec, 57, 158, 261
    AH (Authority Header and, 158
    confidentiality and, 158
    configuration, 159
    FreeBSD configuration, 160

multihoming, 251, 262
    8+8, 251
    geographical addresses, 252
    MHAP (Multihoming Aliasing
        Protocol), 252
    network design and, 88
    protocol-independence and, 88
    SCTP and, 252
Murai, Jun, xxi

N

name resolution, configuration, 127
name service switch file, 114
names
    parsing
        code example, 226
    printing, code example, 226
    resolution, 41
NAT 46/64-PT transition mechanism, 75
NAT (Network Address Translation), 5, 262
native connectivity
    Ethernet and, 91
    incompatible equipment, 188
ND (Neighbor Discovery), 262
Neighbor Advertisements, 37
neighbor cache, 36
neighbor discovery, 35, 126
    address resolution and, 35
Neighbor Solicitation messages, 37
neighbors
    bidirectional contact, 38
    SEND (secure neighbor discovery
        protocol), 39
netmask, network design and, 85
netsh, 108, 120–138, 220
NET-SNMP, 183
netstat, 126
network design, 84
    addresses, 84
    DHCP and, 87
    multihoming, 88
    netmask, 85
    subnet mask, 85
    subnetting, 85
network layers, 8
network management, coexistence and, 91
networks
    management, 182
    monitoring, scripting, 184
    OSI model, 8
    renumbering, 6

NI_MAXHOST, 237
NNTP (Net News Transfer Protocol), 214,
        262
node information queries, 125
nodes
    home addresses, 51
    home networks, Mobile IPv6, 51
notation
    base 10, 24
    binary, 24
    decimal, 24
    elision, 23
    grouping addresses, 23
    hexadecimal, 23
    hexdigit notation, 23
    scope identifiers, 26
NSD
    nameserver, 152
    transport and, 153
NTP (Network Time Protocol), 215, 262
    ntpd, 215
ntpd, 215
NTT/Verio, xxiii
NUD (Neighbor Unreachability
        Detection), 38

O

online guides for coding, 243
OpenSSH, 218
optimization overview, 20
OS X, 110
OSI
    definition, 262
    model, 8
OSPF (Open Shortest Path First), 262
    routers, 54
    routing protocol, 166

P

P2P (Peer to Peer), 262
    applications, 254
PA (Provider Aggregate), 262
    space, 12
packet structure, headers, 20
    fixed-length, 20
packets
    redirection, 38
    Router Advertisement, 38
    Router Solicitation, 38

About the Authors

Niall Richard Murphy has been involved with the Internet since 1995, when he and many others founded the UCD Internet Society. He has worked for many of the core Internet organizations in Ireland, including the INEX, the IEDR, Ireland On-line, and, many moons ago, HEAnet. Niall is the author or coauthor of numerous technical articles and talks, including RFC 3314 and RFC 3574 on 3G and IPv6, and has spoken to audiences at conferences and research institutions.

His current abiding interest is using wireless networking to fix the doldrums that are fixed-line end-user telecomms in Ireland. Don't even get him started about ADSL.

David Malone is a researcher in Maynooth University. David is a mathematician at heart, with a Ph.D from Trinity College Dublin, but he also has an unhealthy interest in computers. He has been involved with Unix systems administration since 1994 and has been a committer on the FreeBSD project since 2000.

David is the author of various articles, talks, rants, and papers. His interests include dilation equations, mathematics of networks, Unix security, timekeeping, and IPv6.

Colophon

Our look is the result of reader comments, our own experimentation, and feedback from distribution channels. Distinctive covers complement our distinctive approach to technical topics, breathing personality and life into potentially dry subjects.

The animal on the cover of *IPv6 Network Administration* is a softshell turtle. There are many species of softshell turtle in North America, all of the family *Apalone*. Some of the most common species include the Florida softshell (*Apalone ferox*) and the Eastern spiny softshell (*Apalone mutica*). They are freshwater turtles, living in streams, ponds, and lakes. Instead of the hard shell that covers many turtles, the softshell turtle is protected by a brown or olive leathery carapace. They use their long, rounded noses for searching out food and as snorkels for breathing in the water.

The English language distinguishes between turtles and tortoises, but the Japanese language does not. Both are *kame* in Japanese. However, Japanese distinguishes between the softshell turtle on the cover (*suppon*) and *kame*. This is probably because *suppon* are a Japanese delicacy.

The tagline "teaching the turtle to dance" comes from the tradition of visiting *http://www.kame.net* to test if your IPv6 connection works. If you visit this web site using IPv6, the turtle icon at the top of the page dances. When you have IPv6 working, you have taught the turtle to dance.

Colleen Gorman was the production editor and proofreader for *IPv6 Network Administration*. Sarah Sherman and Claire Cloutier provided quality control. Lydia Onofrei provided production assistance. Johnna VanHoose Dinse wrote the index.

Ellie Volckhausen designed the cover of this book, based on a series design by Edie Freedman. The cover image is a 19th-century engraving from the Dover Pictorial Archive. Emma Colby produced the cover layout with Adobe InDesign CS using Adobe's ITC Garamond font.

David Futato designed the interior layout. This book was written using LaTeX and CVS over IPv6. It was converted to DocBook Lite using a Perl hack by David Malone. It was then converted by Joe Wizda to FrameMaker 5.5.6 with a format conversion tool created by Erik Ray, Jason McIntosh, Neil Walls, and Mike Sierra that uses Perl and XML technologies. The text font is Linotype Birka; the heading font is Adobe Myriad Condensed; and the code font is LucasFont's TheSans Mono Condensed. The illustrations that appear in the book were produced by Robert Romano, Jessamyn Read, and Lesley Borash using Macromedia FreeHand MX and Adobe Photoshop CS. The tip and warning icons were drawn by Christopher Bing. This colophon was written by Colleen Gorman, David Malone, and Niall Richard Murphy.

Keep in touch with O'Reilly

1. Download examples from our books

To find example files for a book, go to:

www.oreilly.com/catalog

select the book, and follow the "Examples" link.

2. Register your O'Reilly books

Register your book at *register.oreilly.com*

Why register your books?
Once you've registered your O'Reilly books you can:

- Win O'Reilly books, T-shirts or discount coupons in our monthly drawing.
- Get special offers available only to registered O'Reilly customers.
- Get catalogs announcing new books (US and UK only).
- Get email notification of new editions of the O'Reilly books you own.

3. Join our email lists

Sign up to get topic-specific email announcements of new books and conferences, special offers, and O'Reilly Network technology newsletters at:

elists.oreilly.com

It's easy to customize your free elists subscription so you'll get exactly the O'Reilly news you want.

4. Get the latest news, tips, and tools

www.oreilly.com

- "Top 100 Sites on the Web"—PC Magazine
- CIO Magazine's Web Business 50 Awards

Our web site contains a library of comprehensive product information (including book excerpts and tables of contents), downloadable software, background articles, interviews with technology leaders, links to relevant sites, book cover art, and more.

5. Work for O'Reilly

Check out our web site for current employment opportunities:

jobs.oreilly.com

6. Contact us

O'Reilly & Associates, Inc.
1005 Gravenstein Hwy North
Sebastopol, CA 95472 USA

TEL: 707-827-7000 or 800-998-9938
   (6am to 5pm PST)
FAX: 707-829-0104

order@oreilly.com
For answers to problems regarding your order or our products. To place a book order online, visit:

www.oreilly.com/order_new

catalog@oreilly.com
To request a copy of our latest catalog.

booktech@oreilly.com
For book content technical questions or corrections.

corporate@oreilly.com
For educational, library, government, and corporate sales.

proposals@oreilly.com
To submit new book proposals to our editors and product managers.

international@oreilly.com
For information about our international distributors or translation queries. For a list of our distributors outside of North America check out:

international.oreilly.com/distributors.html

adoption@oreilly.com
For information about academic use of O'Reilly books, visit:

academic.oreilly.com

Related Titles Available from O'Reilly

Networking

802.11 Security

802.11 Wireless Networks: The Definitive Guide

BGP

Building Wireless Community Networks, *2nd Edition*

Cisco IOS Access Lists

Cisco IOS in a Nutshell

Designing Large-Scale LANs

DNS & BIND Cookbook

DNS & BIND, 4th Edition

Essential SNMP

Hardening Cisco Routers

Internet Core Protocols

IP Routing

IPv6 Essentials

LDAP System Administration

Managing NFS and NIS, *2nd Edition*

Network Troubleshooting Tools

Networking CD Bookshelf, *Version 2.0*

Postfix: The Definitive Guide

Practical VoIP Using Vocal

qmail: An Alternative to sendmail

RADIUS

Samba Pocket Reference, *2nd Edition*

sendmail 8.13 Companion

sendmail, *3rd Edition*

sendmail Cookbook

Solaris 8 Administrator's Guide

TCP/IP Network
Administration, *3rd Edition*

Unix Backup and Recovery

Using Samba, *2nd Edition*

Using SANs and NAS

O'REILLY®

Our books are available at most retail and online bookstores.
To order direct: 1-800-998-9938 • order@oreilly.com • www.oreilly.com
Online editions of most O'Reilly titles are available by subscription at safari.oreilly.com